Political Leadership in NATO

Westview Special Studies in International Relations

Political Leadership in NATO:
A Study in Multinational Diplomacy
Robert S. Jordan

This unusual history of the first four secretaries-general of NATO and their importance in the postwar politics of Western defense is a study of diplomacy—of individuals and the impact of their personalities on international events. It can perhaps best be described in terms of what it is not. It is not, for example, exclusively a book on NATO, nor is it a text on international organization. It is neither a history of European politics nor an analysis of East-West relations. It is not a specialized study of nuclear politics, and it does not pretend to be a record of the political interplay between the United States and its European allies. Yet all of these themes appear in the work.

In the course of preparing this book, Dr. Jordan came to know the four secretaries-general, as well as many other individuals involved in NATO since its inception. While his analysis is objective and he has thoroughly documented his observations, there is also a valuable personal element in his assessment of the impact the persons who occupied this relatively little known but very important office had on the institution they headed and the international political environment in which they operated.

Robert Jordan has been professor of political science at the State University of New York at Binghamton and is now adjunct professor of political science at Columbia University. He also serves as director of research at the United Nations Institute for Training and Research (UNITAR). He holds doctorates from Princeton and Oxford universities.

Political Leadership in NATO:
A Study in Multinational Diplomacy

Robert S. Jordan
with Michael W. Bloome

Westview Press / Boulder, Colorado

Cover photo courtesy of NATO Information Service

Westview Special Studies in International Relations

Copyright © 1979 by Westview Press, Inc.

Published in 1979 in the United States of America by
   Westview Press, Inc.
   5500 Central Avenue
   Boulder, Colorado 80301
   Frederick A. Praeger, Publisher

Library of Congress Cataloging in Publication Data
Jordan, Robert S., 1929-
   Political leadership in NATO.
   (Westview special studies in international relations)
   Includes bibliographical references and index.
   1. North Atlantic Treaty Organization. I. Title.
JX1393.N67J67   341.72   78-6969
ISBN 0-89158-355-6

Printed and bound in the United States of America

This book is dedicated to the four persons at Oxford who first encouraged me to study the diplomacy and diplomatic methods of secretaries-general:

Max Beloff
W. F. Deakin
Norman Gibbs
Alexander Loveday

Ministerial meeting, NATO tenth anniversary, Washington, D.C., 2 April 1959.

Contents

Acknowledgments

In the course of the preparation of this book I have received invaluable help from many present and former officials of NATO. While I find it impossible to thank each individually, I do wish to make clear my appreciation: without their cooperation this work would never have materialized. I must, however, single out and express a deep sense of gratitude to the late W. Randolph Burgess who, more than any other person, opened doors and pointed me in the right direction.

I should also like to express thanks to the following persons who, in various capacities, have contributed to the completion of this effort: Anne Wallace Scoffier and her late father, Richard Wallace, former director-general of the Atlantic Council of the United States; John Vernon of the NATO Information Service; and graduate students Jacob Bercovitch and John Chiddick (of the London School of Economics and Political Science), David Ewing (of the School of Public and International Affairs, George Washington University), and Parley W. Newman, Jr. (of the Department of Political Science, Columbia University).

Finally, Péter Vukasin, of the State University of New York, and Davidson Nicol, executive director of the United Nations Institute for Training and Research, provided personal encouragement.

Robert S. Jordan
New York, June 1978

Introduction

Perhaps the easiest way to introduce this book is to state what it is not. It is not, for example, a book on NATO, nor is it a book on international organization. It is not a history of European politics nor an analysis of East-West relations. It is not a study of nuclear politics; and it does not pretend to be a record of the political interplay between the United States and its European allies, though all of these themes do appear. Rather, this book represents a study in diplomacy: it is a history of four men—the first four secretaries-general of the North Atlantic Treaty Organization—and their importance in the postwar politics of Western defense. It is a study not of structure but of individuals and the impact of their personalities and vision on international events.

This is also a personal book. In the course of its preparation, I have come to know the four secretaries-general, as well as many of the other individuals involved in NATO since its inception. Although I have attempted to remain objective in my analysis and have employed historical and other published sources to verify my observations, there remains an element in the book that reflects a personal evaluation of these men. For any and all such observations and conclusions, I, of course, assume full responsibility.

Although the primary purpose of this endeavor lies in an exploration of the impact of four men on Western politics, any such discussion must take place within the context of their principal political arena—NATO. Raymond Aron, the distinguished French scholar, once observed that "the Atlantic Pact is a classical reply to a classical demarche."[1] Aron's reference is to the fact that the North Atlantic Treaty constitutes an alliance, and that alliance in turn represents an important element in international politics.

What Is an Alliance?

An alliance may simply be conceived as the power configuration of a state or group of states pitted against that of another state or states. It must be recognized, however, that alliances can assume various forms and be employed for different purposes.[2] Technically, an alliance differs from another contemporary form of military association, the collective security arrangement, in that in the former, states bind themselves to direct their military might against a specific target—an enemy state or states—whereas in the latter, as exemplified by the United Nations Charter, states agree to refrain from the use of force between themselves and to jointly resist aggression by an outside state.

The language of the North Atlantic Treaty suggests that it is a collective security arrangement. Article I provides that:

> The Parties undertake, as set forth in the Charter of the United Nations, to settle any international disputes in which they may be involved by peaceful means in such a manner that international peace and security and justice are not endangered, and to refrain in their international relations from the threat or use of force in any manner inconsistent with the purposes of the United Nations.

NATO, however, is best viewed as an alliance. Though not openly expressed in the Treaty, it is clearly understood that the signatories combined their military forces to oppose a common enemy: the Soviet Union. There were, of course, the political problems that the alliance had to confront, but over which the alliance did not have full authority. The two most important and pervasive have been the problem of nuclear weapons and nuclear strategic doctrine, and the reconstituting of German national independence and German rearmament through the formation of the Federal Republic of Germany.

Another distinction often made is that between offensive and defensive alliances. In an offensive alliance, states are said to combine for the purpose of territorial expansion. The agreement between Hitler and Stalin in August 1939 to divide Poland offers a good example of this form of alliance. In contrast, the members of a defensive alliance coalesce to protect themselves against an external threat. A good example here is the Rio Pact concluded between the United States and most of the states of Central and South America in 1947. In practice, however, such a distinction encounters considerable difficulty. Few states are willing to cast themselves in the role of the aggressor, and thus virtually all alliances claim to be defensive in nature. Even the Molotov-Ribbentrop Pact mentioned above was publicly hailed as a treaty of nonaggression.

The final test, then, is that of intent, which is difficult to apply objectively. For example, both NATO and the Warsaw Pact claim to be defensive alliances, but from its own perspective, each alliance fears that the other may in reality be an offensive alliance. The Warsaw Pact treaty even copies almost word for word the language of the North Atlantic Treaty. Thus, the distinction between offensive and defensive alliances is elusive and should be applied with caution.

Alliances serve other functions in addition to increasing the power of individual states and providing a means for their security. An alliance, interestingly, may be used to control or restrain one or more of its members. This may be accomplished partly through the creation of legal obligations and partly through the actions of other alliance members. For example, at various times NATO has been able to moderate the effect of the disputes between Greece and Turkey over the island of Cyprus.

Another function sometimes claimed for alliances is the maintenance of international order. Through the establishment of a visible configuration of power, it is argued, international politics becomes more regular, orderly, predictable, and therefore safer. But again, in practice, this goal has been difficult to attain. Throughout history alliances have been characterized either by atrophy or by smoldering internal dispute that has ultimately burst into flames to the detriment of all. Alliances may have postponed conflict but have never really managed to prevent it.

The use of alliances has unquestionably been a major element in the traditional international politics of Europe. Whenever one state has threatened to dominate Europe, others have joined together to meet that threat. The political history of Europe for the last two centuries may be viewed, at least in part, as a continual process of alliance formation and dissolution as the great powers and their smaller consorts sought the elusive goals of security and aggrandizement. If in 1812 Britain, Prussia, and Russia could combine to defeat the imperial Napoleon, why in 1949 should not Britain, France, and later West Germany coalesce to oppose the more contemporary threat of Soviet expansionism? True, crucial to the new pact was the United States, culturally if not geographically European, but the method remained the same: to ally in order to meet a common enemy.

Mr. Aron, after his observation on the traditional nature of the North Atlantic Treaty, went on to point out that the creation of an international political organization to institutionalize a defensive arrangement (NATO) constituted a new and unique phenomenon in the history of alliances: no alliance in modern history had created an actual organization to carry out its purposes or had been given such a sense of permanency. Yet this new organization, like the political commitment it served, has had its roots in the soil of classical European politics.

In 1815, following the defeat and permanent banishment of Napoleon, the victorious states gathered, at Metternich's beckoning, in Vienna, where they sought to devise a system that would prevent the occurrence of another such disaster in Europe. Drawing on the advice of Grotius as well as their own precedent of assembling in a "congress of nations," the foreign ministers elaborated a congress system through which a new order was to be created. This congress system called for the periodic assemblage of European congresses wherein the disputes among the great powers might be resolved through bargaining and compromise. While only four congresses and seven years were required to demonstrate the effectiveness of the states' political ambitions in preventing collaboration, the congress system did institute a new form of multilateral diplomacy and set the stage for the appearance of what has come to be styled "conference diplomacy."[3]

A century after the Congress of Vienna, the leaders of Europe, joined by those of the United States and other states affected by the First World War, met again, this time in Versailles, to devise a system that would prevent another devastation of Europe.[4] Drawing on the precedents of the congress system, the Hague conferences of the 1890s, and the efforts of individuals, including the president of the United States, the peacemakers at Versailles created an international political organization that they hoped would regulate the use of force among the states of Europe. In one sense the League of Nations was a more mature expression of nineteenth century desires to promote international cooperation through consultation; in another, it represented the desire to avoid another devastating war.

Even had it not been crippled from birth, when the United States failed to ratify its covenant, the League never possessed the strength necessary to fulfill its mission. Although it provided for methods designed to produce settlements on negotiable issues (such as "cooling-off" periods), the League lacked the ability to come to grips with the essential anarchy underlying the nation-state system as it had evolved in Europe. After earlier disappointments had laid bare the League's weakness—a weakness of will of the great powers—Europe was again unprotected from the ravages of war. Hitler's war was not a war of miscalculation; it was a war based on national policy:

> Out of forty-five million adult men three million fighters have organized themselves: they represent the political leadership of the nation. . . . Into their hands the people in full confidence has placed its destiny. But thereby the organization has undertaken a solemn obligation: it must see to it that this core whose mission it is to safeguard the stability of the political leadership in Germany must be preserved for all time.
>
> Insofar then as we devote ourselves to the care of our own blood—that blood which has been entrusted to us by destiny— we are at the same time doing our best to help to safeguard other peoples from diseases which spring from race to race, from people to people. If in West or Central Europe but one single people were to fall a victim to bolshevism, this poison would continue

its ravages, it would devastate the oldest, the fairest civilization
which can today be found upon this earth.

Germany by taking upon itself this conflict does but fulfill,
as so often before in her history, a truly European mission.[5]

And the League could not deal with what had not been envisioned
—a war deliberately calculated, in which the League was viewed
as a political object to be both manipulated and then discredited
and rejected.

The horrors of major wars spawn new initiatives for institu-
tionalizing peace. Building on the foundation of the League and
the lessons learned from Hitler's methods, the victors of the
Second World War, gathering in San Francisco, founded the
United Nations. This new organization, made effective through
great power cooperation and armed with the might of collective
security, was to dissuade any potential aggressor by bringing to
bear the overwhelming force of a "grand coalition" as represented by the permanent members of the Security Council. And
even if this deterrence should fail, the collective strength of the
states comprising the Security Council would ensure an aggressor's defeat. Yet like the League, much of the premise underlying the United Nations was unsound: by 1947 the great power
consensus, so essential for the United Nations' ability to function in security matters, was dissolving.

The Creation of NATO

In 1948, the states of Western Europe, recognizing the inability of the divided United Nations to preserve peace and fearing the success of Soviet advances in Eastern Europe, banded
together to oppose this new threat. The instrument of their
alliance was the Brussels Treaty, a fifty-year multilateral pact,
which reflected the Europeans' apprehensions and their traditional response to a "demarche." British Foreign Secretary
Ernest Bevin originally conceived of what was to become the
Brussels Pact as a series of treaties—between Britain and France,
Britain and Belgium, Britain and the Netherlands—patterned on
the earlier Anglo-French Treaty of Dunkirk. Although nominal-
ly aimed at Germany, in the spirit of the United Nations Charter, it was understood that the real target of the Dunkirk treaty

was the Soviet Union. Bevin presented his ideas to Secretary of State George Marshall at the London Conference of Foreign Ministers in December 1947. Marshall, in turn, reported Bevin's proposals to other members of the American delegation, including John Hickerson and John Foster Dulles. Dulles, after some thought, felt that a single multilateral treaty, similar to the Rio Treaty and thus provided for in the UN Charter, was preferable to Bevin's series of treaties. When a similar proposal came from Belgian statesman Paul-Henri Spaak, Dulles, through Marshall and Under Secretary of State Robert A. Lovett, was instrumental in persuading Bevin to follow their course. After a month of negotiations, the Brussels Treaty was signed on 17 March 1948.[6]

In April 1949, after intensive bipartisan consultation with congressional leaders by the Truman administration and a year of careful negotiations, the United States, now willing and able to expand the multilateral cooperation of the Marshall Plan into the security arena, joined with Western Europe in the North Atlantic Treaty, thereby combining American substance with European desires.[7] Although widely acclaimed throughout the West as a major diplomatic triumph, some dissension arose from unusual quarters. Conservative Republican Senator Arthur Watkins of Utah joined with the Soviet Union in attacking the North Atlantic Treaty as an instrument aimed at Russia and therefore unduly provocative.[8] Eddie Rickenbacker, air hero of the First World War, argued that the greatest mistake this country could make would be "to place too much faith in the North Atlantic Pact as a factor in world security."[9] His warning was echoed from across the Atlantic by General Charles de Gaulle, who attacked what he labeled the "chloroform team" for pretending that the North Atlantic Treaty guaranteed anybody's security, including that of France.[10] Perhaps the best note was sounded by Sir Winston Churchill, who interpreted British ratification of the North Atlantic Treaty as an "occasion for satisfaction but not triumph or exultation."[11]

In many respects NATO reflects the United Nations that it supplanted as the instrument of European security. The North Atlantic Council, composed of permanent representatives from the member governments, is the body's highest organ; the Military Committee and the Command Groups correspond to an expanded and effective implementation of the United Nations' abortive Military Staff Committee and international forces; and the International Staff/Secretariat carries out functions similar in many ways (but quite dissimilar in others) to those of the United Nations Secretariat.[12]

Originally, NATO consisted of a rather loose arrangement between three principal organs and was viewed more as a planning agency than as a functional international organization. The highest body was, of course, the Council, composed of foreign ministers. In the early years, the Council met periodically in rotation among the national capitals of the members. Below the Council were two specialized organs, the Defense Committee and the Defense Financial and Economic Committee. The Defense Committee, made up of defense ministers, was charged with preparing a defense plan for the alliance. This initial plan was submitted in April 1950. The Financial and Economic Committee, meanwhile, gathered data on defense expenditures and resources and attempted to develop methods for measuring costs and for working out financial arrangements to handle the transfer of military goods.

The original structure, however, proved unsatisfactory. The Council, meeting only periodically, could not provide continuous policy direction and coordination for the two committees. The alliance, as Dean Acheson described it, was "a body— or more accurately twelve bodies—without a head."[13] There had grown up a system of committees, and while these had met, they had "failed to produce continuing or authoritative direction."[14]

By the spring of 1950, when the Military Committee submitted its report, it had become clear that there existed a significant lack of coordination between the civilian and military branches of NATO. As a first attempt to remedy the situation, the Council, at its meeting in London in May 1950, created a permanent civilian organization, the Council of Deputies, to oversee the activities of NATO. Among the many functions of the Council of Deputies was the responsibility to ensure that problems of military forces and financial costs were not treated as separate entities but as one problem. This marked the beginning of an evolution of NATO structure, if the term evolution

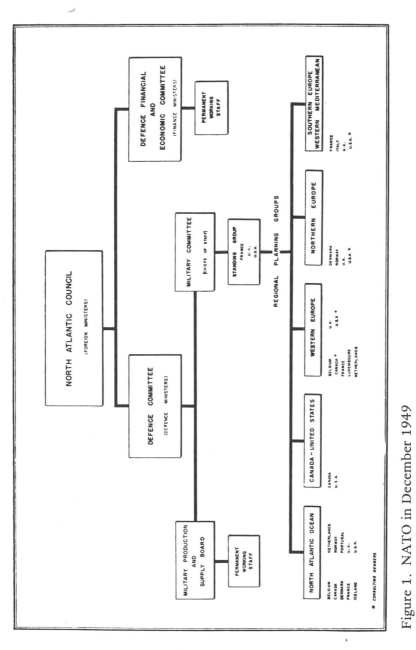

Figure 1. NATO in December 1949

Source: Lord Ismay, *NATO: The First Five Years: 1949-1954,* p. 26.

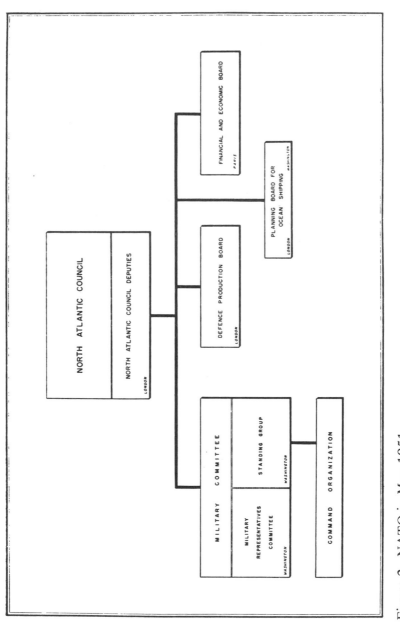

Figure 2. NATO in May 1951

Source: Lord Ismay, NATO: The First Five Years: 1949-1954, p. 42.

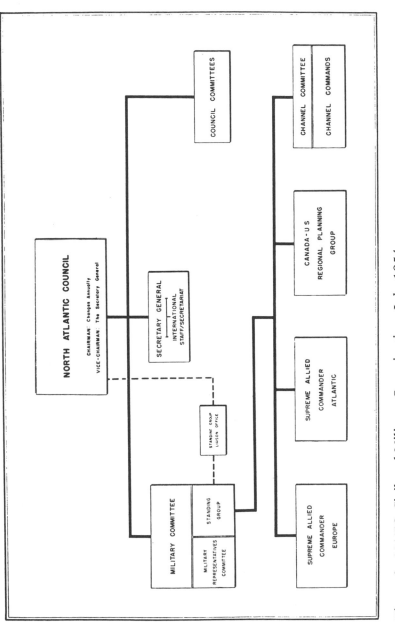

Figure 3. NATO Civil and Military Organization, July 1954
Source: Lord Ismay, *NATO: The First Five Years: 1949-1954*, p. 57.

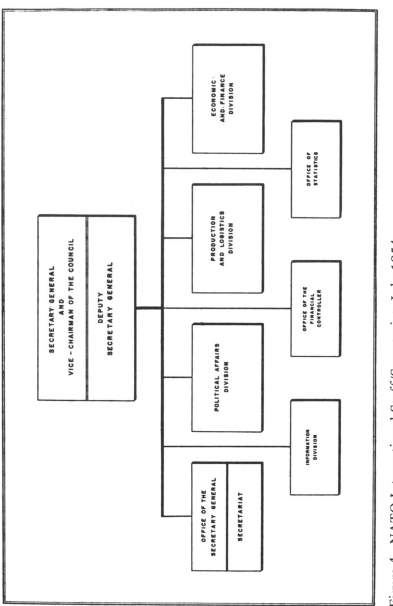

Figure 4. NATO International Staff/Secretariat, July 1954
Source: Lord Ismay, *NATO: The First Five Years: 1949-1954,* p. 63.

appropriately describes a process of bargaining and compromise. The development of NATO does not represent the conscious unfolding of a plan; it is more closely akin to the process by which a committee in attempting to create a horse instead produces a camel.

As the military side of NATO grew, it became increasingly apparent that the administrative organs of the alliance were unable to handle effectively the attendant military, political, and financial problems; further reorganization was necessary. Throughout the spring and summer of 1951 the Council of Deputies and its subsidiary organs undertook much of the preparatory work for this reorganization. At the Ottawa Conference in September 1951, the Council created the Temporary Council Committee (TCC). The TCC, although primarily concerned with the preparation of a comprehensive plan for production rates of military equipment and for force buildups, also examined the structure of the alliance. The TCC's report in December 1951 offered specific proposals for force targets and military standards for adoption by the alliance. It also underlined the need for improving and strengthening the nonmilitary structure of NATO.

These reorganization efforts culminated in the Lisbon Conference in February 1952. To solve the problems posed by lack of continuous policy direction, the Council was reformed. The Council was now to be composed of permanent representatives who would be in continuous session. Paris was selected as headquarters for the new organization. The Council was to be served by a secretary-general and an international staff that would absorb all existing civilian agencies. Under the secretary-general, the staff was divided into three major divisions—Political Affairs, Production and Logistics, and Economics and Finance—and three minor ones—Information, Financial Controller, and Statistics. The responsibility for staffing and defining the scope and direction of these new agencies fell to NATO's first secretary-general, General Lord Ismay.

The creation of the position of secretary-general and the International Staff/Secretariat at Lisbon reflected a compromise between American and British proposals. The United States had recommended a secretary-general who would guide the work of the Council with the rank of vice-chairman. Therefore, the secretary-general would have access to the Council and would have the power to submit recommendations. Beneath the secretary-general would be an international staff, divided into functional sections and composed of specialists approved by their governments. Underlying the American proposal was a desire to provide for a more competent and efficient organization with increased ability to coordinate governmental decisions and administer programs.

The British, on the other hand, did not wish to see the secretary-general participate directly in Council sessions, though they agreed he should have access to that body. They also felt that the staff should be relatively small and divided into two main groups, one to be concerned with military affairs and the other with economics and production. The British did not endorse the concept of a strong central organization and preferred a secretary-general who would not be involved in political matters; he would be restricted instead to the supervision and implementation of nonmilitary activities.

The compromise reached at Lisbon favored the Americans: the office of secretary-general contained within it the possibilities for playing an active role in alliance politics. This potential was increased later when the secretary-general assumed the chairmanship of the Council, replacing the rotating ministerial system for the position. The secretary-general thus found himself required to perform multiple roles: he was spokesman for the alliance, chairman of the Council, initiator of ideas, mediator, conciliator, negotiator, administrator, and international diplomat. How he would chose to fulfill these roles was an important—and open—question.

Multinational Diplomacy as a Function of the Alliance

Although the military aspects of NATO have received the most public attention, the concern of this book lies with the complex problems of multinational diplomacy as embodied in the International Staff/Secretariat and as focused on the secretary-general. Like other contemporary organizations designed to provide peace and security, the tradition of NATO international administration reaches back into the nineteenth century.[15] The International Telegraphic Union, founded in 1865, and the Universal Postal Union, created in 1874, were the first in what became a rapid proliferation of various international agencies whose functions included a diverse set of activities.

The origins of these international agencies may be attributed to a common perception among national leaders of a need for cooperation and coordination in many noncontroversial areas at a level above the nation-state. The success of these agencies derives in large measure from the noncontroversial aspect of their activities. The various international agencies of the late nineteenth century performed functions that, although important, did not protrude into the primary concerns of states—peace and security.

Within these international bodies there developed a form of organization that became the evolutionary parent of the structure of modern international organizations. On one hand, there emerged a permanent staff designed to carry out the purposes of the organization, which gave it a sense of permanency and coherence. On the other, the staffs and their functions became separated from the governing body of the organization, usually with some form of council composed of member states that set policy for the organization. This dual structure carried over into the twentieth century and can be seen today in the United Nations and in NATO. Both organizations are controlled by representatives from the member states and both have an independent administrative body or secretariat. However, the secretary-general of NATO, like his counterpart at the United Nations, differs from the heads of the earlier international organizations in one crucial respect: his functions, far from being nonpolitical, lie directly in the peace and security sector of high politics in the nuclear age.

The first coupling of international administration and international politics occurred in the League of Nations. To Sir Eric Drummond, the first secretary-general of the League, fell the responsibility for directly influencing the future scope and direction of international political administration. Drummond, wishing to avoid the conflict inherent in multinational control of administration, sought and effectively established a truly inter-

national secretariat and civil service based on loyalty to the
organization rather than the country of national origin. Drummond's visible participation in politics was slight; he rarely
entered debates and did not publicize his views. Yet he performed an important political function behind the scenes as
mediator and negotiator between disputing parties. Drummond's
successor, Joseph Avenol, preferred an active role for the
secretary-general but felt constrained by Sir Eric's precedents
and did not expand the scope of the office beyond the boundaries established by his predecessor.

At San Francisco, many envisioned an expanded role for
the secretary-general of the new United Nations. Although his
title was not changed to "chancellor," as the British wanted, or
to Roosevelt's formula of "World's Moderator," the first occu-
pant of the office, Trygve Lie, shared this vision, which he
did not hesitate to put into practice. Article 99 of the UN Charter, which provided that the secretary-general could bring important matters to the attention of the Security Council, gave
him a constitutional grant of power beyond anything possessed
by Drummond. Lie used his office and authority in an expansive manner; he was not content to be a mere civil servant but
strove to become a "force for peace."[16]

Both the nonpartisan and expansive approaches to international administration have been reflected in NATO. Lord
Ismay, like Sir Eric, was a product of the British cabinet system
and saw his role as that of an independent, responsible international civil servant. And like his British counterpart in the
League, Ismay felt his primary responsibility lay in the development of an effective administrative organization built on the
foundation of a genuine international civil service. The sympathies of Ismay's successor, Paul-Henri Spaak, were more closely
allied with those of Trygve Lie. Spaak attempted, with varying
degrees of success, to play an active role in alliance politics. He
did not consider it inappropriate to argue his views before the
Council or even heads of state, although de Gaulle's rebuffs
adequately demonstrated the limits of the secretary-general's
diplomatic effectiveness.

These divergent views and approaches to international politics and administration suggest a number of questions relating

to the secretary-general of NATO and his functions within the alliance. Who, for example, should define the roles of the secretary-general: heads of government, the Council, or perhaps the secretary-general himself? Additionally, what functions should he be assigned and in what areas? Where should he be restricted? What are the justifications of these roles and functions and what are the criticisms? And to go one step further, what historically have been the roles the secretary-general has played? And who have been the supporters and the critics, with what arguments?

Another suggestive set of questions involves the broader context of the alliance system. First, what are the characteristics of the system? What impact do events have on the system? And reciprocally, how does the system influence events? Focusing on the secretary-general, how is the scope of his office related to the system? How do events affect his office? And conversely, what is the impact of his personality on events? Finally, what relationship exists between the personality of the secretary-general and the definition and execution of his functions?

These questions that probe relationships, the source and direction of change, and the definition and justification of roles underlie the account of this book: its thrust is toward an exploration of the secretary-general as multinational political leader, both in a specific and in a general sense. The data are drawn primarily from interviews with the secretaries-general themselves and with many of their NATO colleagues. Memoirs and other historical sources are employed to buttress and amplify these often highly personal, though penetrating, interviews.[17] This particular approach to the secretaries-general permits the acquisition of insights and an understanding of individual interrelationships that, although vitally important in assessing the alliance as a political system, are often not easily perceived by an outside observer.

The study of multinational diplomacy, as developed in this book, represents only one of many possible approaches to the subject. Perhaps most dissimilar to this work are the studies of traditional diplomacy as epitomized by Sir Harold Nicolson.[18] The multinational diplomacy of today differs significantly from traditional diplomatic methods, making it somewhat difficult to analyze the secretary-general in terms of a historical framework that no longer fits. Somewhat more closely associated with this book are those works that focus on national elite decision makers.[19] Although these sources are valuable in terms of method, it must be remembered that there exist significant differences between the domestic and international political arenas. Another useful approach is that employed by Professors Robert Cox, Harold Jacobson, and David Kay in their exploration of the decision-making process within international organizations.[20] The present effort, however, while also concerned with structure and process, places relatively more emphasis on the thoughts and actions of individuals, and especially as they relate to one office and person—that of the secretary-general.

Perhaps this study could be said to derive from two sets of works. The first set comprises those studies that focus on national decision-making processes.[21] The techniques and models utilized in these studies can be effectively extrapolated to NATO and have proved useful in terms of organization and analysis. Second, those studies that examine the bureaucratic functions and politics within the European community have contributed to the attempt to interpret the bureaucratic and political interplay within the NATO system.[22] The major difference is that within the European community no clear leader emerges, whereas the concern here is with the secretary-general's ability to function in the role of a political leader as well as international administrator. The desire is to go beyond an analysis of NATO as a political system, or as a military coalition, in order to portray the secretaries-general as individuals within that system.

Notes

1. Raymond Aron, *Peace and War: A Theory of International Relations* (New York, 1968), p. 382.

2. Two other useful discussions of alliances may be found in Robert E. Osgood, *Alliances and American Foreign Policy* (Baltimore, 1968); and George Liska, *Nations in Alliance: The Limits of Interdependence* (Baltimore, 1968).

3. Cf. René Albrecht-Carrie, *A Diplomatic History of Europe Since the Congress of Vienna*, rev. ed. (New York, 1968); and Henry A. Kissinger, *A World Restored: The Politics of Conservatism in a Revolutionary Age* (New York, 1964).

4. On the development and evolution of the League and United Nations, see Inis L. Claude, Jr., *Swords into Plowshares: The Problems and Progress of International Organization*, 3rd ed. (New York, 1964); and Evan Luard, ed., *The Evolution of International Organizations* (New York, 1966).

5. Speech at Nuremberg, 3 September 1933. Quoted in *Adolph Hitler: My New Order*, ed. Raoul de Roussy de Sales (New York, 1941), p. 1208.

6. This account is developed more fully by Parley W. Newman, Jr., *NATO and the Defense of Europe* (Ph.D. diss., Columbia University, 1977).

7. Regarding American substance, former Secretary of State Dean Acheson makes the following observation:

> The signing ceremony for the NATO was dignified and colorful, with the President and Vice President of the United States standing on either side of me as I signed the treaty. The Marine Band added a note of unexpected realism as we waited for the ceremony to begin by playing two songs from the current popular musical play *Porgy and Bess*—"I've Got Plenty of Nothin' " and "It Ain't Necessarily So."

Dean Acheson, *Present at the Creation: My Years in the State Department* (New York, 1969), p. 284.

8. *New York Times*, 5 March 1949.

9. Ibid., 1 April 1949.

10. *Times* (London), 2 May 1949.

11. Ibid., 13 May 1949. The British had been, however, the closest collaborators with the United States in working out such a relationship. Also, even at this stage, France was the "odd man out"—being brought into the negotiations only after the groundwork had been laid between the British and the Americans.

12. For some comparisons and also a review of the evolution of Second World War coalition relationships into NATO, see Robert S. Jordan, *The NATO International Staff/Secretariat, 1952-57: A Study in International Administration* (London and New York, 1967). On the early structure of NATO see Lord Ismay, *NATO: The First Five Years* (Brussels, n.d.); and NATO Information Service, *NATO: Facts and Figures* (Brussels, 1971).

13. Acheson, *Present at the Creation*, p. 397.

14. Ibid.

15. The evolution of international political administration is briefly described in Part 1 of Jordan, *Staff/Secretariat.*

16. For a discussion of the origins of the secretariat system, see Robert S. Jordan, "The Influence of the British Secretariat Tradition on the Formation of the League of Nations," in *International Administration: Its Evolution and Contemporary Applications,* ed. Robert S. Jordan (London and New York, 1971), pp. 27-50; and Robert Rhodes James, "The Evolving Concept of the International Civil Service," in *International Administration,* pp. 51-73.

17. Of the four secretaries-general studied here, only three have left memoirs, and of those only two are full accounts of their tenure as NATO's chief officer. Lord Ismay's memoirs deal with the events of his life through his service in Churchill's cabinet following the Second World War. He chose to pass over his service to NATO, claiming that he could not effectively relate these experiences as he was still too close to them at the time of writing. The two complete accounts are those of Paul-Henri Spaak and Dirk U. Stikker, the second and third secretaries-general. Spaak's memoirs focus, as did his life, on the theme of European unity, and his account of his tenure as secretary-general is woven around this theme. Other aspects of his duties and responsibilities receive mention, but are not developed to the same extent. (The English version of his memoirs is an abridgment of the French and suffers from a mediocre translation. All quotes from Spaak's memoirs in the text are direct translations from the French edition.) Dirk Stikker devotes nearly a third of his memoirs to NATO, a fact that reflects the importance he attached to the alliance. Stikker's account is filled with detail, but as one of the more "activist" secretaries-general, much of what he says has been balanced against the opinions of others. Manlio Brosio, who is still active in political life, has shown no inclination to write his memoirs. For the account of his tenure as secretary-general, it was necessary to rely more heavily on interviews and other sources.

18. Harold Nicolson, *Diplomacy* (Oxford, 1963).

19. These include the traditional political biographies and the so-called psychobiographies. Perhaps the classic example of the latter is the work by Alexander George and Juliette George, *Woodrow Wilson and Colonel House* (New York, 1956).

20. See, for example, R. W. Cox, Harold Jacobson, et al., *The Anatomy of Influence: Decision-Making in International Organizations* (New Haven, 1973); and David Kay, ed., *The United Nations Political System* (New York, 1967).

21. One example from an extensive literature is Graham Allison,

Essence of Decision: Explaining the Cuban Missile Crisis (Boston, 1971).

22. See, for example, David Coombes, *Politics and Bureaucracy in the European Community* (Beverly Hills, Calif., 1970); and Leon Lindberg and Stuart Scheingold, *Europe's Would-be Polity: Patterns of Change in the European Community* (Englewood Cliffs, N.J., 1970).

Lord Ismay: The "Old Soldier" Turned Diplomat, 1952-1957

Introduction

Lord Ismay belongs to that now legendary group of public officials who developed, administered, and sustained the British Empire—an empire that enabled an island nation to achieve and maintain a position as a world power for four centuries. Born in India to a career civil servant, Ismay did not follow his father's example, choosing instead to serve with the Indian army.[1] After spending a year at the Royal Military College, Sandhurst, and another as a subaltern with the First Batallion of the Gloucestershire Regiment, he was assigned to the 21st Prince Albert's Own Cavalry at Risalpur in the North West Frontier. Seeking to broaden his experience, Ismay obtained a transfer to the Somaliland Camel Corps, arriving in August 1914.

When he learned of the outbreak of war in Europe, Ismay, like most of his fellow officers, applied for service on the Continent, but was refused. Instead, he spent the next five and a half years pursuing the "Mad Mullah" (Mahomed bin Abdulla Hassan) through the African hinterland. In a sense, his stay in Africa was fortunate, as fully half of his companions in the Indian cavalry lost their lives during the Great War.

After an extended leave in England, Ismay returned to duty in India, but his stay was short, as he had successfully completed the entrance examination to the Staff College at Quetta, in present-day Pakistan. For the next dozen or so years, Ismay alternated between staff positions in India and London, among which was a four-year stint beginning in 1926 as assistant secretary to the Committee of Imperial Defense, an assignment that would eventually involve him in the highest councils of state.

24

NATO ministerial meeting, Bonn, 2 May 1957. From left to right: Lord Coleridge, NATO executive secretary; Lord Ismay, NATO secretary-general; Professor Gaetano Martino, foreign minister of Italy, president d'honneur; Baron Adolph Bentinck, NATO deputy secretary-general. (Courtesy NATO Information Service)

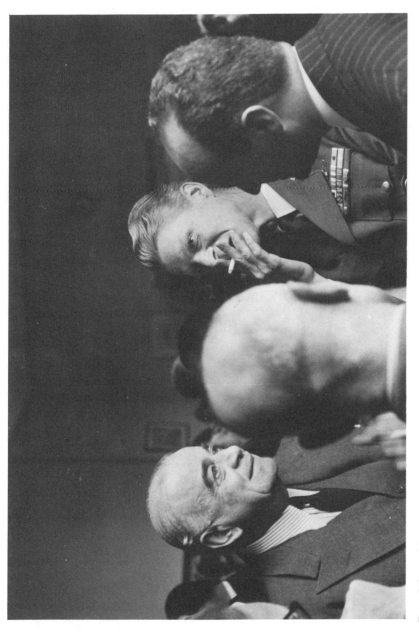

From left to right: Lord Ismay, NATO secretary-general; General Norstad, supreme allied commander Europe; H.E.M. André de Staercke, Belgian permanent representative to NATO. Date unknown. (Courtesy NATO Information Service)

NATO headquarters, Palais de Chaillot, Paris, October 1954. Ministers who had taken part in the Nine Power Conference (Paris Agreements). From left to right: P. H. Spaak, L. Pearson, P. Mendes France, K. Adenauer, G. Martino, J. Bech, J. Beyen, A. Eden, and J. F. Dulles. (Courtesy NATO Information Service)

When Churchill became prime minister and minister of defense in 1940, he made Ismay (or "Pug" as he was known to his global circle of friends) his chief of staff (military) and representative to the Chiefs of Staff Committee. Ismay thus attended most of the wartime conferences, including those at Cairo, Malta, Teheran, Quebec, Moscow, and Yalta, and participated in nearly all the major decisions of the war. "We became," said Churchill speaking of Ismay, "hand-in-glove, and much more."[2] The experience and esteem Ismay gained during the war were major factors in his appointment as the first secretary-general of NATO.[3]

Ismay's ability to work with the leaders of different states, his efficiency in executing complex plans, and his good humored patience contributed to his reputation as an adept administrator-diplomatist. The warmth and tact he displayed while occupying delicate and pivotal positions during the war years won him great personal respect and affection. He came to know well the military and civilian leaders of the major allied powers, among whom were many destined to inherit the responsibility for the welfare of the West in the postwar years: Eisenhower, Attlee, de Gaulle, Harriman, Bevin, Marshall, Eden, Montgomery, Mountbatten, Forrestal, and Beaverbrook.[4] With the establishment of NATO, these same men who had won the war were now in the forefront of preserving the peace against the new threats of a former ally.

With the conclusion of the Second World War, Ismay retired from military service and returned to two previous themes in his career: administration and India. He took charge of the reorganization of the British defense machinery, which he molded into a centralized ministry of defense, and he served as Lord Mountbatten's chief staff officer in the negotiations for the British withdrawal from India during 1947-1948. He also accepted other assignments from the Labor government, though as a private citizen and not as a member of a political party. When Sir Winston Churchill and the Conservatives were returned to power in October 1951, Ismay's old boss appointed him secretary of state for commonwealth relations.

Although his cabinet position required him to deal with new problems and to bear broader responsibilities, Ismay nonetheless maintained a close relationship with the prime minister as a consultant on defense affairs, on which he kept himself informed.[5] When Churchill came to Washington in January 1951 to discuss the Korean War and other problems of defense with his American counterparts, Ismay was among those who accompanied him.[6] "He knows the Prime Minister's mind," wrote the *New York Times,* "is fully conversant with the strategic situation and knows many of the men with whom he will be dealing in Washington."[7] The closeness of the wartime association between Ismay and Churchill seemed destined to carry over.

Before assuming public office, Ismay had spoken out, both

in the House of Lords and in print, putting forth his ideas on the requirements for stemming what was perceived at that time as an ever-expanding Soviet threat. He thought NATO insufficient, too narrow in scope, and inadequately organized to meet the global challenge of Soviet power. "Rather a lot of harness and too little horse" was the way he described the alliance.[8] Ismay wondered "whether some close adaptation of the Combined Chiefs of Staff organization would not be equally serviceable for the needs of the free world in our present situation,"[9] and called for a Combined Chiefs of Staff whose first task should be to "draw up an over-all unified strategic plan" to be used in the event of war with Russia."[10] This supreme council of war, he felt, was even more necessary after the conclusion of the Second World War when it could serve a preventive function, maintaining the peace and security of the world.[11]

Two years later, Ismay would look favorably on the policy of John Foster Dulles, as the American secretary of state sought to form a series of regional defense pacts to contain the Soviet Union. But in 1951 Ismay was troubled by the unilateral actions of the United States, especially in its prosecution of the war in Korea.[12] Ismay felt the allies must act in concert if they were to preserve their freedom. The lessons of the Second World War were clear on this point.[13]

Ismay strongly supported the appointment of General Dwight D. Eisenhower in late 1950 as the first NATO supreme commander, Europe (SACEUR). Eisenhower, Ismay felt, possessed unique prestige, qualifications, and experience. Shortly after Eisenhower's arrival in Paris, Ismay paid him a visit and came away "impressed by the team spirit which animated the members of the international [military] staff."[14] Eisenhower's ability to activate and to harmonize a multinational force, as demonstrated in the Second World War, was widely known and boded well for the future development of NATO's military arm into an effective defense mechanism. While Ismay heartily welcomed this development, he nevertheless noted that the alliance was still a group of sovereign states that retained their right to comply or not with the requests of the interallied command.

Given Ismay's experience, outlook, and ideas, his appointment as the first secretary-general of NATO would appear an obvious selection. In fact, however, the choice proved to be not such an easy process. At the beginning of 1952, a general reorganization of NATO's structure was in the offing. The Council of Deputies had been unable to fulfill its role as an expeditor, due to its lack of authority over the multiplicity of boards and groups, committees and subcommittees scattered among London, Paris, and Washington. As Ismay himself described the 1950-1951 period: "The increasing responsibilities assigned to NATO by member governments necessitated the centralization and simplification of the civilian agencies still too complex and scattered."[15] General agreement had been reached by mid-January that these bodies be amalgamated into a single international secretariat to be headed by a secretary-general. It was also agreed that the Council of Deputies should be replaced by a permanent and higher-ranking body with greater authority. The restructuring of NATO was to be completed at the meeting of the Council of Ministers scheduled for February in Lisbon.[16]

Churchill sent Ismay, as acting minister of defense, along with Foreign Minister Anthony Eden. Ismay's assignment was to handle military questions while Eden's was to deal with the political aspects of the conference. Prior to the conference there existed considerable skepticism in London as to whether twelve countries meeting around a table could effectively coordinate their military and foreign relations. As Ismay phrased it: "I thought it unlikely that any useful results would be achieved in a milling mob of this kind."[17] Although the Lisbon Conference did produce many important results, the particular style of mass diplomacy did not appeal to Ismay. The wrangling, he felt, was disagreeable, and he left Portugal remarking: "This is the first that I have seen of NATO, and thank heavens it's the last."[18]

Agreement on structural reform of the nonmilitary side of the alliance, however, left two problems still unresolved: where the headquarters of the new organization would be located and who would be selected as the first secretary-general. During the Lisbon Conference, Anthony Eden suggested London as the site for the permanent headquarters of NATO. His argument, based upon a centrality of location between America and Europe, reflected the British wish to maintain a semidetached relationship with the continental states. The continental states, on the other hand, feared that a London-based NATO implied a lack of American concern and, worse, an absence of commitment to a vigorous defense of Europe in the event of war. For this reason, most of the continental member states opposed London and favored Paris. The United States, wishing to placate European fears, gave its support to Paris. And with that support, Paris was duly selected.[19]

Seeking to compensate United Kingdom officials for their disappointment over the administrative compromise that favored the Americans and the choice of Paris over London, Secretary of State Acheson suggested Sir Oliver Franks, British ambassador to the United States, as secretary-general.[20] The invitation to Sir Oliver, however, was made public before ascertaining the ambassador's desires. When he declined the offer, the ministers were placed in an awkward position: whomever they picked would be unflatteringly labeled a second choice. The appointment of Canadian Foreign Minister Lester Pearson would have been a graceful way out, as it was common knowledge that he had initially been favored for the position. However, this became impossible when his government refused to make him available. It also would not have fitted the quid pro quo agreed to at Lisbon.[21]

The solution to the dilemma appeared when Prime Minister Churchill offered NATO his secretary of state for commonwealth affairs, Lord Ismay. Upon being offered the post by Eden, Ismay expressed his reluctance to leave the cabinet. Besides giving up his important position in the cabinet, part of Ismay's hesitancy may have stemmed from his desire to retire from public life. "I was tired of being a rolling stone," he later wrote, "and comforted myself with the thought that when my present job in the Cabinet came to an end, it was absolutely certain that I would not be required to roll any more."[22] And perhaps he was also influenced by the public knowledge that others had already refused the appointment.[23]

But true to the ideals of the public-spirited citizen, Ismay responded to his prime minister's plea to head the revamped organization.[24] "My arguments," he said, "were demolished one by one, and there was nothing for it but to surrender. Was the Prime Minister prepared, I asked, to state categorically that it was my duty to accept? 'It is your duty to accept, Pug,' was the immediate reply. That settled it."[25] Ismay was then sixty-six.

Ismay's appointment as secretary-general was widely welcomed. Among military men, his general's rank accorded him authority; diplomats remembered his blunt yet tactful charm; and political leaders expressed admiration for his executive talents. General Alfred Gruenther, NATO chief of staff, who would later be appointed SACEUR, called Ismay an "ideal choice."[26]

Ismay assumed office on NATO's third anniversary, 4 April 1952. The numerous committees and other subsidiary bodies to be located in Paris (except the Standing Group that remained in Washington) were gathered together under his direction. He also headed the International Staff/Secretariat which was to serve the newly created Council of Permanent Representatives.[27] As chief executive officer, Ismay was responsible for providing support to the Council and its committees. Further, he was to submit periodic reports on the progress of the alliance.[28]

Lord Ismay as Administrator

In addition to administrative and executive functions, Ismay had a sensitive political task to perform as vice-chairman of the Council, the organization's highest body, to which he was responsible. As the only nonnational member of the Council, but with powers to prepare papers and to take initiatives, he occupied an ambiguous place in organizational charts. With direct access to governments and NATO agencies, he hoped to take advantage of his position to act as a link between the alliance's civil and military wings. After assuming office, Ismay made a deliberate effort to pay official visits to all member governments for the purpose of opening the channels of access and generating the personal contacts he would need in his new role.[29] His aptitude for mediation between those who plan and those who execute would be well tested.

Ismay held definite feelings about the development of NATO. He wanted to see the organization expand into a policy-making institution for the so-called free world.[30] This growth was meant to encompass cooperation in the nonmilitary social, economic and political areas as provided in Article II of the North Atlantic Treaty.[31] This cooperation, Ismay felt, required a high level of representation on the Council; members of the Council should be cabinet ministers or political leaders. To supplement the structure, Ismay also envisioned the establishment of a regular NATO parliamentary meeting at which NATO decisions would be debated by the quasi-legislative body, just as defense questions were debated by the House of Commons in Britain.[32]

Ismay was further given the task of transforming the framework agreed to on paper at Lisbon into an effective working structure. This he did "with charm and great skill."[33] Assembling a staff, which he desired to keep as small as possible, was Ismay's first requirement.[34] Having insisted on complete power over staff appointments—he was quoted as saying, "you might as well get fourteen people to choose your wife for you"—he proceeded to put together in a short time a staff that emphasized as much as possible both geographic balance and quality.[35] Ismay also acted to create the position of deputy secretary-general. This was contrary to the expectations held at the Lisbon Conference, but for Ismay this step constituted a necessary response to the needs of the smaller member states to participate at the highest levels.[36] Jonkeer Henri van Vredenburch of the Netherlands was selected for this position, and the precedent of giving an influential role in the Staff/Secretariat to a smaller power has generally been honored.

Ismay's appointments reflected his desire to recruit a capable staff while avoiding the Anglo-American dominance that characterized the earlier structure. Although there was "no hard and fast rule as to the proportion of appointments to be held by each country . . . every effort [was] made to ensure an equitable distribution."[37] It is a curious fact that to this day many have expressed the opinion that "the Anglo-Saxons ran the show as an extension of the war-time Combined Chiefs-of-Staff."[38] Although as early as July 1954 there were about the same number of French and Belgians (seventy-two) in senior grades as Americans and British (seventy-five),[39] the *perception* of a "club" persisted. In the time of Brosio, an effort was made to redress the balance. Keeping the French actively committed to NATO was, of course, a primary task for all the secretaries-general.

Below the level of secretary-general and deputy secretary-general, Ismay's plans called for three major administrative divisions: political, economic, and production and logistics. An assistant secretary-general was to head each division. These three offices, following Ismay's desire to ensure national balance, were to be filled with appointees from the major powers, the United Kingdom excluded. Sergio Fenoaltea of Italy was nominated to head the Political Affairs Division. Fenoaltea, former Italian ambassador to China, had been a well-known figure in Italian politics for many years. The Production and Logistics Division went to an American, David L. Hopkins, a Baltimore banker who had become known for his philanthropic work. The French appointee was René Sergent as head of the Economic and Finance Division. Sergent, before his appointment, had been the financial attaché to the French embassy in London.[40] Of the three assistant secretaries-general, the latter was probably the most notable. Sergent, who later became head of the Organization for European Economic Co-operation (OEEC), successfully established a mutually beneficial link with that organization. OEEC statistical data proved useful to NATO for the evaluation of the economic and financial implications of its defense programs for the member states.[41] When Sergent resigned in March 1955, François-Didier Gregh, also of France and formerly with the World Bank, returned to Paris to take over the Economic Division.[42] Gregh became an important figure in NATO during his slightly more than twelve-year tenure.

Ismay took Captain Richard (later Lord) Coleridge along as his executive secretary. Coleridge, who had worked under Ismay during the war on secondment from the Royal Navy, was a highly dedicated, hardworking administrator. He also had the advantage of being strictly apolitical in the execution of his responsibilities. Coleridge took charge of the Office of the Secretary-General and the supervision of support for the Council and its committees, which included all secretarial assistance and the administrative services of the Staff/Secretariat itself.[43]

Some of the credit given to Lord Ismay for building an efficient
secretariat must be shared with Coleridge for an excellent effort
in assembling and running the organization.[44] Ismay, naturally,
was one of the first to recognize Coleridge's contribution to
NATO.[45]

As an administrator and organizational leader Ismay received
high marks. He was highly accessible, and his disarming style
enabled others to speak freely to him. He was generally well
liked and trusted, an indispensable trait for a multinational
diplomat at the head of a loose coalition of states. "His experience, his good nature, the affection and respect in which he
was held," wrote Ismay's successor, Paul-Henri Spaak, "enabled
him to overcome a great many obstacles."[46] The confidence
Ismay instilled in the staff and the respect he commanded from
governments and their leaders demonstrated his keen and continuing insight into their problems.

An illustrative example of Ismay's brand of effective administration (involving the derivation of a formula for sharing infrastructure costs) is, perhaps, best recounted in the secretary-
general's own words:

> They dumped the whole problem in my lap, so I called in three
> assistant secretaries-general, and each of us drew up our own list
> of what we thought the percentage of sharing should be, and then
> we averaged them out. I couldn't for the life of me possibly say
> on what basis I acted, except I tried to take into account all
> sorts of things like the ability to pay and whether the building
> would be going on in a country so that it would benefit from the
> construction and the money spent. The outcome was that in
> Council everyone agreed to take the percentage of costs assigned
> to his country for within 1.8 per cent, which was simply divided
> up among the fourteen members.[47]

For all the sensitive and important positions he held, Ismay
was a modest and charming man. His leadership of the Council
reflected his unpretentious manner. In speech and action, Ismay
always insisted he was the Council's servant. He eschewed any
posture of pressuring the ministers or their governments. His
method was to present his views quietly prior to Council sessions, and then employ a national representative to put his

proposals on the floor, although under Council rules he was empowered to do so himself.

Often Ismay's most important function at Council meetings, which he endeavored to keep short (he also favored short papers), was to sum up the discussion. Speaking succinctly and emphasizing points of agreement, Ismay would help steer the Council to a conclusion without relying on philosophical discourse. Ismay's relations with the Council clearly reflected his own experience with, and preference for, the subtle interplay between ministers and career civil servants that characterizes the British cabinet system.

At numerous formal and informal occasions, Ismay's outgoing personality and friendly understanding helped reduce the friction within the newly assembled NATO bureaucracy. For example, during his first year in office, Ismay undertook to visit the United States, Greece, Canada, and most of the other member states, where he made arrangements for liaison between the civil and military authorities of NATO and member governments. He did this while always keeping the Council fully informed of his activities.[48] The congenial atmosphere Ismay fostered in the Council itself facilitated full and frank discussion.[49] Thus, when in the summer of 1952 economic and political conditions in the United States, the United Kingdom, France, and the Netherlands led these states to reassess their defense budgets and contributions to the alliance, a revised plan was agreed to by the Council amicably and without rancor.[50]

To avoid bitterness when questions of politics, finance, or administration were before the Council, decisions were made unanimously. This procedure was also dictated by good sense and the political necessity of running an association of sovereign states. Ismay presided, and when agreement was difficult, he would invite the representatives of the dissenting parties to lunch at his home to settle their differences in a more informal and relaxed setting. One observer described the effectiveness of this tactic in the following words: "It is hard at all times to reject a compromise which Lord Ismay considers reasonable; after an hour or two of his hospitality, it becomes almost impossible."[51]

By adopting the report of the Committee of Three on Nonmilitary Cooperation in December of 1956, the members of the alliance agreed to make the secretary-general chairman of the Council. They also created the largely ceremonial position of president of the Council that permitted the continuation of the tradition that a foreign minister, selected in rotation, retained national direction of the organization through this titular position. Along with this increased responsibility came increased authority for the secretary-general. That the member states were confident in placing this authority in the hands of the secretary-general testifies to the skill and adeptness with which Ismay had presided over the Council's deliberations.

NATO Diplomacy under Lord Ismay

At the initial ministerial meeting of Ismay's incumbency, held in Paris during December 1952, Ismay submitted his first report on the progress of NATO activities outside the military field. Preparations for effectively widening the scope of the alliance, as provided in Article II of the North Atlantic Treaty, had occupied a major portion of the Council's time during the fall of 1951.[52] The Council was particularly concerned about political consultation and the establishment of concrete measures to increase political and economic cooperation.[53] Behind these concerns lay an awareness, which Ismay shared, of the unwanted but real possibility of NATO's becoming a static body. "It's hard," he said, "to keep up your enthusiasm when you are only on the defensive. And NATO must remain on the defensive."[54] The adoption of his report and the provisions for further detailed studies with a view toward promoting social progress, especially in application of Article II of the treaty, represented a preliminary movement in the direction of cooperation outside strictly military affairs.[55]

The December ministerial meeting also saw the Council's first effort at dealing with a situation outside the North Atlantic area. The Council adopted a resolution stating that the French forces in Indochina deserved the support of the allied governments, as their aims and ideals were in harmony with those of the Atlantic community.[56] Lord Ismay, concerned about the efficacy of NATO, viewed this development as a step in the

direction of a global defense posture that he felt was necessary
to contain effectively the threat of communism.

An example of Ismay's desire to see NATO become involved
in international affairs outside the North Atlantic area can be
seen in his attempt to deal with the dispute between Greece and
Turkey over Cyprus in 1956. When this long-standing feud
showed signs of turning hot, Ismay called a meeting of the
Council and suggested that mediatory efforts within the organization should be set in motion. Both the United Kingdom and
Turkey, however, opposed NATO's intervention, while the
Greeks insisted on the terms of a recent United Nations resolution calling for Cypriot self-determination. Because the United
States was unwilling to pressure the British, and because France
was embroiled in troubles in North Africa, Ismay was unable
to take any effective action within NATO and the issue had to
be dropped.[57]

The year 1956 also saw Khrushchev's momentous speech at
the Twentieth Party Congress. With Stalin dead three years and
the Russian succession now secure, signals emanating from the
Kremlin seemed to augur well for peace in Europe. But the
hope generated in Eastern Europe by the first secretary's pronouncements led only to unsuccessful demonstrations in Poland
and the quick suppression of a revolt in Hungary in the fall of
1956. The Soviet Union, it appeared, was more liberal in word
than in deed.

The NATO allies did not react particularly effectively to the
Soviet actions in Hungary, due largely to the suddenness of
events and their deep involvement in another crisis: the Suez.[58]
Acting to protect their interests, which had been threatened by
the Egyptian nationalization of the Suez Canal, and misreading
the American pullout of the Aswan Dam project, Israel, Britain,
and France in October of 1956 mounted an invasion of Egypt
in an attempt to seize the Canal. This action occurred without
any prior formal consultation of the NATO partners, although
there had been rumors. The failure of the attack, due in large
measure to the stern United States sanction in the United Nations Security Council against the invasion and the subsequent
strain on British-American relations because of bilateral pressures, served to underline the need for stronger consultation in

NATO among the member states prior to taking military initiatives outside the NATO area.

Because the strength of the alliance depended as much on the political unity of the members as on their military might, the North Atlantic Council, acting in response to the Suez crisis, sought to identify and define the means required to safeguard their cohesion. The Council created a committee of three foreign ministers, Lester Pearson of Canada, Halvard Lange of Norway, and Gaetano Martino of Italy, which was asked to "recommend measures designed to improve and develop our cooperation in various non-military fields and to strengthen unity within the Atlantic Council."[59] The report of the "Three Wise Men," submitted to the Council in December 1956, called for consultation to be initiated in the planning stages of policy formation when the interests of the alliance should be taken into account. The report also established the right of governments and the secretary-general to open for discussion any subject of common interest to the NATO partners.[60]

In line with these recommendations, the secretary-general was empowered to form a watchdog committee to settle disputes among the allies or to provide machinery for conciliation, mediation, or arbitration of such disputes. Furthermore, members of the alliance were expected to make use of the NATO framework to settle their disagreements before resorting to any other international body.[61]

Agreement to such prior consultation, however, did not come easily. For example, Secretary of State John Foster Dulles firmly opposed subjecting American policies concerning the defense of Taiwan to prior consultation. In effect, Dulles wanted to set limits on efforts to make NATO a political as well as a military body.[62] The European governments held different views. Heinrich von Brentano, West German foreign minister, proposed the creation of a bimonthly meeting of under secretaries of state whose purpose would be to coordinate policies. The British foreign secretary, Selwyn Lloyd, suggested the formation of an "Atlantic Assembly" similar to national parliaments. This was reminiscent of Ismay's earlier notion. But unable to produce anything more universally acceptable, the ministers unanimously adopted the report of the "Three Wise Men."[63]

One of the most important political questions facing the allies in the early 1950s was that of the participation of West Germany in Western defense. Although it was a question directly affecting NATO as a whole, special responsibility for Germany rested with the United States, the United Kingdom, and France (as occupying powers), and therefore many of the discussions concerning Germany took place outside of NATO. The heavy economic and military burden that the Korean conflict placed on the allies, most of all the United States, was the immediate event that precipitated these discussions. The United States government wanted Germany to provide twelve divisions for the defense of Europe in order to free American troops for use in Korea. But the French balked at the reestablishment of a German army, and the Germans wanted their sovereignty restored, if they were to contribute in the West's defense.

At a meeting of the North Atlantic Council in September 1950, Secretary of State Dean Acheson presented a package for meeting these objections; he proposed that West Germany contribute to a general strengthening of NATO forces and that a centralized command structure be established under which the German army would serve. French Foreign Minister Robert Schuman and British Foreign Secretary Ernest Bevin, however, had serious misgivings—Schuman remarking that French public and parliamentary opinion were totally opposed to any idea of German rearmament scarcely five years after the war's end. It was therefore decided to study the problem further until the next Council meeting.

The next month French Prime Minister René Pleven outlined a plan for a European army under a European minister of defense, and on 26 October 1950 the French National Assembly adopted the Pleven plan. A few days later, at a meeting of the Military Committee of NATO, there was agreement on the appointment of a supreme commander of allied forces in Europe and on the size of forces to be contributed to the collective defense, but there was none on the question of a West German contribution. In December, the North Atlantic Council invited the governments of France, the United Kingdom, and the United States to explore the matter with Germany. Subsequently negotiations were begun at Petersburg between the allied high commissioners and Chancellor Adenauer.

These negotiations were, however, superseded by the convening in Paris of a conference on the establishment of a European army. In April 1951, France, West Germany, Italy, and the Benelux states signed a treaty creating the European Coal and Steel Community, which provided for the joint development of these basic industrial resources. In July, the Petersburg negotiations were formally suspended and instead the Paris conferees approved a report recommending the establishment of a European Defense Community (EDC). By the beginning of 1952, the United States and the United Kingdom had both accepted the French idea as an acceptable way of bringing West Germany in to strengthen Western European defenses.[64] Besides creating a European army, the EDC would control overall defense production, letting out contracts for arms and supplies to individual member states.

The proposed EDC was a major topic of conversation among the foreign ministers of the alliance at their meeting in Lisbon in February 1952. A consensus was reached on the three interrelated subjects of the future of the Occupation Statute of Germany, West Germany's place in the EDC, and the EDC's relationship with NATO.[65] Anthony Eden spoke for the British government on those subjects, while, as mentioned earlier, Ismay was burdened with the long—sixteen hours total—and tangled negotiations on infrastructure needs and costs for the new integrated NATO command. It was, of course, at Lisbon that the reorganization of NATO's civilian structure was decided on, including the establishment of the office of secretary-general. By the time Ismay was appointed and took up his duties in Paris, the question of West Germany's participation in Western defense had been pretty well settled.

At its second weekly meeting after Ismay's arrival, the Council on 6 May 1952 adopted the text of the draft protocol on reciprocal guarantees to be established between the EDC and NATO. The protocol, which extended the guarantee of Article V of the North Atlantic Treaty to West Germany, could not be signed until the work on the EDC Treaty had been completed and it had been signed.[66] This occurred on 27 May, when also the Occupation Statute was abolished, West German sovereignty was restored, and ambassadorial relations between West Germany and the NATO allies were established.[67] Ismay's part in all of this had been restricted to working out the technical problems.[68] Once the treaty and protocol had been signed, he and NATO had to wait for the state signatories to ratify the conventions. The sooner the EDC Treaty was ratified, the happier he would be.[69]

Western defense policy hung on the ratification of the EDC for the next two years. Ismay was a supporter of the EDC as the best means for incorporating German forces in the defense of Western Europe and would seek another solution only if the EDC failed.[70] This was the common attitude among Western leaders and so no official alternative program planning was done, even though by the end of 1953 signs of French coolness to the idea of a supranational army had definitely surfaced. The Ministerial Council at its meeting in Paris in April 1954 re-affirmed NATO's support of the EDC Treaty.[71]

However, with the emergence of strong nationalist anti-EDC sentiment in France, it became apparent that the EDC was not likely to be ratified, and other alternatives began to be seriously considered. During Ismay's official visit to the United Kingdom in the early summer, the secretary-general discussed with British officials the possibility of direct West German membership in NATO.[72] After the French National Assembly rejected the EDC Treaty during the night of 29 August 1954, a solution to the problem of German participation in Western European defense through direct NATO membership appeared to be the most likely course. The demise of the EDC thus set in motion a series of events to accomplish the same goal, but through a less politically cumbersome method. Furthermore, the divergencies of 1950 among the major Western powers had largely evaporated: the desire of the United States to replace its troops with German units had subsided after a Korean truce was signed; French fears of a revitalized Wehrmacht had diminished in the four years since the idea had been broached; and the German wish to be treated as an equal was received more favorably as political and economic progress proceeded smoothly under Konrad Adenauer's strong leadership.

The negotiations on the conditions of West German participation took place primarily outside the Council. The six EDC signatories, along with the United States, the United Kingdom, and Canada, each represented by its foreign minister, met in London to work out a settlement. After a brief adjournment to secure final authorization and support from their respective governments, the participants concluded their work with the signing of the London and Paris Agreements on 23 October 1954. Under the agreements the German occupation regime was ended with an invitation to the Federal Republic of Germany to join NATO. The Brussels Treaty Organization was revived and retitled the Western European Union, and Britain and the United States agreed to guarantee French security against a rearmed Germany.

In short, the process of political normalization in Western Europe had begun. The termination of the Austrian occupation and the neutralization of Austria through the Austrian Treaty of 1955 can be directly attributed to the West's settlement of defense arrangements the year before. In addition, the agreement to hold a four-power summit conference in Geneva on 5 July 1955 seemed to bode well for the future of Europe as a whole, and it appeared that a new era in NATO's development was similarly possible.

After the Federal Republic of Germany acceded to the North Atlantic Treaty in the spring of 1955, Ismay visited Bonn to welcome the Germans to the alliance and to acquaint their government with its operation. Positions in the International Staff/Secretariat had been kept vacant for German nationals for six months in anticipation of West German membership. Similar arrangements at SHAPE had been reached with General Gruenther.[73] With this official reconciliatory embrace of the former belligerent, a new phase in the postwar era was opened; the political mistakes following the First World War had been avoided. Yet the NATO partners were to face numerous problems and conflicts of an entirely different nature. The so-called West German *ostpolitik* of the 1960s, the problem of how NATO could cope in the American-Soviet détente, and the negotiations in the 1970s leading to a conference of European security and cooperation can be seen as the further evolution of the process begun during Lord Ismay's tenure at NATO.

Lord Ismay's Relations with the Military

Many of the problems the allies were to face in NATO stemmed from the impact of technological innovation on the conduct of war. The establishment of a unified, multinational command structure (SHAPE) with General Dwight D. Eisenhower at its helm (SACEUR), represented a first and not unsuccessful response to the realization that security was no longer divisible. Eisenhower's wartime leadership made him a unique figure in postwar allied circles. His experience in working with an international staff was well suited to the tasks of welding together a peacetime military force and of setting up a European command headquarters. When Eisenhower departed after less than eighteen months to become involved in the race for the American presidency, the hero of the Korean War, General Matthew B. Ridgway, was called to replace him. After only fourteen months of service, General Ridgway was succeeded, in turn, by General Alfred M. Gruenther, who had served as chief of staff to both Eisenhower and Ridgway, and had been Eisenhower's choice to succeed him.

Ismay's relationships with NATO's military leaders were consistently good. He and Eisenhower had been wartime colleagues. When Eisenhower arrived in Paris in the spring of 1951 to assume command, Ismay spent a week with him renewing their acquaintance.[74] At that time Ismay was impressed by the team spirit that Eisenhower had instilled among the members of his multinational staff. Probably because of Ismay's own military background, the staff officers at SHAPE headquarters found it easy to do business with him even after Eisenhower left. Ismay was also quite successful in developing mutual understanding between the political and military branches of NATO. He sought to familiarize Council members with the military side of the alliance by bringing them to SHAPE headquarters frequently, by arranging for them to attend field exercises when possible, and by otherwise making sure that they acquired a knowledge of military problems. On the whole, it was felt to be most useful, from the military's point of view, for the politically oriented Council members to observe firsthand the operations of a major military command.[75] Indeed this close Council-SHAPE relationship caused some concern on the part of the Standing Group (U.S.–United Kingdom–France) and the Military Committee (located in Washington), which felt it was being left out.[76]

However, misunderstandings between the Council and SHAPE did occur from time to time. One such misunderstanding arose as a result of the exercise "Mainbrace" in which some NATO naval units might have come too close to Soviet territorial waters. Admiral Sir Patrick Brind (commander in chief, allied forces Northern Europe) had informed the individual governments of the extent of the exercise, but the question had not been referred to the Council. The normal procedure would have been to notify first the Standing Group in Washington, which would have then consulted the Council, but Admiral Lynde McCormick (supreme allied commander, Atlantic), the commander of the maneuvers, did not do this. After this episode, Ismay took steps to ensure that the Council would be consulted prior to any large-scale maneuvers.[77] To further facilitate political-military liaison, a joint meeting of the Council and the Standing Group was held under Lord Ismay's chairmanship. Ismay had tried to bring the two bodies together to form a more orderly system of coordination, conceiving their relationship as similar to that of a government and its chiefs of staff.[78]

Ismay's role as a conciliator and a behind-the-scenes expeditor is well illustrated in the selection of Eisenhower's successor. When Ismay learned of Eisenhower's desire to retire from SHAPE, he held several talks with U.S. Permanent Representative William H. Draper, as it was evident that the next SACEUR would also be an American general nominated by the president of the United States. Ismay followed up these discussions with a series of informal talks with each of the other thirteen allied representatives to ensure that their governments would agree to ask the United States to appoint a new commander and that there would be no objection to the individual selected. Ismay maintained continuous contact with Draper and the other permanent representatives, so that when President Truman nominated Ridgway, he was smoothly and unanimously approved.[79] The important point in this episode is that Ismay had been in office only four weeks.

In the area of alliance strategy, Ismay did not substantially change the views he had developed during the Second World War. Remembering the worldwide vision held by the Combined Chiefs of Staff, he advocated in 1951 that NATO likewise adopt this broad perspective: "Democracies should form the habit, have the means, of thinking together and acting together in all matters, be they great or small, in the interests of any of their number that are threatened, and further that the enemy should know without a shadow of a doubt that they are so aligned."[80]

He acknowledged that NATO as it was presently constituted could consider Far Eastern questions, for instance, only insofar as they referred to member states. As he said: "I am convinced the present solution is only a partial one, aimed at guarding the heart. It must grow until the whole free world gets under one umbrella."[81] The first step, Ismay believed, came within the ANZUS Treaty.[82] The treaty, which was a mutual security pact among Australia, New Zealand, and the United States resembling the North Atlantic Treaty, went into force on 29 April 1952.[83] In speaking of the need for coordination between NATO and the ANZUS Pact's Pacific Council, he told a joint meeting of the North Atlantic Council and Standing Group that "we cannot do our business except on a global basis."[84]

In a trip to the United States the next week Ismay would again try to persuade President Eisenhower and his advisors to accept responsibility for planning with its allies and friends on a worldwide scale, instead of piecemeal. In the Far East, the United States was leading the United Nations action in Korea, the United Kingdom was battling communist guerrillas in Malaya, and France was fighting the Vietminh in Indochina. Surely the democracies could devise some sort of cooperative arrangement against the growing communist menace.[85] As pointed out earlier, the United States as the global power was reluctant to place curbs on its independence of action and thus resisted any coordination that implied joint policymaking. As far as Washington was concerned, American foreign policy was to be made only there. Because many of the NATO member states supported the creation of a common strategic political body, Ismay persisted in seeking to persuade President Eisenhower of the advantages of a joint planning program. "Certainly, we must think out our defense on a global plan [sic]; nevertheless NATO groups the nations who are at the centre of the danger," he averred later in the year.[86] Ismay's plea, however, found little support in any branch of the American government, although the thrust of his proposal was not lost on the other NATO members.

With the reluctance of the United States to cooperate in allied global planning, Ismay toned down his proposals. When Dulles successfully engineered the formation of a South East Asia Treaty Organization (SEATO) on the model of NATO, Ismay merely offered to help the fledgling organization get started.[87] And when the Franco-British intervention in Egypt shattered allied unity, Ismay was not one to engage in post facto recriminations over the failure to have previously established joint policy planning mechanisms.

Ismay had more success in strengthening NATO's internal force planning procedures. The preparation of the Annual Review was a responsibility assigned to the secretary-general when the office was created in 1952. With his typical thoroughness, Ismay sent a questionnaire, which was about 200 pages long, to all member governments and based his report on a careful study of their replies. While not hesitating to report those states that had failed to reach their military targets, he was nonetheless careful not to single out any member for reproof.[88]

In the area of nuclear policy, there was considerable uncertainty as to the process by which the alliance should decide, or participate in the decision, to authorize the use of nuclear weapons in the event of hostilities. Such a decision was certainly political as well as military. "Everyone realizes," said Ismay, "that the use of the A-bomb is a political decision. No commander could take it without consulting his government."[89] For NATO, the decision presumably would be made unanimously by the Council. But the man in Europe directly in control of these weapons was the supreme allied commander, a member of the American armed forces, and there existed no provisions whereby the Council could control the SACEUR in this area. By inaction, the responsibility of decision was left to national authorities, and the secretary-general, given the sensitivity and intractability of the issue, was unwilling to press for a solution in favor of NATO. The virtual American monopoly on strategic and later tactical nuclear weapons, coupled with its unwillingness to share the control of these weapons, contributed to the difficulty of the situation.[90] It remained for Ismay's successors, and especially Dirk Stikker, to bring NATO to grips with this problem.

One major defense issue dominated Ismay's last days as secretary-general. The initial allied defense plans were largely drawn from the experience of the Second World War. NATO's defense strategy had always been to hold the enemy as far east as possible, and West German entry into the alliance required that the forward defense line be firmly established along the East German border. The concept remained essentially the same: maintain as large an armed force as far to the east as possible, in order to meet and hold in check a possible invasion by a numerically superior Soviet-led army.[91] Ismay, who along with the allied military commanders had experienced the Second World War, was comfortable with this idea. Thus, a buildup of NATO forces proceeded, albeit at a pace that fluctuated in response to the international political environment of the 1950s: in 1949, twelve divisions and four hundred aircraft; in 1950, fifteen divisions and twelve hundred aircraft; in 1954, ninety divisions and upwards of four thousand aircraft.[92]

The place of atomic and hydrogen weapons was given careful study by Supreme Headquarters and by national civilian and military officials. Yet no estimate of the effect of nuclear weapons on the military strategy of the alliance was included in force planning until 1954. Then, following rejection of the EDC Treaty and as part of the terms adopted in admitting West Germany to NATO, a reevaluation of troop requirements was undertaken. Two additional factors were included in NATO calculations: the contribution of the Bundeswehr and the introduction of tactical nuclear weapons. This latter, in turn, reflected the Eisenhower administration's desire to cut defense costs by getting "more bang for the buck."[93] Instead of the proposed ninety divisions, an "adequate minimum" of thirty was accepted. As part of the Paris Agreement, the United States and the United Kingdom undertook to provide and maintain as long as necessary—with certain stipulated reservations in case

of emergency, or financial difficulties in the case of Britain—
a certain number of their forces on the European Continent as
their contribution to the "shield."[94]

But, as often happens in international politics, unforeseen
circumstances led the governments party to the agreements to
alter their commitments. Upon the outbreak of fighting in
Algeria, the French reassigned five divisions from SHAPE to
North Africa. The Adenauer government in West Germany
decided to postpone conscription in response to domestic
opposition, with the result that the twelve German divisions
did not materialize on schedule. And in late 1956 the British
presented a plan to withdraw about one-third of its Army of
the Rhine from the Continent. This last move was opposed by
the new SACEUR, General Lauris Norstad, and it created a
minor crisis within the alliance.

General Norstad, formerly first air deputy at SHAPE, had
been named SACEUR in November 1956. A general at forty-
five, he came to the highest position in NATO with a reputation
as an outstanding military planner. Eisenhower described
Norstad as "the best organizer he had ever met."[95] And the
soon-to-be-appointed secretary-general, Paul-Henri Spaak, concluded that of all the SACEURs, Norstad was "one of the best."[96]
Norstad was also to demonstrate considerable political acumen.

As the SACEUR's advice was crucial for releasing Britain
from her treaty obligation, Norstad took a leading role in the
discussions among the allies. He cited military justifications for
retaining the British divisions: "The defensive forces deployed
on the eastern frontiers were an essential part of the deterrent."[97]
He also brought in political considerations: "The presence on
European soil of British troops . . . is a symbol. To Europe, it
signifies that Britain is with them right from the start."[98]

In speeches on both sides of the Atlantic, in press releases,
in his invitation to the permanent representatives to attend a
major military exercise of SHAPE, and in his formal report to
the Council of the Western European Union, Norstad sought
to forestall the British move. All the while Norstad was making
headlines and trying to influence the policy of a major alliance
power, Lord Ismay's voice was scarcely heard in public. Taking
a position directly opposed to the declared national policy of a

member of the alliance, especially his native country, was not his style. Furthermore, by the time the troop cuts were announced, Ismay had already let it be known that he would resign his post in the spring of 1957. As his successor had already been picked, Ismay no longer commanded the full authority of his position. He did, however, express one strong opinion: if economic reasons underlay the British decision to retrench, those reasons and no others should be advanced. If Britain were to try to soften the blow by raising the possibility of supplanting troops with an equal amount of firepower, then the signal might well be given for other NATO members to employ the same argument, in which case the ground troops composing the NATO shield would melt away.[99]

A compromise was eventually reached under which some withdrawals would occur, others would be postponed for further study, and some forces stationed in England would be earmarked for service on the Continent, if needed.[100] Just as he had not been a central figure in the efforts to forestall the British decision to cut its forces, Ismay was not directly involved in the bargaining that brought about a compromise, because this took place primarily within the Council of the Western European Union. Rather, much of the credit for that accomplishment must go to Paul-Henri Spaak, then Belgian foreign minister and soon to assume the secretary-generalship of NATO.[101] To do Ismay justice, however, it should be noted that the major reason cited for the troop cuts was that of economic exigency.

At the close of his term as secretary-general, Ismay could genuinely claim success in the primary tasks for which he had been appointed. He managed to build an efficient nonmilitary organization and, with the report of the "Three Wise Men," to launch it toward broader political and economic purposes. That same report indicated the need for the unified, imaginative political leadership Ismay always considered essential for NATO. Ismay also earned high marks for assembling an able staff and for his defense of the interests of the smaller member states. Both as an international civil servant and as chairman of the Council, Ismay won much personal affection and respect for the office he held. His personal warmth infused those with whom he worked and animated the organization he led. Though he never billed himself as "Mr. NATO" and preferred quiet persuasion to public display, Ismay nonetheless helped make the ideal of a peacetime defensive alliance a living entity.

Notes

1. The account of Ismay's early years is taken from his autobiography *The Memoirs of General Lord Ismay* (New York, 1960), hereinafter cited as *Memoirs*.

2. Winston S. Churchill, *The Second World War: The Gathering Storm,* 8 vols. (Boston, 1948), I:644.

3. One observer described Ismay as a "tactful go between, as 'an interpreter, one among a thousand'; he explained, he soothed, he suggested, he harmonized." J.R.M. Butler, *Grand Strategy,* 4 vols. (London, 1957), 2:250.

4. Eisenhower paid Ismay this tribute: "Ismay's position . . . was, from the American point of view, a critical one because it was through him that any subject could at any moment be brought to the attention of the Prime Minister and his principal assistants. It was fortunate, therefore, that . . . his personality was such as to win the confidence and friendship of his American associates." Dwight Eisenhower, *Crusade in Europe* (London, 1948), p. 487.

5. Ismay, *Memoirs,* pp. 452-53.

6. *Times* (London), 11 January 1952.

7. *New York Times,* 13 November 1951.

8. *Times* (London), 22 February 1951.

9. Ibid., 28 July 1950.

10. Ibid., 14 September 1950.

11. *Daily Telegraph,* 16 August 1951.

12. Ibid.

13. *Scotsman,* 24 June 1951.

14. Ismay, *Memoirs,* p. 456.

15. Lord Ismay, *NATO: The First Five Years, 1949-1954* (Brussels, n.d.), p. 48. For a fuller account, see Ismay, *Memoirs,* p. 28. See also the introduction to this book.

16. Ismay, *Memoirs,* pp. 458-60; NATO Information Service, *NATO: Facts and Figures* (Brussels, 1971), pp. 32-33. For a fuller discussion see chapter IV of Jordan, *Staff/Secretariat.*

17. Ismay, *Memoirs,* p. 458.

18. Ibid., pp. 459-60.

19. There were, of course, other considerations including prestige, advantage of access, and domestic influence. For a fuller discussion, see

Dirk U. Stikker, *Men of Responsibility: A Memoir* (New York, 1965), pp. 309-10; and Jordan, *Staff/Secretariat*, pp. 34-37.

20. At Lisbon, it had been felt previously that the position of secretary-general should be filled by a national of one of the smaller powers who would then be in a position to mediate between the large powers. This idea, however, was abandoned in favor of selecting a Briton. See Jordan, *Staff/Secretariat*, pp. 39-40; and *New York Times*, 15 March 1952.

21. Other candidates included Sir Edmund Hall-Patch, British ambassador to the OEEC, Dirk Stikker, Dutch foreign minister, and Halvard Lange, foreign minister of Norway. Lange, like Pearson, was not made available by his government. See Stikker, *Men of Responsibility*, p. 309; Jordan, *Staff/Secretariat*, p. 40; and *Financial Times*, 28 February 1952.

22. Ismay, *Memoirs*, p. 461.

23. *Manchester Guardian*, 7 March 1952, branded the search for a secretary-general as a "farce" and speculated as to who would accept the post "now after so many have rejected it."

24. One cannot help being struck by the remark on the first page of Ismay's memoirs: "in those days, commerce was not considered a suitable employment for a gentleman." Public service was.

25. Ismay, *Memoirs*, p. 462.

26. *New York Times*, 5 April 1952.

27. See chapter VI Jordan, *Staff/Secretariat*; and NATO Press Release, 4 April 1952. See also the introduction to this book.

28. Ismay, *The First Five Years*, pp. 55, 62-65; *New York Times*, 5 April 1952.

29. Ismay, *The First Five Years*, p. 62.

30. *Daily Telegraph*, 16 August 1951.

31. *Manchester Guardian*, 30 October 1952. This is also alluded to in Ismay, *Memoirs*, p. 456.

32. *New York Herald Tribune*, 3 April 1955.

33. Stikker, *Men of Responsibility*, p. 310.

34. *Manchester Guardian*, 4 April 1953.

35. *Times* (London), 19 April 1952.

36. See Ismay, *Memoirs*, p. 461; *New York Times*, 13 February 1952; and Jordan, *Staff/Secretariat*, p. 118.

37. Ismay, *The First Five Years*, p. 62.

38. 30 (3) and 33 (5).*

39. Ismay, *The First Five Years*, p. 67. This attitude probably had

---

*Notes coded in this manner refer to personal interviews conducted by the author. Individuals consented to interviews as long as their remarks would be unattributed. A wide sample as to nationality, role in NATO, and relationship to the secretary-general was obtained.

more substance on the military side, in regard to the distribution of command posts.

40. Jordan, *Staff/Secretariat*, p. 119; and *New York Times*, 10 May 1952.

41. See Jordan, *Staff/Secretariat*, p. 212.

42. *Times* (London), 14 March 1955.

43. Ismay, *The First Five Years*, pp. 62-64.

44. 24 (1).

45. See, for example, Lord Ismay's letter to Robert S. Jordan, printed in Jordan, *Staff/Secretariat*, p. viii.

46. Paul-Henri Spaak, *Combats Inachevés*, 2 vols. (Paris, 1969), 2:109; 24 (1).

47. Quoted in Alastair Buchan, *NATO in the 1960's* (London, 1960), p. 13.

48. *Manchester Guardian*, 23 April 1953 and 29 May 1953.

49. 27 (1).

50. *Financial Times*, 21 August 1952.

51. *Daily Telegraph*, 10 May 1957.

52. Ismay felt this article was unique to the North Atlantic Treaty and deserved careful attention and implementation. Ismay, *Memoirs*, p. 456.

53. *New York Times*, 19 September 1952; and *Manchester Guardian*, 30 October 1952.

54. *New York Times*, 22 May 1952. See also, Ismay's remarks later the same year advocating "pooled sovereignty." *Times* (London), 19 September 1952.

55. *NATO Facts and Figures*, p. 28.

56. Ibid.

57. *Scotsman*, 23 April 1952.

58. For a fuller description of the Suez Crisis and its effects on NATO, see Jordan, *Staff/Secretariat*, pp. 71-79; Spaak, *Combats*, 2:255-61; and Stikker, *Men of Responsibility*, pp. 263-70.

59. Spaak, *Combats*, 2:106.

60. For the full text of the report, see *NATO: Facts and Figures*, pp. 335-57.

61. Ibid.

62. See, for example, Secretary Dulles' speech of 8 May 1956 (NATO Speech Series, no. 78, NATO Information Service).

63. For a fuller discussion, see Jordan, *Staff/Secretariat*, pp. 72-75. As developed in the next chapter, this report was initially seen as an important tool by Ismay's successor, Paul-Henri Spaak.

64. *Times* (London), 11 January 1952.

65. *Times* (London), 22 February 1952; and 28 February 1952.

66. *Times* (London), 7 May 1952.

67. *Times* (London), 27 May 1952.

68. See, for example, *Times* (London), 13 May 1952.

69. *Times* (London), 27 October 1952.

70. *New York Times,* 19 April 1953.

71. *Times* (London), 24 April 1954.

72. *Times* (London), 30 June 1954.

73. *New York Times,* 5 July 1955; and 6 July 1955.

74. Ismay, *Memoirs,* pp. 456-57.

75. 27 (2).

76. *Times* (London), 9 October 1952; and 27 (2).

77. *Manchester Guardian,* 9 October 1952.

78. *Times* (London), 28 October 1952.

79. *New York Times,* 29 April 1952.

80. Quoted in the *New York Times,* 26 February 1953. Ismay's opinion echoed that of his friend and patron, Churchill, who thought it a great pity that "the Combined Chiefs of Staff Committee was allowed to lapse" in the first place. Speech to House of Commons, 30 November 1950, in *Winston Churchill: His Complete Speeches, 1897-1963,* 12 vols., ed. Robert Rhodes James (New York, 1974), 8:8134.

81. *Manchester Guardian,* 9 October 1952.

82. *Times* (London), 30 October 1952.

83. Draft text in *Department of State Bulletin* 25 (23 July 1951): 148-49.

84. *Times* (London), 20 February 1953; and *Daily Telegraph,* 20 February 1953.

85. *New York Times,* 26 February 1953.

86. *Times* (London), 4 April 1953.

87. *Times* (London), 6 July 1954.

88. The preparation of the first Annual Report put a heavy strain on the Staff/Secretariat, and its successful conclusion represented a significant milestone in NATO administration. See Ismay, *The First Five Years,* pp. 92-97; and Jordan, *Staff/Secretariat,* pp. 214-224. The procedures used were derived from the earlier Marshall Plan experience.

89. *New York Herald Tribune,* 31 October 1956.

90. For a good discussion of the problems surrounding nuclear sharing and control, see the relevant chapter in section II of Timothy W. Stanley, *NATO in Transition* (New York, 1965).

91. The Soviet army stationed in East Europe had been about 175 divisions since 1947. In addition, in 1957 there were about 20 satellite divisions and 6,000 aircraft.

92. Ismay, *The First Five Years,* pp. 101-12.

93. For an excellent study of the evolution of the Eisenhower "New Look" policy, see Samuel P. Huntington, *The Common Defense: Strategic Programs in National Politics* (New York, 1961). For a stinging criticism of the "New Look," see General Maxwell D. Taylor, *The Uncertain Trumpet* (New York, 1960).

94. See Protocol No. II (on Forces) Modifying and Completing the Brussels Treaty of the Western European Union, 23 October 1954 (NATO Information Service).

95. Quoted in Spaak, *Combats,* 2:263.

96. Ibid.

97. *Manchester Guardian,* 30 January 1957; see also *Times* (London), 30 January 1957.

98. Ibid., 11 February 1957.

99. *Times* (London), 15 February 1957.

100. The full text of the communiqué of the WEU specifying the precise terms of the agreement can be found in the *New York Times,* 20 March 1957.

101. *Times* (London), 19 March 1957.

Paul-Henri Spaak's Effort at Forging an Alliance Diplomacy, 1957-1961

Introduction

The second secretary-general of NATO, Belgian statesman Paul-Henri Spaak, presented a striking contrast to his predecessor. "I'm a politician," he quipped in answer to an attempt to engage him on a technical matter, "a politician, not a diplomat; never a civil servant."[1] Unlike the more retiring Lord Ismay, Spaak enjoyed the excitement and challenge that came from being in the spotlight. He displayed great zeal, personal magnetism, and not a little brilliance in the many political roles he filled in the more than forty years of his public career—roles he often played with theatricality.

Born in 1899, Spaak received a classical education, learning to admire rhetoric and logic. From his training he developed a marked ability as a persuasive and moving speaker, and was once described as "perhaps the most accomplished orator" in Belgium.[2] From his father, Paul, who left a profitable law practice to devote full time to the stage as a playwright, Spaak inherited his dramatic flair.[3] His mother, Marie, may be credited for endowing her son with his passion for political life. From an eminent liberal family—her father, Paul Janson, was a leader of the Liberal Party—she moved left into the Socialist Party where, starting as a suffragette, she remained active as a senator beyond her eighty-third birthday.[4]

Never one to miss a chance to get into the fray, Spaak, at sixteen and cheating on his age, sought to escape occupied Belgium during the First World War in order to join his country's army on the Yser. Captured before crossing the border, he spent two years in a German prison camp. Yet in spite of this hard-ship and delay, Spaak managed to earn a law degree and was registered to practice by the age of twenty-two. However, he soon abandoned the bar for politics, which he had entered while at the university and where he earned a reputation as a leftist agitator. In 1925, he worked as secretary to a socialist cabinet minister, but resigned the next year rather than participate in a grand coalition government led by the right-wing opposition. He spent the next few years as the editor of the doctrinaire Marxist fortnightly *Bataille Socialiste.*[5]

In 1932 Spaak won election to parliament as a leader of a militant faction, Action Socialiste. But with increased respon-sibility and age, Spaak moderated his views.[6] In 1935 he first entered the cabinet. Telephoning his mother, he announced: "This is your son. If anything happens to your telephone, let me know. I am now Minister of Transportation and Com-munications."[7] A year later he became foreign minister and in 1938 prime minister. He held one or the other or both of the two offices almost continuously until he accepted the invita-tion to become NATO secretary-general in 1957.

Spaak pursued his political career—bedeviling opponents, exhorting followers, leading demonstrations—with an intense energy that carried over into his private life. As a youth he was a tennis player of international rank, noted for the ferocity and guile of his game. In later years, a preference for more sedate games such as bridge and table tennis, combined with a fond-ness for good food and wine, of which he was an excellent judge, transformed his athletic profile into the rotund figure so well known to the world. Spaak also enjoyed watching soccer and the ladies. His favorite slogan, *"Je m'obstine"* ("I persevere"), indicates his propensity for tenacious and bold action.[8]

After the Second World War, Spaak directed his energies into the movement for Western European unity. Coming from a small state twice ravaged by war in his lifetime, it was under-standable that he should advocate regional integration. As a member of the Belgian government-in-exile in London during the Second World War, Spaak was able to observe at firsthand the destructive possibilities of unbridled nationalism and hence the potential benefits of international cooperation. Spaak felt

NATO headquarters, Paris. Date unknown. From left to right: A. Douglas Home, foreign minister of the United Kingdom; P. H. Spaak, NATO secretary-general; Dean Rusk, American secretary of state. (Courtesy NATO Information Service)

NATO headquarters, Paris. Press conference, December 1959. From left to right: C. E. Shuckburgh, assistant secretary-general for political affairs; V. Massenet, NATO assistant press officer; P. H. Spaak, NATO secretary-general; H. Lange, Norwegian foreign minister, president of the North Atlantic Council; E. Key, NATO press officer. (Courtesy NATO Information Service)

NATO headquarters, Paris. Date unknown. S.E.M.P. de Leusse, French ambassador to NATO (left) and P. H. Spaak, NATO secretary-general. (Courtesy NATO Information Service)

that the only sure method to prevent another war in Europe
was to unite Europe politically, and so he dedicated the next
twenty years of his life to that effort. Of all the undertakings
in which he had been engaged, Spaak later wrote, "that which
led to the founding of a politically and economically united
Europe is that which most animated me, that to which I gave
the most heart, dedication and will."⁹

Even before the end of hostilities, Spaak began his efforts
toward creating unity. In February 1945, he held economic and
commercial talks with his counterpart in Paris. Even in these
early talks Spaak was looking toward the development of a
more multilateral plan, which many felt involved at least a
customs union.¹⁰

The international community first became aware of Spaak
at the United Nations Conference in San Francisco. As the most
articulate spokesman of the smaller powers, he led the assault
on the veto. Though unable to dislodge it from the Charter,
his efforts were rewarded by his election as president of the first
United Nations General Assembly held in London in 1946.¹¹

Spaak's vision of Western integration and international cooperation gave coherence and meaning to many of the compromises
he sought and the bargains he struck. His initial splash in international affairs on the world scene at the San Francisco conference
revealed his internationalist views; Spaak ardently supported
those Charter provisions that would establish order under some
variant of world government through the application of international law underwritten by an international army. Spaak described the ideal international society as "one wherein all nations
will be named equal under the law, ready to accept international
law as conceived by the majority and upheld by powerful armed
forces."¹² Hostility to the veto represented a logical corollary,
and further reflected Spaak's insistent, almost religious, belief
that global survival in the atomic age rested on the ebbing of
national sovereignties. Yet at San Francisco Spaak properly
distinguished between the ideal and the possible. The small
powers, he said, "must bear in mind two points of view equally
important: to do nothing to make more difficult an agreement
between the great powers and to defend at the same time the
essential interests, moral and material, which they represent."¹³

After his tenure at the United Nations, for which he showed impatience and disappointment, Spaak returned to Europe where he began anew his efforts to create what he deeply desired—a United States of Europe.[14] Setbacks did not affect his indefatigable diplomacy nor weaken his firm conviction that every strand of integration adds to the fabric of unity. Spaak had begun to explore, perhaps as much as any other individual, the possibilities of supranational authority before the Second World War ended. Immediately thereafter, he was one of the architects of the Benelux Union, which for many purposes acts as a single unit. He presided over the Council of Europe for two years, resigning in 1950 because of the Council's failure to extend its powers beyond consultation.[15] He labored for the Organization for European Economic Cooperation (OEEC) and the Brussels Treaty Organization, or Western Union (WU), and was deeply involved in bringing the Six (Benelux, France, Italy, and West Germany) together in the European Coal and Steel Community (ECSC). The defeat of the European Defense Community proposal saddened Spaak, but his hopes soon rebounded with the reestablishment of momentum provided by the negotiations for a European Economic Community (EEC) and an atomic energy pool (EURATOM).

As "the non-partisan, hard-driving chairman of the intergovernmental committee" responsible for the EEC and EURATOM treaties, Spaak earned much praise.[16] His deft handling of the negotiations was rewarded with the rapid approval of the treaties by the Six. For Spaak, this represented a personal victory as the treaties committed the signatories to surrender eventually aspects of their sovereign power to a supranational body, a step that with some foresight he feared might never happen. "There must be success here," he was quoted as saying. "This is Europe's last chance."[17]

Spaak also hoped for changes in the decision-making structure of the community. Specifically, he wanted the community's parliament to be directly elected by citizens all across the Continent, rather than appointed by the parliaments of the member states as they were at that time.[18] Only in this manner could the European Economic Community acquire legitimate political authority and aspire to supersede its constituent member states.

With the inauguration of the EEC on 25 March 1957 in Rome, Spaak turned his energies to yet a larger political arena: NATO. As Belgian foreign minister, Spaak represented one nation of nine million people; as a molder of the EEC, he had influenced the lives of some one-hundred and sixty million people in six countries; as secretary-general of NATO, he was to serve fifteen governments embracing four hundred and fifty million people.[19] The rejuvenation of the alliance, the coordination of foreign policies, the maintenance of defense programs, and the mobilization of support for a wide range of multinational activities presented a set of vastly complex problems that Spaak found most attractive.

"I like changing jobs and facing fresh challenges," Spaak wrote: "These changes make one's life so much richer."[20] Yet it was not only the thought of new challenges and personal growth that attracted Spaak to NATO: after the strains of the Suez Crisis of 1956, he deeply felt the alliance needed help. Spaak believed his "overriding mission [was] to restore vitality and strength to the alliance between the United States and Western Europe that guarantees the principles on which Western civilization rests."[21]

Spaak's concern for NATO lay more on the political than on the military aspects of the alliance. "An alliance," he told the Conference on the North Atlantic Community, "which is and which continues to be, whatever its success, a purely military alliance would in the ultimate analysis be weak and in danger."[22] Thus Spaak directed his efforts as secretary-general primarily toward strengthening political cooperation and consultation within the alliance. "This task, of reinforcing the political side of NATO, of coordinating policies and avoiding crises—of preserving the Atlantic commonwealth—this is the larger one," is the way Spaak phrased it.[23]

Yet it is doubtful that Spaak would have accepted the secretary-generalship without the provisions of the report of the "Three Wise Men," which concluded that:

> The fundamental fact is that the nation-state, by itself and relying exclusively on national policy and national power, is inadequate for progress or even survival in the nuclear age. . . . No state, however powerful, can generate its security and its welfare

by national action alone. .... [T]he transformation of the Atlantic
Community into a vital and vigorous political reality is as important as any purely national purpose.[24]

The foreign ministers of NATO had adopted the report's
prescription—to strengthen relations, eliminate conflict, and promote conditions of stability among their countries—during the
same Council session at which Spaak was appointed. The means
recommended involved increased cooperation on the political,
economic, scientific, and cultural planes. The authority that the
report gave the secretary-general to deal with these issues constituted one of the principal justifications for Spaak's acceptance
of the post.[25] "It was a matter of record," wrote one observer,
"that the Council first issued the mandate calling into being
the Committee on Nonmilitary Cooperation and that it was
fulfilled before Spaak was elected. But so congenial was the
coincidence between its conclusions and the man, that the order
might have been reversed."[26]

Another positive aspect of the report's provisions, as far as
Spaak was concerned, lay in the prominence accorded economics.
Political cooperation and economic conflict were not reconcil-
able. It was in NATO's interest to seek the resolution of economic disputes among its members before they resulted in
political or strategic repercussions damaging to the alliance, as,
for example, in the case of Suez. Therefore, the economic as
well as the political field required a genuine desire among the
members of the alliance to work together and a readiness to
take into consideration, in the planning stage if possible, the
interests and views of other governments.

The report included an expansion of the secretary-general's
authority to enable him to carry out his responsibilities more
effectively. The secretary-general was given the right and duty
(already given to member governments) to bring to the attention of the organization any matter that, in his opinion, may
have threatened the solidarity and effectiveness of the alliance.
He was also empowered to offer his good offices at any time to
the parties of a dispute, and, with their consent, to initiate or
facilitate procedures of inquiry, mediation, conciliation, or
arbitration. (Lord Ismay had originally taken advantage of this

prerogative in the case of the dispute over Cyprus.) Though impressive on paper, the means at the disposal of the secretary-general were decidedly limited compared to the centrifugal forces tearing at the alliance: divisions on colonial policies, strains imposed by defense requirements, doubts about American intentions, and the demands of the French, to name but a few.

Spaak came to NATO with definite ideas about the role the Atlantic alliance should play in world affairs and the lines along which it should evolve. Although he had advocated neutralism during his political adolescence, Spaak had since vehemently eschewed that policy. He favored taking firm but not intransigent stands vis-à-vis the Soviet Union. A self-proclaimed independent and free thinker, he claimed kinship to the staunchly anticommunist, socialist-humanitarian tradition, which traces its lineage back to Bernstein and the utopian socialists. Spaak believed the communists had abdicated the right to be leftist, meaning the belief in social progress and the advancement of the welfare of the working class.[27] In his view, communism had evolved into a form of totalitarian tyranny whose aims of world domination were a danger to peace everywhere. But its threat was not merely economic or social; its ambition was to be the wellspring of a new civilization in which the essential foundation of the West's intellectual, moral, political, and spiritual life would be negated. Spaak put it this way: "Our whole spiritual inheritance which is, after all, our most important possession, is threatened by this system which claims to be a universal doctrine borne on the tide of history."[28] The overriding mission of the alliance remained, therefore, the same as when it was founded in 1949: to maintain the security of the North Atlantic area, and to guarantee the principles on which Western civilization rested—respect for individual rights and human dignity and the exercise of government through the consent of the governed.

Military preparedness was still the key to keeping these values safe, and this included the stationing of American ground forces in Europe. The maintenance of aircraft and missile bases on the Continent was an insufficient guarantee for most allied governments, for without a covering strategic deterrent force, which included United States forces in Europe as part of the "tripwire," Europeans might feel themselves to be primary targets of Soviet missiles and aircraft without an assured American involvement in the event of attack.[29]

But the fact that NATO was reaching beyond defense measures, as the Committee of Three's report indicated, was of crucial importance to Spaak. His hope clearly embraced the construction of a broader North Atlantic community in which the United States and Western Europe would continue to work together. He did not rule out an eventual confederal arrangement; in the short-term it would likely begin with closer economic ties, a free trade area and perhaps aid-sharing programs. It was with an eye toward the goal of helping integrate further the Western world that Spaak took up the gavel as NATO's secretary-general.[30]

Spaak embarked on his new assignment with an assist from an old friend and trusted colleague, André de Staercke. De Staercke, the Belgian permanent representative at NATO, was already at the end of 1956 the doyen of the Council and would remain so throughout the period covered in this book. Well acquainted with Spaak's style and philosophy, de Staercke was one of the first to tempt him with the possibility of taking up the challenges of the job of secretary-general. When Spaak decided to leave the confines of national politics, de Staercke conducted the negotiations that led to Spaak's appointment.[31] Spaak assumed office on 16 May 1957. His qualities of perceptiveness, indefatigability and originality were seen as the right combination for the times.

It has been said that if Spaak had been from a larger country he would have been a molder of history.[32] Doubtless aware of his potential, Spaak attempted to fulfill a similar role as the primary political leader of the alliance.[33] This he did without flamboyant appeal, for, although possessing a compelling personality, he was largely indifferent to the ceremonial and social aspects of his office, preferring to concentrate on substantive issues. Sometimes plagued by gout, he entertained relatively infrequently.[34] In contrast to Lord Ismay, who made the Villa Said—the secretary-general's official residence—a center of hospitality, Spaak hosted few parties and also paid little attention to protocol.[35]

This is not to imply that Spaak was unsociable. On the contrary, he enjoyed pleasant personal relationships with his colleagues. He was usually available to greet visitors and was never reluctant to give them, or anyone else, his opinion. Spaak enjoyed talking, preferring French to English.[36] He delivered most of his speeches in French but attempted otherwise to strike a balance between the two official NATO languages.[37] He once remarked while touring the United States that he looked like Churchill and spoke like Charles Boyer, but would prefer resembling Boyer in figure and Churchill in speech.[38]

Spaak had a quick, restless mind, preferring movement and action to contemplation. He relished the constant give and take of politics. A long-time practitioner of the art of compromise, he became one of the best. As one observer expressed it, "if M. Spaak has not actually formulated a theory of compromise, he is one of its greatest practitioners on the diplomatic playing fields.[39] "Of course," added a student of Spaak's diplomatic style, "he doesn't believe in compromise as an end in itself, but regards it as a vehicle for reaching the goal that is greater than the principles of dispute standing in the way."[40]

Indeed, one of Spaak's strengths as secretary-general was his ability to serve as the mediator in a dispute. When acting in this capacity he did not hesitate to put aside precedent or bend principle if it would help the parties find common ground. Because he was not an expert in any one field—not even economics—his solutions often minimized technical factors. Some of the victims of a Spaak compromise have uncharitably commented that his indifference to technical matters masked plain ignorance.[41] Perhaps more justly Spaak should be viewed as an imaginative, flexible, and effective negotiator who ceaselessly sought grounds for an accommodation between disputing parties.

Spaak's frankness was tempered with a pragmatism that could at times turn him reticent.[42] For example, during the late 1950s the balance-of-payments deficits that the United States had been running since 1951 began to cause concern in international financial and political circles.[43] At this time, United States monetary and political officials began pressing for a reduction in the large U.S. contribution to Western defense and urged European members of the alliance to pay their "fair share" of the costs. Spaak, however, was unwilling to become involved in the technical and ticklish debate as to precisely what constituted an equitable burden. Fortunately, the West Germans, mindful of the economic and military benefits of having American troops on their soil, were willing to contribute enough financially to offset, if temporarily and partially, Washington's requirements. In late 1959, with Secretary of State Christian Herter's reassurance that the United States had no intention of abandoning its commitment to Europe, the Bonn government agreed to provide a contribution of $250 million beyond its previous budgeted allotment, together with an increase in West German payments for equipment.[44]

A characteristic of men like Spaak, who see the wider sweep of history and are able to communicate their vision to animate others, is often little interest in administration and the details of day-to-day operations.[45] For example, when taken with the idea of developing NATO's relations with the Soviet Union, he wanted to see to it himself rather than utilize the normal diplomatic channels.[46] One probably exaggerated story had it that Spaak seldom read a cable or memorandum and relied entirely on newspapers and his intuition.[47]

Bilateralism, Multilateralism, and Summit Meetings

It was fortunate for Spaak that he came into office at a time of reinterpretation of the functions of the alliance. Reference has already been made to the report of the "Three Wise Men." This broad-gauge report was completed at the end of 1956, so that Spaak found it waiting for him when he moved to Paris in May 1957.

The next step was to put the recommendations of the report into action, and that involved a great deal more than having the NATO Council solemnly accept the report, or indeed than having the foreign ministers act on it at one of their regular meetings. To get the maximum effect it was decided to call a "summit" meeting of the heads of government of all the NATO states, the first such meeting at that level. To give time for preparation, the date was fixed for December 1957. It was a NATO Council meeting but at the highest level.

The feature of the report of the "Three Wise Men" given the greatest attention at the summit meeting was *consultation* in all its implications, and the meeting gave Spaak exactly what he needed to apply his political talents. The history of postwar "summitry" is long and varied, but this one was a clear success. One of the detailed conclusions reached, helpful to Spaak, was that the NATO secretary-general was to be the presiding officer at all NATO meetings at whatever level. Another innovation was the creation of an economic committee, though its functions were not well defined, nor were its relations with other international economic organs such as the OEEC made clear. As one indication of American support for a broader NATO political consultative role, it was announced that the U.S. permanent representative on the Council, at that time W. Randolph Burgess, would attend meetings of the president's cabinet and the National Security Council when he was in Washington.[48]

As can well be appreciated, under these arrangements Spaak's style of leadership in the Council contrasted sharply with that of his predecessor. His style was highly personal; unlike Ismay, Spaak felt free to interject his thoughts on items under consideration.[49] When a permanent representative first broached a subject or reopened an old one, Spaak would encourage full debate, in which he took an equal part.[50] He was happy to lead discussions on a wide range of issues, including for example, mainland China and the offshore islands, the Congo, and Southeast Asia.[51] During the first half of Spaak's tenure, the Council held over seventy special sessions to discuss political problems.[52] A long-time observer of the NATO scene was convinced that NATO would have been nothing without the added political consultations Spaak instituted.[53] The political atmosphere in Paris was simultaneously more pragmatic and speculative than it had been during Lord Ismay's time.

The Council's greater involvement in global questions called for a number of changes in its routine and in the supporting work of the Staff/Secretariat. Political affairs were usually handled directly through the secretary-general's office, while economic, military, and administrative affairs were shared by

François-Didier Gregh, deputy secretary-general for defense coordination and assistant secretary-general for economics and finance, and Lord Coleridge, executive secretary. Sometimes this arrangement resulted in a bypass of the Political Affairs Division, if a matter required quick or secret action by Spaak. As the secretary-general felt high politics to be his personal domain, it was not unusual for him to keep his chief subordinates less than fully informed in the interests of confidentiality.[54] On occasion this created a problem for Sir Evelyn Shuckburgh, assistant secretary-general for political affairs, and André Saint Mleux, Spaak's *chef de cabinet.*[55]

The Council's involvement in subject areas previously reserved for national or big power forums introduced a high-level note into its regular sessions.[56] Spaak, as in his treatment of the Cyprus affair, demonstrated that he was competent to handle matters of major international political importance.[57] He bristled against the notion that NATO was merely a collection of sovereign states that were obliged to consult the organization only when one of them needed extra support, and he opposed any attempt by the larger members to dictate policy on the expectation of its automatic adoption. The great powers merited positions of leadership but should not of their own accord authorize alliance policy.[58] Spaak felt debate and the airing of dissenting opinions to be vital functions of the Council. If the former were the case, the smaller member states would eventually find the dictation of policy so annoying as to encourage them to abandon the enterprise. The smaller states were, in fact, capable of opposing independent action by the larger members. This Norway demonstrated at the 1957 heads-of-government conference, when it refused to accept those portions of the communiqué that had been drafted without its participation.

Spaak was convinced that the ultimate aims of the alliance were best served when consultation was fully practiced. The process he championed worked well during the Berlin crisis of 1958-1959 and the Middle East flare-up of 1958.[59] Regarding the latter incident, Spaak declared that "Britain and the United States were absolutely right when they sent troops into Lebanon and Jordan earlier this year. They had acted after full consultation with their Atlantic partners in the NATO Council."[60] In the former instance, although the Western answer to Premier Khrushchev's demand that the occupying powers withdraw from West Berlin was worked out among the foreign ministers of the Big Four, their conclusions were afterwards discussed and endorsed by the entire NATO Council.[61] Spaak believed that an Atlantic policy could evolve only when such procedures for consultation were routinely followed.

To gain acceptance for this conception, Spaak obviously needed the cooperation of the permanent representatives and their governments. He realized that he could neither issue instructions to representatives nor expect governments to make policy solely on the basis of the advice of their NATO diplomats.[62] But Spaak did feel that a collective judgment was far superior to a collection of judgments. His efforts to produce a collective judgment were on occasion, however, hindered by his own strong beliefs and frank retorts.[63] And on occasion governments would react adversely to his prodding, or, worse yet, would give only minimal acknowledgment to his designs.[64]

The inclination of the big powers to bypass NATO and deal bilaterally, much to Spaak's chagrin, increased with the interest in bilateral summit diplomacy displayed during the latter 1950s and early 1960s. In February 1959, British Prime Minister Harold Macmillan and Foreign Secretary Selwyn Lloyd were received in Moscow, where they hoped to ease the pressure of Khrushchev's 27 May deadline for the transfer of Soviet control of East Berlin to the East German government. From May through the summer of 1959, the foreign ministers of the occupying powers met in Geneva for talks on Germany. In August the vice-president of the United States, Richard Nixon, visited the Soviet Union, and in September the Soviet premier accepted the invitation of President Eisenhower to visit that country. (The "spirit of Camp David" generated by that visit was the high point of this period of summit diplomacy.) February 1960 found the Italian president in Moscow, and in March Khrushchev journeyed to Paris. The summit conference scheduled for May 1960 in Moscow was to be the culmination of these visits, but it was never held because of the U-2 incident. With its failure, an end came to the round of high-level contacts until a new American administration took office the following year.

While heads of government were caught up in the whirl of jet age summitry, Spaak expended considerable effort in an attempt to persuade the major powers to shift their gaze from the summit to the foundation. Thanks largely to Spaak's efforts, the members of the Council were kept informed and were allowed an input on East-West issues. Spaak, ever the political realist even in the promotion of his own ideas, did not expect NATO to be able to unify all the conflicting policies of its members on contentious issues. But on European concerns he was demanding. At the ministerial meeting, held in Washington in April 1959 to commemorate NATO's tenth anniversary, the Council received a report and a personal briefing on the principles that the foreign ministers of the Big Three and West Germany had agreed on as guidelines for their May conference in Geneva with the Russians. At this session the Council devoted most of its time to a discussion of the Western position on the related problems of Berlin, Germany, and European security.[65]

Spaak's persistence and persuasiveness helped in achieving continued consultation between the Council and the foreign ministers of the Big Three through the end of the 1959 Geneva meetings on Germany. Consultation, however, declined during the year preceding the ill-fated East-West summit of 1960.[66] Spaak became extremely upset when he learned that the heads of government of the United Kingdom, France, the United States, and West Germany planned to meet in Paris in December 1959 to complete plans for a united front for their May encounter with the Soviets. He insisted that a report be made to the full Council. Originally, the government leaders were scheduled to meet following the Council's adjournment, but thanks largely to Spaak, arrangements were made to sandwich the Western summit between Council sessions in order to permit the Big Four to hear the views of the smaller powers on any potential settlement in Europe.[67]

Afterwards, Spaak could say with some satisfaction that "we have begun again to consult fully and this is a very good procedure."[68] Spaak's efforts were also meant to assuage the fears of such middle powers as Italy and Canada that they were being crowded into the background. Beyond that, the smaller member states were much concerned over the terms of a settlement that would affect them as much as it would those who negotiated it. Spaak's suggestions for the institutionalization of consultation was in part an effort to formalize the role of the smaller members.

Another, and more personal, project that Spaak tried to advance called for the conjunction of national efforts to aid the less-developed countries. "It is in Africa and Asia that the destiny of the free world will be decided," Spaak told an audience late in 1960.[69] At a minimum, a long-term NATO policy should be formed to help those less-developed states that were resisting communist domination. This policy would be conceived in a "spirit of collective generosity" to counteract Russian economic penetration in the Middle East and Africa.[70]

Spaak asserted that the Soviet Union's success could be attributed to two basic factors. The primary factor lay in their emphasis on commercial rather than altruistic standards in aid dealings. The Soviet Union did not simply give aid, which implied a patron-client relationship; rather, it bought and sold, albeit offering generous credits or barter terms at exchange values above those prevailing on the world market. The Soviets employed long-term contracts to insulate these transactions from the fluctuations of the world market. They were skilled in the art of drawing maximum advantage from their economic agreements and thus averting adverse political and psychological reactions while still advancing their own interests.[71] Second, their efforts were concentrated on those developing states most susceptible to their influence. They were careful not to dissipate their resources by spreading them too widely.

Initially Spaak's idea for a concerted Western economic policy toward the developing states was enthusiastically received. In the United States it received the editorial endorsement of the influential *New York Times*.[72] On the other side of the Atlantic, Antony Nutting, British minister of state for foreign affairs until the Suez debacle, was lavish in his praise for the plan and for Spaak, "a statesman who understood the Soviet economic threat." Nutting thought that Spaak was best qualified to lead an international agency that would harness Western capacity to compete economically with the Soviets and that would settle disputes arising from national competition or jealousy among the allies.[73] Nutting's scheme was more ambitious than the one Spaak proposed; yet Spaak probably approved of the former's deductions. President Eisenhower gave Spaak's suggestion some support at the heads-of-government meeting in Paris.[74] Belgian foreign minister Victor Larock similarly urged the establishment of a comprehensive Atlantic Economic Union.[75] And many others recognized that a coordinated economic policy would go far toward solving NATO's essential dilemma: the greater NATO's success in deterring aggression, the more susceptible it would become to internal dissension. An active role in promoting economic development would minimize the negative role placed on the organization as a defensive military alliance.[76]

Spaak's plan, however, soon met opposition from the United States. W. Randolph Burgess, the U.S. permanent representative to NATO,[77] had great respect for Spaak's talent as a politician, negotiator, and leader, but was simultaneously concerned by the secretary-general's weakness in the field of international economics, especially regarding NATO, Western Europe, and Atlantic economic policymaking. Spaak and Burgess spoke often with one another with the result that their views on a possible economic function for NATO, even though somewhat divergent, did not affect other important matters. Spaak wanted NATO to acquire sole authority in the area. Burgess wanted NATO to deal only with economic affairs related to the alliance, while the primary authority would remain in the OEEC. This difference in viewpoints persisted throughout Spaak's relationship with the United States.

The outcome of the first consideration of alliance economic policy produced a mild victory for Spaak. At the ministerial council in Copenhagen in May 1958, the foreign ministers reached a compromise on the issue. In the communiqué it was recognized that consultations on methods and machinery for closer economic cooperation would take place, although there was little commitment to concrete action. The Council created an economic committee that was to meet regularly under the chairmanship of the assistant secretary-general for economics and finance. The committee was mandated to consider factors that would affect economic growth in member states with a view to garnering support for their defense efforts and to providing a framework for discussions of problems of common interest.[78] This constituted a gesture towards implementation of Article II of the treaty. Thus an acknowledgment was made of Spaak's point that a purely defensive military organization could not effectively survive in peacetime. In the discussions at Copenhagen, the United States had been unenthusiastic, although it did approve of the limited resolution.[79]

It appears, however, that the only substantive issues discussed in the economic committee were those relating to East-West economic relations and the economies of the Eastern bloc states.[80] There was, in fact, no specific charge given to the committee to take up the problems of the developing countries, but alternatively there was no bar to the investigation of such questions. The actual topics considered by the economic committee, and then perhaps referred to the Council for action, would be settled by the preferences of its members. Spaak must have hoped that once the committee was established, he would be effective in fostering efforts to enlarge the committee's tasks.

This period marked a Western European preoccupation with international economic cooperation: the Common Market and the European Free Trade Association (EFTA) were both barely under way, and there was thus a certain amount of spillover of economic subjects into NATO's affairs. The British, who were opposed at that time to the concept of a common market, were trying to foster the idea of an Atlantic free trade area under the auspices of the OEEC. Reginald Maulding of the United Kingdom made a strong bid for extending the OEEC to absorb the common market, which ran counter to Spaak's desire to have NATO become the central organ of Western unity, economic as well as political.

Therefore, Spaak continued to lobby for his plan after the meeting in Copenhagen. He had gained status with the adoption of his suggestion to lessen secrecy about alliance affairs and to provide more information to the press. This suggestion was aimed at attracting more headlines for NATO in order to revive interest in it among the publics of Western Europe and North America. The argument that the Cold War was as much a battle of ideas and interest as of anything else could help Spaak to convince the foreign ministers to give greater public access to NATO affairs.[81]

Spaak, who was then enjoying great prestige, pressed his plan for a NATO economic function at the NATO parliamentarians conference in November 1957 and continued his efforts the following spring at the ministerial meeting in Washington.[82] Summarizing NATO's achievements on the occasion of its tenth anniversary, Spaak was able to use the platform to contrast those achievements with its deficiencies in the economic field; he warned that the alliance "has seriously compromised . . . [its] success in the military and political fields" by neglecting to take steps in the economic field.[83]

Soon after, however, Spaak was decisively outmaneuvered by the United States. After laying the groundwork in the autumn of 1959, the Americans persuaded the European members at the December ministerial session of the Council to consent to a restructuring of the OEEC. A working group of four was appointed early the next year to recommend more precise details of the overhaul. Ambassador Burgess was made the group's chairman. The formation of a broad committee within a restructured OEEC, to consult on policies for aiding the less-developed states (independently of Cold War connotations), had been a complementary aim of the United States and thus became a part of the agreements that resulted in the expansion of OEEC into the Organization for Economic Cooperation and Development (OECD). The OECD, expanded in membership to include Canada and the United States, then incorporated within it the Development Assistance Group (later the Development Assistance Committee [DAC] of the OECD), which included neutral states like Sweden and Switzerland, and which had been in operation pending a final decision on reorganization of the OEEC.

Spaak was naturally upset with these developments, for the appearance of the OECD and particularly the creation of the DAC made any NATO-centered Western economic organization appear remote. But his conception of such an organization was

also not popular with many Europeans, because it appeared to
them to have a Cold War political overtone, especially as he was
prepared to exclude Switzerland and Sweden.[84]

With the signing of the OECD agreement on 14 December
1960, the battle seemed lost, but Spaak was not one to surrender
easily. He scaled down his proposal and presented it to the
ministerial meeting later the same week. His revised proposal
recognized that the alliance was not the appropriate agency for
administering aid programs; it should instead consider the
political aspects of the programs engaged in by its members.
Spaak stressed that the Soviets had adapted their Cold War
tactics to include economic relations toward less-developed
countries. The OECD, he added, should be technical or operational, leaving NATO to be advisory and political in economic
matters.[85] But the merits of the revised plan were clearly inferior to those of the original; there were now sound arguments
to be made against it on the basis of duplication of effort. The
birth of the OECD had stolen away its raison d'être. The United
States therefore had no compunction against staunchly resisting
any effort that would challenge its policy of excluding NATO
from any involvement in Western aid programs to the developing states. There already existed a tension in the aid process,
because the donor, if he attempted to influence unduly the
recipient, would be left open to the charge of interfering politically in the affairs of the recipient government. The United
States wanted to avoid any further risk of alienating those
neutrals in the Third World it was seeking to court. The revised
Spaak plan thus received its final setback at what was his final
ministerial meeting as secretary-general.

De Gaulle and the September Memorandum

In retrospect Spaak's term as secretary-general can be
divided into two periods, with the ascension to power of
General Charles de Gaulle marking the turning point.[86] If
Spaak's role in the Cyprus crisis typified his diplomatic method,
and if his concept of an Atlantic community with a global
economic outreach represented his political aspirations for
NATO, then de Gaulle's directorate proposal and *force de frappe*

symbolized respectively the obverse of these concepts. The French leader and the NATO secretary-general were to remain proponents of conflicting ideals for years after Spaak left NATO. The singular importance of the general's ascension was quickly revealed, when, on 17 September 1958, de Gaulle sent a letter outlining his attitude toward NATO to President Eisenhower and Prime Minister Macmillan. The simple fact that de Gaulle had chosen to address himself to the two leading members of the alliance without informing the other members was testimony to the respect he accorded them.[87] De Gaulle's memorandum pointed out the anomalous condition that had arisen since the inception of the alliance: in 1949, the United States held a monopoly on nuclear weapons and was the unchallenged leader of the so-called Free World. Because of the emergent Soviet threat to the West, NATO had been founded to ensure the security of Western Europe and North America. Since the ratification of the North Atlantic Treaty, however, the United States had slipped from its dominant position, and thus her authority to make the crucial decisions about the defense of the West was open to question. France, de Gaulle avowed, could no longer acquiesce in the obsolete arrangements of NATO. It no longer made sense that decisions central to French security should be made on another continent. To him, the speed and range of modern weapons rendered that concept absurd. De Gaulle concluded that the West's strategic nuclear policy should be jointly decided by the United States, Great Britain, and France, and that a system should be instituted whereby the three powers would take responsibility for planning and effecting military action—nuclear and conventional—on a global basis. Spheres of operations would be defined among the three as circumstances dictated. De Gaulle made France's continued participation in NATO contingent on the acceptance of this triumvirate arrangement.[88]

Spaak was shocked. He had spoken with de Gaulle at length late in June 1958, and the general had not hinted at the radical demands he was about to propound. Spaak intimated that de Gaulle was poorly informed about international affairs, but this seemed unlikely as the general had been receiving regular briefings from diplomatic and intelligence sources throughout his seclusion.[89] Spaak's reaction was above all political. He sounded out the views of Secretary of State Dulles in a meeting they both attended in Boston and also sought to learn the reception given the general's proposal by the other allied governments. Dulles, Spaak said, did not oppose an expansion of the French role within NATO, but he did seriously object to the substitution of a "directorate" for an alliance of fifteen.[90]

One month later, the secretary-general responded officially to de Gaulle's memorandum. Associating himself with the basic criticisms that de Gaulle had articulated, he did not summarily reject the general's proposal. Instead he emphasized the success that had been achieved, with his encouragement, in overcoming the geographical limits previously imposed on the Council's deliberations. Spaak stressed the idea that the economic and political interests of many alliance members—such as Portugal, the Netherlands, Belgium, Turkey, and the United Kingdom—in problems outside Europe ensured that the Council could not possibly remain indifferent to worldwide developments. He therefore thought it a deplorable idea to create a three-power directorate to set a global foreign policy for the West. The Italians and West Germans would be sorely tempted to withdraw from NATO and resume independent policies rather than be subjected to directives decided on without their participation. Also, if NATO lost most vestiges of cooperative multilateral action, it would become a hollow enterprise for the smaller states, and they might very well adopt a neutralist stance within the East-West context. In sum, Spaak felt the plan was not well conceived and was bound to find opposition in London and Washington.[91]

As mentioned earlier, Spaak's theory of diplomacy was based on frank exchange and a mutual understanding of substance and motive. A state, he felt, should strive to advance its interests whenever the occasion presented itself and negotiation was the proper vehicle of advancement. But failure in the course of negotiations to pursue all avenues of possible agreement was foolish, an invitation to misunderstanding and conflict. Where prospects for settlement were not bright, the parties should talk matters out, if only to avoid exacerbating the situation; a formula for saving face and reaching some accommodation in the process might turn up.[92] The United States government and de Gaulle, however, did not seem to share Spaak's view of the proper conduct of interstate relations.

Spaak had advised the United States to take up those points it could agree with in the memorandum as a basis for discussions within a NATO framework. The topics that Spaak believed deserved such consideration embraced political, economic, and military elements. More specifically, they involved participation by the European member states in the preparation of NATO military strategy and operations and the expansion of the geographical area covered by the North Atlantic Treaty. Because he estimated acceptance of the Gaullist global directorate would mean the dissolution of the alliance, Spaak offered a counterproposal. Groups of experts might be established to study problems of particular regions, and Council subcommittees, restricted to those with an interest in a concerned area, might also be created. Due to strong American and French resistance, the Council did not take up these suggestions although Spaak claimed that he had been authorized to create special committees as the need arose.[93]

Unfortunately, at least as far as Spaak was concerned, the initial American response to de Gaulle's proposal was negative. On 20 October 1958 President Eisenhower formally notified de Gaulle that while consultations

> must further be broadened . . . this cannot be forced. . . . We cannot afford to adopt any system which would give to our other Allies, or other free world countries, the impression that basic decisions affecting their own vital interests are being made without their participation.[94]

The doubt in Washington as to whether the general's proposal represented genuine policy or was simply part of a diplomatic maneuver was answered in December.[95] At that time, during a discussion among the United States, Great Britain, and France at the ambassadorial level, the French confirmed that they did indeed want tripartite global planning.[96] That same month, Secretary Dulles informed General de Gaulle that the United States was willing to extend consultations but could not establish a directorate over NATO or any other state.[97]

The other members of NATO echoed the American rejection of de Gaulle's proposal. The smaller states were incensed by both the general's procedure and his plan. The Scandinavians, Turks, Italians, and Dutch resented the implications of political inequality contained in the directorate.[98] It meant reversion to wartime procedures, the elimination of the progress—incremental though it had been—made in the development of consultation among the allies. The West German government, not wanting to alienate either France or the United States, maintained a judicious silence. Despite the encouragement the Bonn government lent to the rebuilding of a strong and confident France, de Gaulle's demand—or at least the sentimental nationalist context in which it was presumably put—was deeply unpopular in West Germany. It was seen as an effort to restore an archaic French supremacy on a continent that in 1958 was dedicated to cooperation without discrimination or hierarchy. In private and public conversation, it was frequently remarked that the French desire reflected their leader's mania for greatness.[99]

A directorate was so clearly contrary to the current of Western European thought and action in the postwar era that nowhere outside France did it receive much support. Spaak speculated that considering the memorandum's misjudgments, it had been drafted without the help of the Quai d'Orsay. This particularly concerned him as it signified that the foreign policy of a major power was being determined virtually by one man alone.[100]

Given the negative response from the Americans and the British, Spaak concluded that "all seemed finished. DeGaulle," Spaak said, "never again spoke of his propositions."[101] The truth, however, is that de Gaulle never again spoke of his propositions to Spaak. As the secretary-general had taken a position against him, de Gaulle simply elected not to inform Spaak any further but rather communicated directly with the American permanent representative; the SACEUR was similarly ignored. De Gaulle continued to press Eisenhower, and the two heads of state exchanged memoranda on the subject from 1960 to the end of Eisenhower's term. In 1961, when President Kennedy visited Paris, he reviewed with de Gaulle the entire series of exchanges between Eisenhower and de Gaulle. Nonetheless, de Gaulle believed he never received satisfaction, a factor that contributed to his later decision to "withdraw" from NATO.[102]

The alliance, and especially its secretary-general, had still to suffer the consequences of de Gaulle's beliefs. The general had little but disdain for politicians, who, in his view, were animated by narrow, partisan motives. He placed the blame for the abysmal French military defeat in 1940 on the leaders of the Third Republic. The sorry condition of the French state in 1958 he attributed to the politicians of the Fourth Republic. Politicians as a group, he felt, did not inherently possess the wisdom, vision, and conviction necessary for the leader of a great nation like France. To de Gaulle, Spaak was from the same mold.[103] Thus de Gaulle had little regard for the secretary-general. Furthermore, as the champion of the nation-state, de Gaulle was annoyed by this spokesman for supranationality.

In their personal relationship, Spaak sought to move directly to concrete issues and hard negotiations, while de Gaulle remained cool and aloof.[104] "I was attaching an importance to the office of Secretary-General which de Gaulle would not accord," he wrote.[105] There was never much in the way of fruitful discussion between the two; no real exchanges came about from their talks.[106] In fact, their meetings have been described as political rows.[107]

In sum, Spaak's direct diplomacy and continual attempts at compromise evoked no responsive chord whatever in de Gaulle and little support from the rest of NATO.[108] It was a frustrating experience for Spaak—one that must have made him question his open diplomatic style and certainly dampened his optimism. De Gaulle's concept of Europe and NATO was indeed extremely troubling to Spaak, who was a leader in the struggle for joining the states of Western Europe and North America in a supranational Atlantic community. De Gaulle, of course, objected to both Atlantic confederation and Western European federation. The 17 September memorandum proved to be only the opening round in their ideological and political struggle; the situation could and did become more difficult for Spaak.

SHAPE, Defense Policy and Nuclear Weapons

It was Spaak's suggestion that led to the preparation of an authoritative compilation of military establishments around the world by the Institute for Strategic Studies (ISS). Such a compilation was necessary because of the many inaccuracies in the press on the comparative size and composition of Soviet and American forces. It proved impossible to work on such a project within NATO: an open debate in Paris on American defense requirements could be exploited for domestic political purposes. In addition, NATO-compiled figures could easily be dismissed as biased and self-serving. So Spaak and Sir Evelyn Shuckburgh arranged for the ISS to undertake the task.

Lacking Lord Ismay's solid wartime military connections and record, Spaak's relations with the military fluctuated from issue to issue. For example, in 1957 when British plans to withdraw forces from the Continent upset the West Germans, the NATO dialogue with Chancellor Adenauer centered primarily on West German rearmament and related financial matters, where there was no basic divergence between Spaak and the military authorities.[109] The specific responsibilities for implementing the 1954 London and Paris Agreements had been worked out by the former SACEUR, General Alfred Gruenther, and Spaak did not choose to reexamine them.

The secretary-general and General Lauris Norstad, who had succeeded General Gruenther, enjoyed a cordial relationship, largely because Spaak willingly deferred to the SACEUR in military matters.[110] Spaak wrote that he "decided to follow [Norstad's] opinion in all that concerned defense. Technically, I could only bow before his competence and I was soon convinced of his complete loyalty to the Atlantic Alliance."[111]

Norstad had carved out for himself an indispensable position in Europe. He, more than Generals Gruenther or Ridgway, filled the gap left by Eisenhower's departure and became the foremost pro-European American spokesman in NATO. General Lord Montgomery, although the deputy SACEUR from 1951 to 1958, developed a reputation of never really understanding the NATO operation.[112] Norstad, on the other hand, quickly mastered it.[113] He possessed an adept political mind and good instincts for the relationships necessary for the cultivation of power. "General Norstad," wrote one commentator, "epitomizes the new generation of United States soldier-statesmen-diplomats."[114]

Norstad made it a practice to hold weekly meetings with France's NATO diplomats, and General de Gaulle would see Norstad independently of the American NATO diplomatic mission, which forced the American permanent representative to inform himself through a third party. Norstad also frequently helped Spaak in the latter's relations with the United States and helped the United States in its relations with Spaak.[115] He also inaugurated the practice of briefing the permanent representatives to educate them on nuclear affairs.[116] Involved in rebuilding the Bundeswehr, Norstad and Chancellor Adenauer became friends and developed a close working relationship.[117] Norstad, by encouraging direct diplomatic dealings with SHAPE, acquired a prominent voice in NATO's political affairs.

When Spaak attempted to restrict the public statements of military officials in order to reinforce his role as NATO's chief political spokesman, most Council members, as well as SHAPE, opposed the effort.[118] Norstad simply ignored it. This led to some tension between the secretary-general and the SACEUR, but André de Staercke prevented the appearance of a serious division between NATO's two top figures.[119]

Even though Spaak sought to effect a coherent NATO defense policy, Norstad had substantial and even decisive influence. For example, whenever anything leaked to the *New York Times* that caused jitters in Western capitals about some aspect of United States policy, or Khrushchev made a truculent statement, West Germany, Italy, and Belgium would seek reassurance from Norstad rather than from Spaak. The European governments of course reviewed their defense programs with the SACEUR.[120]

The secretary-general's primary concern was his belief that the Eastern bloc posed a grave menace to the world's democracies.[121] For this reason, Spaak opposed the liquidation or reduction of any of the military bases on the periphery of the NATO geographical area on the grounds that such actions seriously weakened NATO's retaliatory capability. In Spaak's view, the more bases there were and the more widely they were dispersed, the better the chances of avoiding war.[122] However, he happily left the preparation of the final details of any defense plans to Norstad, SHAPE, and the national delegations. It was only when disagreements over strategic policy called into question the alliance's political integrity that he allowed himself to become entangled in military affairs. This was the case with regard to the French challenge to the fundamental defense arrangements of NATO from 1959 on, until they withdrew from its military organization.

Military integration was the NATO military orthodoxy of the late 1950s and was a view that Spaak supported fully. Speaking before his first NATO parliamentarians conference in 1957, the secretary-general presented the case for a unified allied army. The current system of separate military organizations for each state, he argued, invited disjointed development. If one state modified its defense posture, then others would be tempted to follow. Thus there existed a disincentive for a single member state to alter its proportion of defense expenditures; Spaak pointed out that reductions in the length of conscription taking place at that time in several member states aptly illustrated his point. Furthermore, Spaak foresaw that the process of domestic retrenchment in defense outlays would accelerate unless qualitative improvements were made in the alliance's basic military doctrine. Recalling the EDC concept, Spaak insisted that if each member state had a specialized function to fulfill in an integrated military structure, the national governments and legislatures would think twice before making cuts in their respective defense budgets, because to do so might jeopardize the entire alliance.[123] In other words, he believed that military integration would reinforce collective political responsibility.

Spaak also advocated an integrative approach to scientific and technological problems. After the Soviet technological coup of Sputnik, Spaak advocated the pooling of advanced Western scientific research. Here was another area where the Atlantic community could contribute more than the sum of the individual efforts of its constituent states. He argued that a multilateral program of scientific research could reverse the dispersion and duplication of effort that was wasting the critical human and financial resources of all. "Then and only then will we be able to compete with the single-minded [scientific] effort of the Soviet Union," he said.[124] Looking at it pragmatically, Spaak hoped that joint research and development ventures would lead to the termination of restrictive and outdated legislation such as the U.S. McMahon Act, which prohibited the sharing of atomic and nuclear information possessing military applications. Spaak believed that such scientific knowledge should be shared among the allies when it was obvious that the prospective enemy already possessed it.

Spaak attacked a scheme in which four alliance member states would compete in a contest to see which would be chosen to produce a new fighter plane for NATO. "This means four expensive lines of identical expenditures for developing a single product! What waste and duplication! If this goes on we in NATO might have to choose between Sputnik and washing machines. Either way, the choice would make us all second-rate powers."[125] Here the secretary-general pointed out the true character of Western European–North American interdependence. Not only would it be folly for a small state like Belgium to invest huge sums on sophisticated weaponry, but Western European–North American competition was also wasteful and dangerous.

Yet most of all, Spaak gave expression to the need for the leaders of the alliance, especially the United States, to include their partners in strategic planning. He viewed the dissemination of nuclear secrets and the dispersal of advanced weapons technology as necessary steps toward a more equal distribution of influence within the allied councils. Even though Spaak eloquently voiced Western European displeasure over what they regarded as the subordinate treatment they were receiving at the hands of "les Saxons," as already pointed out it was de Gaulle who headed the movement against what was viewed as the hegemonic tendencies of the United States.

But General de Gaulle had firm convictions about the place of France in world politics that involved assumptions inconsistent with those of NATO's secretary-general. To the general, France was a great power and therefore entitled to the perquisites of one.[126] A state was distinguished by its ability to define, and secure by force of arms if necessary, its territorial domain. In the nuclear era most states had lost this ability and had thus been reduced to the level of "legal artifacts," dependent on another state for their physical survival. States that could no longer control their borders were open to penetration and potential domination by an alien state. For France, according to de Gaulle, this was intolerable; she must remain the master of her destiny. The first requirement for France, therefore, was security. This could only be ensured in the contemporary age by national control over a nuclear deterrent. From this premise there followed two alternatives: (1) the transfer to French control of a deterrent by a second state, most likely the United States; or (2) the establishment of its own independent *force de frappe*. When de Gaulle first attempted to implement his policy within NATO the foremost issue centered on sharing in the control of the American deterrent.

After the United States failed to come up with an arrangement capable of meeting de Gaulle's conditions, the French moved even more vigorously than before to acquire their own nuclear strike force. This action changed the impact of the Gaullist dissent on NATO, even though it was as early as 1954-1955 that the French government took the first steps in the development of a nuclear weapons program.[127]

To counter this French challenge, Spaak felt compelled to take a more active role in the defense politics of the alliance. Gaullist dissatisfaction with European security arrangements that depended on a U.S. military guarantee drew support from a large body of nationalist opinion on the Continent. The French were not the only Western Europeans discontented with a strategic doctrine that seemed to place a "president of Europe" on the other side of the Atlantic. The postwar economic recovery had been swift; Europeans now felt that political normalization required the replacement of subordination with partnership. Furthermore, they were also concerned with the possibility that the United States would withdraw its military forces from Europe or make a bargain on its own with the Soviet Union.

Only highly skilled multinational diplomacy coupled with good faith on both sides of the Atlantic could possibly identify and solve the essential political problems of the alliance. Such skillful diplomacy, however, was not to prevail in 1958. As described above, the initial American reaction to de Gaulle's September memorandum was perhaps more negative than was necessary, and Spaak's offers of mediation were politely ignored. Thereafter, French alliance behavior in military affairs became less cooperative. For example, French representatives in SHAPE began what in effect constituted a boycott by refusing to approve military plans. Earlier they refused to allow the introduction of missiles or the construction of launching sites on their territory unless the United States included the warheads along with the delivery vehicles. Such a transfer, however, was opposed by the United States. Other NATO members— Norway and Denmark for instance—had similarly barred nuclear missiles from their soil, although in a more restrained manner and without attaching unacceptable conditions.[128] The United States, on the other hand, was reasonably satisfied with locating missiles in Italy, Britain, and Turkey, where the SACEUR retained authority for their use.[129]

By the fall of 1958 relations between the United States and France had deteriorated badly. The French vetoed the U.S. plan for meeting the costs of the new missile sites through the collective NATO infrastructure budget.[130] Then in the spring of 1959, the French escalated their protest another dramatic step with the abrupt removal of one-third of their Mediterranean fleet from NATO command. In June, de Gaulle refused to allow the United States to stockpile nuclear bombs in France unless his government fully participated in the decision to use them.[131] Finally, in December, the French derailed the scheme for the integration of fighter air forces under the SACEUR. The United States saw this last action as particularly harsh, for it crippled the air defenses of Western Europe. These steps, obviously, ran counter to Spaak's conception of greater rather than less military integration.

In reply to what was increasingly viewed as French obstructionism, General Norstad, acting with the firm backing of the United States, ordered the withdrawal of two hundred fighter-bombers from air fields in France.[132] At the same time his American deputy, General Charles D. Palmer, stressed that the reassignment of the nine air squadrons "would not affect the power or the integrity of the Atlantic Alliance."[133] The United States was forced to act, because the negative French attitude toward nuclear stockpiling was causing "a serious situation" that "forbade any precaution being overlooked."[134] Thus Norstad was deftly trying to pass the ball into de Gaulle's court, but it was Spaak who picked it up first.

In a forum that promised a full debate on the long-simmering quarrel—a French parliamentary committee—Spaak reviewed the state of affairs in NATO. While criticizing the decision of the United States to withdraw its air squadrons, he characterized the French refusal to integrate France's air defense system as petty and foolish. Spaak then raised the question of the directorate. He listed the proposal's inherent faults, and yet he admitted there was something fundamentally sound in the French view.[135] As he later phrased it: "France is also right when . . . she affirms the necessity that she be associated, in the case of a world war, with the determination of global strategy."[136]

Spaak, without conceding to France an exclusive right to decide alliance strategy, pointed to the improved arrangements for consultation within NATO after Suez and repeated his conviction that ad hoc committees of limited membership, composed only of the nuclear powers for example, could operate within a NATO framework. Of course, such special committees could not commit the alliance without the consent of the other members, he added.

Spaak's rhetorical question, referring to nuclear weapons research especially, "must Europe re-invent all that the United States has already invented," drew a loud round of applause.[137] The otherwise unsympathetic audience could not help but be impressed by many of his arguments. By such a balanced performance, he hoped to lay the groundwork for mutual Franco-American concessions. But at a meeting with de Gaulle the following week, the general gave no hint of compromise.[138] And the United States likewise failed to endorse Spaak's analysis. The United States could see little justification in the French stand, which seemed highly presumptuous for a country that, after all, had narrowly avoided civil war only the year before, and for more than a decade had apparently been wasting its resources in a futile series of colonial wars. With more than a touch of irony, the United States pointed to the fact revealed in the 1958 NATO Annual Review that for the first time West Germany was making a larger contribution to NATO's strength than France.

By the end of 1959, Washington had become deeply irritated by the French. In December of that year, General Nathan F. Twining, chairman of the U.S. Joint Chiefs of Staff, delivered to the NATO Military Committee a stinging indictment of what to him appeared to be the French obstruction of NATO military progress. When Twining's censure was leaked to the press, Spaak publicly welcomed airing of the criticism in the hope that it would aid reconciliation.[139] Since the facts were well known, perhaps the chances of frank discussion would be improved. Simultaneously, the secretary-general downplayed reports of a serious malaise in the alliance; he did not think that General de Gaulle had been referring to military integration in NATO when he asserted that integration had had its day. Spaak, however, was caught in a delicate position. He had a duty as the political head of NATO to discourage excess antagonism or division. At the same time he did not want these problems ignored, for they were palpably affecting NATO and needed full discussion.[140]

But there was no abatement of the Franco-American hostility. Making matters even worse than they were, de Gaulle openly announced to the world that France, within a year or two, would conduct a series of atomic tests in the Sahara. Opposition in the United Nations General Assembly did not dissuade him; his response was to emphasize the present nuclear inequality. France, de Gaulle explained, would not abandon nuclear weapons under world conditions that would leave her permanently inferior.[141]

Following Secretary of State Dulles' illness and death in the spring of 1959, President Eisenhower appointed Christian Herter as secretary of state. Herter, unlike Dulles, was hesitant to tackle directly the problems France posed for the alliance. Hence, the Eisenhower–de Gaulle meetings of September and December had little effect in overcoming the Franco-American split. And a plan by Secretary of Defense Thomas Gates took

into account little of the substance of the French criticism.
Meanwhile, Spaak actively lobbied with the American government for the acceptance of proposals to circumvent the Mac-
Mahon Act. He hoped that assistance could be given to the
development of French nuclear technology, but found no
softening in the American position. Characteristically, Spaak
took his case to the highest levels, appealing directly to the new
secretary of state and meeting again with de Gaulle. When no
positive results were forthcoming, Spaak became disheartened.[142]

Once again General Norstad became a key figure in generating an innovative approach toward breaking the deadlock. He
devised a scheme for making NATO a fourth nuclear power by
giving it its own arsenal of nuclear weapons. Supranational
control of the weapons would be exercised through a procedure
that combined the Council and SHAPE, the details of which
were to be worked out later. Chancellor Adenauer, who had
confidence in Norstad, warmly received the idea.[143] Adenauer
had previously admired the resurgence of French nationalism,
but by 1960 had become cool toward de Gaulle's more national-
istically extremist policies.[144]

The Norstad plan also caught Spaak's imagination. In it he
saw a possibility for healing the Franco-American rift.[145] Cost,
he felt, was not a problem as NATO had successfully financed
many joint infrastructure projects. Thus there seemed no inherent reason why the alliance could not have its own nuclear
force. At the NATO parliamentarians assembly in November
1960 Spaak managed to obtain the cautious support of Lyndon B.
Johnson, the vice-president–elect, and Senator J. William
Fulbright for the NATO force.[146] Shortly thereafter, Spaak
went to Washington to press for official approval in the hope
of discouraging the French from proceeding with their independent nuclear force.[147] At the ministerial meeting in December, the secretary-general and the SACEUR worked in concert
for what became known as the Norstad Plan.

Their efforts, however, met with little success. The smaller
NATO member states were not enthusiastic; those governments
that had earlier rejected missile bases had no greater desire to
accept the responsibility for a mutual nuclear deterrent.[148]
Furthermore, it was comforting and comfortable to continue

to rely on the U.S. nuclear deterrent. It was, of course, U.S. support for the plan that was critical, and this support never materialized. Washington made a counterproposal by offering to place five Polaris submarines at the disposal of NATO. This constituted a severe blow for the Norstad Plan, and so the ministers at their December 1960 meeting decided to defer any decision until the spring, when the new president would be able to give an indication of the direction of his policy.[149]

The shelving of the Norstad Plan came on top of Spaak's frustrating efforts to implement Secretary of State Herter's proposal for a ten-year planning program. Herter had initiated this proposal at the ministerial meeting in December of 1959. The program, which was intended to symbolize long-term American commitment to NATO, called for the charting of alliance activities until 1969 when Article XII of the North Atlantic Treaty, which provided that NATO members could withdraw on one year's notice, became operative. Detailed elaboration of this plan for NATO's development was left to the Council and the secretary-general. But Spaak's patience was severely strained in attempting to plot the future course of an association whose members no longer seemed to agree on basic assumptions.

This task, coming as it did on top of other frustrations, marked a low point in his years at NATO. Spaak's scheme for coordinating Western economic policy toward the less-developed countries in NATO had gone unheeded and was superseded when the OECD began operations in early 1961. Even the practice of political consultation was breaking down as the Franco-American crisis slowed or halted all progress in this area. For example, when there was no reply to a plea by the Portuguese foreign minister on behalf of his country's colonial policy, Spaak was discouraged: "This silence was much more disturbing than any reply, however negative or critical, would have been."[150] With the results of all his efforts in serious doubt, Spaak began to fear for the future of the alliance.

During the Congo crisis of 1960 the secretary-general had expressed concern at what he perceived as the over-readiness of some alliance members to alienate their Belgian partner.[151] Nevertheless, he recognized the dilemma: "Can we remain united in one part of the world and work at cross-purposes, or even as adversaries, in another?" he asked. "Can we, thanks to NATO, maintain a common policy on European questions and at the UN oppose each other on all others?"[152] Lord Ismay could not have put the matter better at the time of Suez.

Disconsolate, Spaak informed the permanent representatives in December 1960 of his wish to resign. Amid protests he reconsidered. Rumors of his resignation had been floated before, perhaps to spur the allies toward greater efforts on behalf of Atlantic solidarity. Still, Spaak sensed that more than ever the tone and content of his arguments were falling on unsympathetic ears and that his relationship with the Council was deteriorating.[153] Also, the Council was not keeping pace with the growing influence of SHAPE. Norstad had been successful in establishing himself as an independent political authority, while Spaak, who was a proponent of the orthodoxy of total response, had achieved little progress in overcoming the stalemate on strategic matters.[154] It was Norstad who moved toward a more flexible position by calling for increased conventional military capabilities to strengthen the credibility of the deterrent.[155] The disagreement between them had not been acrimonious, but it did serve to weaken further Spaak's prestige with the military.

Finally, the secretary-general's relationship with the major powers had also degenerated. He had expended his credit with de Gaulle and was discouraged by his inability to reconcile the French to the rest of the alliance.[156] As a leading figure at the Messina Conference, when the final negotiations for the Treaty of Rome took place, Spaak had developed rather ambiguous feelings toward Britain. The last vestiges of the Anglo-American "special relationship" gave him doubts as to the British commitment to the alliance. Also the British, like the Americans, had resisted a NATO nuclear force.[157] While the Americans had honored Spaak personally as a distinguished European statesman, they had given small weight to his policy initiatives. All three states conveyed the feeling that they would consult in the Council only when it suited them and were unwilling to allow NATO any substantial influence on their policymaking.[158] Spaak initially hoped the Kennedy administration would reverse the trend, but he was disenchanted when, by the end of January 1961, the new president had failed to back either Norstad's idea of a NATO deterrent force or his own plans to expand the scope of the organization.

Lacking a mandate, Spaak was disappointed with himself as much as with others.[159] The international political scene that he had desired to enlarge had remained narrow and restricted, and his efforts to change it had not succeeded. Prospects of attaining a true Atlantic community appeared dim. Admittedly, the chances for a recurrence of a debacle like Suez were low, but Spaak's advocacy of consultation across a broad spectrum of issues had not produced the desired results. Much of this, of course, lay in reasons beyond Spaak's influence. The British felt they had their own network for consultation in the Commonwealth and their relationship with the United States. Neither France nor the United States desired to consult on any but purely alliance affairs and continued to argue with one another with little reference to the secretary-general.

On 26 January 1961, Spaak informed the permanent representatives of his decision to resign the office of secretary-general in order to rejoin his party for the Belgian national elections that spring. This time, the decision was final. Irrespective of any personal ill-feelings for Spaak, there was a general sadness at his departure. His experience was highly valued, his energy an unquestioned resource, and his personal prestige a continuing asset to NATO.

Two stories heard in diplomatic circles concerning Spaak's preference for a successor illustrate well two different aspects of his tenure in Paris. The first story highlights his relationship with the Council. According to this account, Spaak suggested Sir Frank Roberts, the permanent representative of the United Kingdom as the next secretary-general. The rumor fed suspicions among the representatives that Spaak sought to enhance his own stature by seeking the appointment of lesser figures as secretary-general.[160] According to the second, and better-confirmed story, Spaak pushed for the appointment of an American, because he felt the prestige of the United States was required to build up NATO's political machinery. Spaak is supposed to have proposed Dean Acheson, former secretary of state, as his replacement.[161]

The circumstances surrounding Spaak's sudden departure left doubts in some minds as to the sincerity of his stated desire to return to Belgian politics. Spaak, however, was almost certainly expressing a genuine sentiment. Belgium was then in political turmoil, having experienced strikes and riots before Christmas in protest against the severity of the government's *loi unique,* a comprehensive economic reform measure.[162] The opposition, including Spaak's Socialist Party, was racked by divisions that had exploded in the strikes led by trade union activists unhappy with the timid response of the party hierarchy. Spaak was needed to help heal the party division and participate in the coming elections. Party leaders, in fact, had been seen trying to prevail on him to reenter national politics, but he had set exacting conditions for his return: a free hand within the party and a ministry if the socialists formed a government.[163]

Previously, Spaak had privately voiced the sentiment that if your party wants you, then you must go or abandon politics, and he had no intention of giving up national politics just yet.[164] Spaak himself had more than once professed that he was a political man more than a diplomat or international civil servant and that "it is impossible for me to resist my animus."[165]

Although the call from Brussels was genuine enough, it could not be evaluated in isolation. Spaak was willing to leave the more international NATO post (and take a loss in pay), because he felt NATO was sliding away from the ideals for which he had so much hoped in 1956. More importantly, he saw that he could do little to prevent the trend. Spaak's departure in 1961 did not signify a task completed, but rather an admission that the forces of nationalism that separated the members of the alliance were greater than those of the personality that sought to unite them.

Notes

1. 3 (4).

2. *New York Times,* 25 July 1945; and 30 (3).

3. Both of Spaak's brothers and his daughter were also involved in the theater.

4. *Observer,* 15 December 1957.

5. This period in Spaak's life has been appropriately labeled "the years of defiance" by J. H. Huizinga in chapter V of his *Mr. Europe: A Political Biography of Paul-Henri Spaak* (New York, 1961).

6. Ironically, his last vote in parliament, in which he supported the move of NATO's headquarters to Brussels, breached party discipline by ignoring the decision of his party's General Council, of which he had been the most prominent member. Spaak, *Combats,* 2:417-21.

7. Quoted in Walter Waggoner, "Mr. Europe Surveys the Future," *New York Times,* 7 April 1957.

8. C. L. Sulzberger, *New York Times,* 1 June 1957.

9. Spaak, *Combats,* 2:11. Much has been made over the contradiction between Spaak's prewar neutralist leanings and his postwar supranational advocacy. His pacifist sympathies should be interpreted in light of his commitment to radical socialist dogma, his inexperience in foreign affairs, and, most important of all, the insoluble problem posed for powerless Belgium in the late thirties. Spaak confided that he entered the foreign ministry with great surprise and not a little trepidation. He was not familiar with the problems, let alone the range of possible solutions, that he would have to face as foreign minister. He had not met a single foreign diplomat, prior to June 1936, and the diplomats in the department were nearly unknown to him. See Spaak, *Combats,* 1:37. He groped about during those difficult years of the late thirties as foreign minister and then briefly as prime minister for answers to puzzles that few European statesmen were able to solve.

10. *New York Times,* 1 March 1945.

11. *Observer,* 15 December 1957.

12. *New York Times,* 8 April 1945.

13. Ibid.

14. "Never," he wrote, "have I felt, as I did in the Assembly of the United Nations, in its composition and its present spirit, the impossibility for the triumph of a rational thesis. Never have I had the feeling of throwing myself against so many prejudices, so much passion, so many fixed positions. Neither legal arguments, reasonable arguments, the spirit of compromise yet indispensable, nor impartial justice, could triumph in that Assembly. As long as the United Nations is not directed by an organ where impartiality is the superior law, where each member has the same passion for the general interest as that which it manifests for its own interest, it is impossible to hope that the ideal of collective security and global solidarity will ever be achieved." Spaak, *Combats,* 1:220.

15. Spaak, *Combats,* 2:49-54.

16. Waggoner, *New York Times,* 7 April 1957.

17. Ibid.

18. William Stringer, "Spaak of NATO," *Christian Science Monitor,* 10 February 1959. This proposal, by 1975, was still being debated in the European Parliament; see especially the Bertrand Report.

19. See Waggoner, *New York Times,* 7 April 1957.

20. Spaak, *Combats,* 2:109.

21. Waggoner, *New York Times,* 7 April 1957.

22. Delivered at Bruges, 14 September 1957. See NATO Speech Series no. 90 (NATO Information Service).

23. Quoted in Waggoner, *New York Times,* 7 April 1957.

24. *NATO: Facts and Figures,* p. 340.

25. Waggoner, *New York Times,* 7 April 1957.

26. Ibid.

27. Ibid.

28. Quoted in Springer, *Christian Science Monitor,* 10 February 1959.

29. C. L. Sulzberger, *New York Times,* 1 June 1957.

30. See, for example, his speech of January 1957, reported in the *Christian Science Monitor,* 18 December 1957.

31. Spaak, *Combats,* 2:109-110.

32. 23 (2).

33. 24 (1).

34. 3 (1).

35. 23 (2). His wife, not well, remained in Brussels; she died in 1960.

36. 3 (1).

37. 3 (4).

38. Waggoner, *New York Times,* 7 April 1957.

39. Ibid.

40. Ibid.

41. Ibid.

42. 3 (2-3).

43. Robert Triffin was one of the first to warn of the internal contradictions of the international monetary system and predicted its breakdown in two articles published in the *Banca Nazionale de Lavoro Quarterly Review* in 1959.

44. *New York Times,* 16 December 1959.

45. 9 (1) and 6 (1). He left the details of running the Staff/Secretariat largely to others.

46. 24 (1).

47. 24 (2).

48. Andrew H. Berding, *Dulles on Diplomacy* (Princeton, N.J., 1965), pp. 75-76.

49. 23 (2).

50. 6 (1).

51. 3 (2).

52. See Stringer, *Christian Science Monitor,* 10 February 1959.

53. 9 (1).

54. 24 (2).

55. 24 (2). See Jordan, *Staff/Secretariat,* for a discussion of the contrast between the British and Continental methods of staff administration. See also the Appendix for an outline of NATO organization. Spaak, being Continental, had Mr. Saint-Mleux perform as a true *chef de cabinet* (also titled *directeur de cabinet),* whereas Lord Coleridge, in Ismay's time, in practice had assumed many of these functions.

56. 24 (1).

57. For a full account, see Spaak, *Combats,* 2: chapter 43.

58. 9 (5).

59. 24 (1).

60. *Manchester Guardian,* 21 November 1958.

61. *New York Herald Tribune,* 13-14 December 1958.

62. 25 (1).

63. Ibid.

64. 23 (2).

65. *Times* (London), 4 April 1959; *Observer,* 5 April 1959; and *New York Times,* 5 April 1959.

66. *Times* (London), 15 December 1959.

67. *New York Times,* 6 November 1959.

68. *Times* (London), 15 December 1959.

69. Speech at Fletcher School of Law and Diplomacy, reported in the *Christian Science Monitor,* 25 November 1960.

70. *New York Times,* 8 December 1957; and *New York Herald Tribune,* 8 December 1957. Egypt, the Sudan, and Lebanon had already signed trade agreements with the Soviet Union. *Le Combat,* 23 February 1959.

71. *New York Herald Tribune,* 26 November 1957. The terms of long-term agreements benefitted the Soviets by tying the fortunes of the LDC's with theirs. They shared in protection against adverse developments in international trade; and barter items allowed them to undermine Western dominance of the international economy and conserve their supply of hard currency.

72. *New York Times,* 19 December 1957.

73. *New York Herald Tribune,* 10 December 1957.

74. See the text of President Eisenhower's speech reported in the *New York Times,* 17 December 1957.

75. *New York Times,* 8 May 1958.

76. A similar suggestion regarding West Germany has been made from

time-to-time. See, for example, Waldemar Besson's chapter in Robert S. Jordan, ed., *Europe and the Superpowers* (Boston, 1971).

77. Burgess, an open and easygoing person, had previously served as an educator, banker, and financial official. Although this was his first diplomatic position, he had handled a variety of responsibilities with intelligence and thoroughness. In addition, his wife served as his more than able aid. 23 (3).

78. *NATO: Facts and Figures*, p. 41.

79. *New York Times*, 8 May 1958.

80. Several commentators have strongly intimated that the embargo of strategic goods to the Eastern bloc of the late 1940s and the early 1950s was created inside NATO. It was also reported that beginning in 1958 with the Economic Committee's creation, policy was made within NATO on the control of credits to the East when trade restrictions no longer seemed a viable policy. See Gunnar Adler-Karlson, *Western Economic Warfare: 1947-1967* (Stockholm, 1968), pp. 49-52, 128-37, 225, 239-41. See also the *Economist*, 2 February 1964, p. 719.

81. *New York Times*, 6 May 1958.

82. *Times* (London), 21 November 1958; and *Manchester Guardian*, 21 November 1958.

83. *New York Times*, 4 April 1959.

84. 24 (3).

85. *New York Times*, 4 December 1960.

86. Spaak, *Combats*, 2:163.

87. Ibid., p. 180.

88. Ibid., pp. 181-82.

89. Stanley Karnow, "An Odd Bit of History: De Gaulle's CIA Aide," *The New Republic* 170, no. 26 (29 June 1974):17.

90. Spaak, *Combats*, 2:183.

91. Ibid., pp. 182-85.

92. 23 (1).

93. *Times* (London), 19 December 1958.

94. Quotation in *NATO Letter* 14, no. 10 (October 1966):29.

95. 23 (1).

96. Eric Stein and Dominique Carreau, "Law and Peaceful Change in a Subsystem: 'Withdrawal' of France from the North Atlantic Treaty Organization," *American Journal of International Law* 62 (July 1968):582.

97. Ibid.

98. 23 (1).

99. Alain Clement, *Le Monde*, 9 July 1959.

100. Spaak, *Combats*, 2:185.

101. Ibid., p. 186.

102. See Elliot R. Goodman, "De Gaulle's NATO Policy in Perspective," *Internationale Spectator* 20 (8 July 1966):934-48.

103. 24 (2).

104. 23 (1).

105. Spaak, *Combats*, 2:191.

106. 23 (1).

107. 24 (2).

108. Spaak, *Combats*, 2:191.

109. See 72-74 above.

110. 12 (2).

111. Spaak, *Combats*, 2:114.

112. 24 (1).

113. 2 (1). General Gruenther once said that, mentally, Norstad was "the fastest thing I've seen." Quoted in Robert C. Doty, "Norstad of NATO: 'Philosopher in Uniform,' " *New York Times*, 26 May 1957.

114. Ibid.

115. 3 (4).

116. 2 (5).

117. Spaak, *Combats*, 2:203-4, 209-10; and 9 (5).

118. 4 (2).

119. Spaak, *Combats*, 2:114.

120. Ibid.; and Doty, *New York Times*, 26 May 1957. Also 2 (1).

121. As previously noted, Spaak was not so pessimistic as to believe the communist danger would never recede. In fact, Spaak and de Staercke were engaged in building a relationship with the Russian ambassador in Paris, and subsequent to his departure from NATO Spaak made two major trips to Moscow as Belgian foreign minister. These visits represented some of the earliest explorations of the possibilities of détente. 24 (1,2).

122. *Le Combat*, 23 February 1959.

123. *Christian Science Monitor*, 14 November 1957.

124. *New York Herald Tribune*, 26 November 1957.

125. *Christian Science Monitor*, 14 November 1957.

126. On the character of de Gaulle and his vision of France, see Charles de Gaulle, *Le fil de l'épée* (Paris, 1961) and *Memoirs of Hope: Renewal and Endeavor* (New York, 1971); André Malraux, *Les chênes qu'on abat* (Paris, 1971) and *Anti-Memoirs* (Paris, 1967); David Schoenbraun, *The Three Lives of Charles de Gaulle* (New York, 1966); and Alexander Werth, *De Gaulle: A Political Biography* (Baltimore, 1967).

127. See Lawrence Scheinman, *Atomic Energy Policy In France Under the Fourth Republic* (Princeton, 1965).

128. *New York Times*, 6 January 1959.

129. Ibid., 23 January, 1 March, and 11 October 1959.

130. Nora Beloff, *Observer,* 14 December 1958.

131. *New York Times,* 10 June 1959.

132. Ibid., 9 June and 9 July 1959.

133. *Times* (London), 10 July 1959.

134. Ibid.

135. Ibid.

136. Spaak, *Combats,* 2:191.

137. *Times* (London), 10 July 1959.

138. Spaak, *Combats,* 2:191.

139. *New York Times,* 15 December 1959.

140. *New York Herald Tribune* (European edition), 15 December 1959.

141. *New York Times,* 11 November 1959.

142. Spaak, *Combats,* 2:192-200.

143. After listening to a strong critique from Adenauer on American foreign policy, Norstad "suggested the creation of a NATO atomic force whose use would be placed under the authority of the Council and which would be at the disposition of the Supreme Commander of the alliance. The Chancellor, who had listened attentively, proclaimed his enchantment and enthusiastically gave his agreement to the formula." Spaak, *Combats,* 2:210.

144. One incident that Adenauer related to Spaak is particularly revealing. Franz Josef Strauss, German minister of defense, paid an official visit to General Norstad without also requesting an interview with de Gaulle. When de Gaulle learned of this, he expressed his severe disapproval because of the implication that NATO was conducting sovereign affairs within France. Adenauer believed this was carrying nationalism to an unnecessary extreme. Spaak, *Combats,* 2:209-10.

145. C. L. Sulzberger, *New York Times,* 4 March 1961.

146. *Manchester Guardian,* 1 February 1961.

147. *Christian Science Monitor,* 26 November 1960.

148. Ironically, the French gave at least partial endorsement to the plan. Ibid., 4 March 1961.

149. *New York Times,* 14 April 1960.

150. Spaak, *Combats,* 2:217.

151. *Le Soir,* 1 February 1961. It is perhaps interesting to note that part of these difficulties arose from the fact that Belgium had not sufficiently consulted her partners before decisions on the national level were taken and implemented. When subsequently Belgian policy had no success, her alliance partners were understandably irritated.

152. Ibid., 3 March 1961.

153. 9 (6).

154. *Manchester Guardian,* 1 February 1961.

155. *Times* (London), 1 February 1961.

156. Not surprisingly, the French expressed no regrets at Spaak's departure. 23 (2).

157. 2 (2).

158. *Times* (London), 1 February 1961.

159. 24 (1).

160. 1 (2).

161. *Manchester Guardian,* 8 February 1961. President Kennedy later appointed Dean Acheson as his personal advisor on NATO affairs and head of a study group on Atlantic affairs, in part because of the European support for Spaak's suggestion.

162. *Economist,* 31 December 1960.

163. C. L. Sulzberger, *New York Times,* 28 January 1961; and *Times* (London), 31 January and 1 February 1961.

164. 3 (1).

165. *Le Soir,* 3 March 1961.

3

Dirk Stikker: Caught Between Détente, France, and Europe, 1961-1964

Introduction

To Dirk U. Stikker, who succeeded Paul-Henri Spaak as secretary-general, the concept of transatlantic cooperation was almost second nature. He, earlier than most, appreciated the significance of the common history, institutions, and values shared by Western Europe and North America. As the citizen of a small merchant state, divided equally between Catholics and Protestants, Stikker was intimately acquainted with the functioning of a pluralist, democratic polity. The Netherlands was—and is—one of the world's most internationalist societies, retaining strong overseas political, commercial, religious, artistic, and linguistic links. In his career as a banker and businessman, Stikker's international outlook was substantially reinforced. In the interwar period he became managing director of Heineken Breweries and presided over an expansion of its interests abroad. To establish the company's overseas network, he frequently traveled outside Europe, voyaging to the United States, the Middle East, Africa, and the East and West Indies.[1] Stikker, unlike most diplomats, thus gained extensive knowledge of the operation of a multinational corporation. This was experience that put him in a favorable position to appreciate the implications of the spectacular growth of such enterprises after the Second World War for the international politics of the Atlantic area.

Stikker was raised in comfortable circumstances in Groningen, a busy port and industrial city in the Protestant northeastern section of the Netherlands. His father came from a family of landowners and farmers; his mother's family was comprised of merchants, shipowners, and shipbuilders. Stikker was an indifferent student, not very good at the classics, nor especially stimulated by history. Possessed of a highly pragmatic temperament, he was not given to speculative or theoretical diversions. This practical bent probably explains his lack of diligence, seemingly out of character, at school.[2] When motivated, Stikker was capable of displaying a powerful tenacity and discipline. For example, in an effort to keep up on a bicycle tour of Switzerland, he overexerted himself to the extent that he required more than a year to recover.[3] Stikker did, however, master languages, attaining fluency in English, French, and German. This proved invaluable during his business trips around the world and later in his diplomatic career.[4]

After receiving a degree in law from the University of Groningen, Stikker entered banking, where his drive became evident. His determination and acuity won him advancement and recognition. By the time he was thirty, Stikker had become the youngest managing director at the important Twentsche Bank. He was thirty-eight when he took over the direction of one of Holland's largest corporations—Heineken Breweries. Stikker continued as its chief executive officer until 1948, when he resigned to enter the government. Although he returned to business sixteen years later, Stikker has often said that he derived the greater satisfaction from his career in public life, particularly in diplomacy.[5]

Stikker, like other businessmen, was profoundly affected by the Second World War. As the head of the country's largest brewery, he guided the Dutch cartelized industry in its efforts to protect itself against Nazi economic interests. In this new role, Stikker found himself suddenly thrust into politics; for in dealing with the Germans, economics became politics. More importantly, economic power became a tool of resistance that Stikker shrewdly used. He established an ingenious system for financing underground activities throughout the country by misrepresenting supplies and diverting material away from the military.[6] For a man who previously had taken no interest in political life and had not even attended a single political meeting, his wartime experiences were decisive in radically changing his personal outlook.[7]

Visit of NATO secretary-general to Federal Republic of Germany, 26 June 1961. From left to right: General Foertsch, inspector general of German armed forces; Chancellor K. Adenauer; NATO Secretary-General D. Stikker. (Courtesy NATO Information Service)

106

NATO headquarters, Paris, 21 November 1961. D. Stikker, NATO secretary-general (left) and Lyndon Johnson, vice-president of the United States. (Courtesy NATO Information Service)

NATO headquarters, Paris, 29 July 1964. Dirk Stikker (right), NATO secretary-general, takes leave of the North Atlantic Council; Manlio Brosio succeeds him. (Courtesy NATO Information Service)

After the war, Stikker began to take an active part in Dutch national politics. He helped found the Party of Freedom and Democracy (Liberal) and served as its first chairman. He headed the Foundation of Labor, a joint worker-management organization for the promotion of harmonious industrial relations, and sat in the upper house of Parliament.[8] When in the summer of 1948 the Beel government fell due to the crisis provoked by the grant of independence to the Dutch East Indies, a new coalition was put together and Stikker became foreign minister in return for the support and participation of his small party.[9]

The international experience that Stikker had acquired in the 1930s was to a large extent not relevant to the major problems with which he was now faced in the 1940s. His new government, installed in August 1948, had already witnessed the Soviet coup in Czechoslovakia and the Berlin blockade. The states of Western Europe were in the midst of forming a mutual security policy to counter the Russian threat, and Stikker remained closely involved with the planning and implementation of that policy through the entire course of his diplomatic career. He participated in the early meetings of the Brussels Treaty Organization, which had come into being only weeks before he entered the cabinet, and in the formation of NATO. In fact, he signed the North Atlantic Treaty for the Netherlands.[10] Shortly thereafter Stikker was named chairman of the Organization for European Economic Cooperation, a position he held until 1952. In a short period Stikker earned a reputation as an outstanding diplomat: he was well organized, decisive, and commanded a far-reaching grasp of the intricacies of many issues.[11] These qualities were also recognized within the Netherlands. Accordingly, when the coalition government fell in 1952, rather than lose his abilities, the new government appointed him ambassador to the United Kingdom.

During his six-year stay in London, Stikker was never far from the problems surrounding the constant need to adapt Western security policy to changing world conditions. The extended and often bitter exchange over the EDC, the hastily convened conference of 1954 to amend the Brussels treaty in order to admit West Germany to NATO, and the Suez debacle with its consequences for Western unity were the most prominent matters with which he dealt as the Dutch ambassador. In 1958 he traveled across the Channel to assume a dual position as the permanent representative of the Netherlands to the North Atlantic Council and to the OEEC.

During the early postwar years, Stikker established contacts among the leaders of Western Europe and North America, some of which were later to have a decisive bearing on his future. As foreign minister and ambassador, he came to know well Dean Acheson and Paul Hoffmann, Halvard Lange and Lester Pearson, Anthony Eden and Ernest Bevin, Maurice Couve de Murville and Robert Marjolin, among others. His close friendship with Konrad Adenauer proved to be the most significant, as they were personal as well as political acquaintances, occupying at times neighboring villas on Lake Como.[12] Besides the West German chancellor, Stikker entertained a number of guests at his Menagio home, including Dean Acheson, former U.S. secretary of state, General Norstad, and the redoubtable Paul-Henri Spaak.[13] At these diplomatic-social gatherings, leisure hours were often spent in a discussion of the political and economic events of the day over cognac and coffee. Stikker enjoyed his work and often became so thoroughly involved in it that there existed little distinction between leisure and labor.

Stikker always committed himself fully to whatever job he had to do and would spend long hours absorbing the details of a subject, frequently gaining a better grasp of the issues than his staff.[14] A former associate in the Dutch Foreign Ministry once described him as a "forceful businessman with an astounding capacity for work, a man who knows how to direct a staff, a big powerful man who is not easy to deflect from his opinion of the job to be done."[15] He would personally read everything—books, memoranda, reports—that related to a problem and liked to maintain a firm hold on the reins of responsibility: he insisted that organizational judgments be his. When Stikker made a decision, it was the result of an ordered process of collecting, examining, and evaluating the data. Once convinced, he held fast to an opinion. He liked to refer to himself as pragmatic and certainly deserved the reputation as a solid and impelling administrator.[16]

His pronounced intelligence, forcefulness, and thoroughness—qualities vitally important for the leadership of multi-national political organizations—resulted in his name being put forward for leading positions in international organizations. For example, he rejected suggestions that he become a candidate for the first secretary-general of the OECD.[17] He preferred not to accept the top post at the OECD, for he was convinced the organization would become no more than a consulting forum. His name was also frequently mentioned in connection with the secretary-generalship of NATO.[18] Stikker, along with Halvard Lange of Norway and Lester Pearson of Canada, was among the prospective candidates to be the first secretary-general. At Lisbon, Stikker at first had had the support of British Foreign Secretary Eden. Had he been offered the secretary-generalship, Stikker would have accepted. For with the formation of a new government in the Netherlands in 1951, it was likely that he would soon leave the cabinet, which he did in September of 1952.

When Eden was forced to withdraw his support due to French agreement on the appointment of a Briton, Stikker took this as a personal rebuff.[19] He continued to desire the NATO post. When he finally attained it, he considered it the crowning point of his career. Ironically, it was during his tenure that NATO's position as the keystone of the Atlantic community began to be called into question. Stikker tried to halt this diminution of NATO by attempting to come to grips with the problem of the control of the nuclear deterrent.

In his public personality, Stikker was businesslike, unemotional, almost phlegmatic, although at times he would exclaim about the incompetence of subordinates or the intransigence of opponents.[20] Such occurrences were rare, however, and were restricted to his office or private meetings. In general he maintained a calm and somewhat formal demeanor, but he was very much an individualist. For example, even though he was a founder of the Liberal party, Stikker did not set a good example as a loyal party member, as he had no compunction about disagreeing publicly with its stands. He was roundly criticized, for instance, for his opposition to the transfer of the sovereignty of the Dutch East Indies to Indonesia.[21]

Stikker's independent nature did not fit well the requirements of popular elective politics.[22] Furthermore, he preferred to work out the subtleties of complex situations that truly challenged and engaged him—hence, his interest in nuclear affairs. Yet he found these nuances difficult to communicate to a large audience. Unlike Spaak, he was not a skilled orator. But like his predecessor, he felt that solutions should transcend ideology.

Stikker did not associate easily with people he did not really know and like, preferring to exercise power quietly, away from the public glare, where his intellect and force could most effectively be brought to bear.[23] One example of his participation in the private rather than the public web of influence can be seen in the fact that the day before he officially accepted the foreign minister's portfolio, he signed some seventy letters of resignation as a director in a myriad assortment of business corporations, charities, and private associations. It is thus not surprising to learn that as a man more accustomed to the dialogue of board rooms than the debate of a parliamentary chamber, Stikker had mixed feelings about his years in political office. While pleased to have had the opportunity to exercise power rationally and with restraint, he felt burdened by the not inconsiderable tasks—both political and ceremonial—of a senior cabinet minister. Responsibilities weighed more heavily on him as the representative of the junior partner in a coalition. After two ventures in electoral politics Stikker was thus quite ready, even pleased, to enter Her Majesty's diplomatic corps.[24]

In contrast, Stikker found his six years in London experience better suited to his temperament. His job was to communicate, convey, explain, and influence; the responsibility of decision was left to the new government and its foreign minister. His task was more straightforward, the answers more definite. In addition, Stikker enjoyed living in England.[25]

As the representative of a small state, Stikker wore several hats. Besides his primary capacity as ambassador to the United Kingdom, he served as ambassador to Iceland, Dutch representative on the Permanent Council of the Western European Union (WEU), and chief of his country's delegation to the United Nations Economic and Social Council for 1955-1956.[26] Through his activities in ECOSOC, Stikker developed an abiding interest in the poorer countries of the world, a concern he pursued years later as a consultant to the Asian Development Bank, the United Nations Conference on Trade and Development (UNCTAD), and as an author and advisor on private investment in less-developed countries.[27] As a member of the WEU Council, Stikker remained involved with the crucial problems of West German rearmament and potential contribution to Western defense. The negotiations, which culminated in the Paris Agreement of October 1954 and which provided for membership of the Federal Republic of Germany in NATO, in fact took place in London.

Also, during part of this period Stikker was peripherally involved in the debates over Western European integration. He had been a supporter, though not a leading advocate, of the early schemes for regional integration—the EDC and the Coal and Steel Community.[28] When efforts to persuade the British to join the European Economic Community failed, Stikker spoke in favor of the Anglo-American proposals for nondiscriminatory liberalization of trade barriers throughout the West.[29] While this may have been the most pragmatic position to take under the circumstances, it nonetheless called into question Stikker's devotion to an independent European policy. The dedicated Europeanist Paul-Henri Spaak described Stikker's actions during this period as "excessive timidity."[30]

But Stikker's residence in London placed him outside the mainstream of the European integration movement. Following the ratification of the Treaty of Rome, the EEC set up headquarters in Brussels, and London became even further removed from Western Europe's incipient political center. At this juncture, Stikker was contemplating retirement. When the dual post of permanent representative of the Netherlands to NATO and to the OEEC became available, however, Stikker readily accepted it. In choosing to go to NATO, Stikker had to turn down the prospect of serving on the Economic and Social Committee of the EEC, thus expressing a preference for the broader Atlantic arena. "I was keenly interested," he wrote, "in developments in NATO, which I had been following since 1952 from a distance. To my mind, NATO was, and still is, the center for Atlantic policy. To take part in its daily functioning . . . was to be the most desirable post I could obtain."[31]

This shift to Paris, with which he was quite satisfied, confronted Stikker with a wide range of problems. But with his special talents he quickly established himself as a respected member of the Council: efficient, forthright, realistic and a devourer of thick files.[32] When Spaak resigned as secretary-general a little more than two years after his arrival, Stikker's name headed the short list of those deemed qualified to fill the position.[33] As a prominent politician from a small, enlightened state—much as Spaak had been, although he possessed little of the character of NATO's second secretary-general—Stikker was viewed as Spaak's heir apparent.[34] Like Ismay, Stikker got along quite well with the Americans and, like the first secretary-general, was expected to adopt a less politically aggressive, yet more administrative approach to the position.

The one negative aspect to Stikker's candidacy centered around a genuine concern for his physical capacity to serve as secretary-general—a demanding position in which he would be required to travel frequently and to speak often on behalf of NATO, as well as preside over the intergovernmental organs and the Staff/Secretariat. Illness had slowed Stikker more than once during the 1950s; most recently, in 1959, he had suffered a heart attack that had incapacitated him throughout the winter. By 1961, however, he appeared greatly improved and received a clean bill of health in a medical checkup, which allayed apprehensions in official quarters.[35] When Stikker's friend, General Lauris Norstad, was reappointed SACEUR by the new Kennedy administration, his own appointment as secretary-general seemed assured.[36] Norstad, a highly effective political general, was in a strong position to lobby with the NATO governments on behalf of Stikker.[37]

In early March 1961, just as Spaak was leaving and a successor would have been installed, Stikker's candidacy came suddenly to a halt. The French, who were suspected of opposing Stikker's designation because of his pro-Atlantic views, began floating the names of several prominent alternative candidates in hopes of drawing support from other member states. When the other governments showed no inclination to abandon their support for Stikker's nomination, the French came out in the open by backing the Italian ambassador in Washington, Manlio Brosio. It had been previously understood, when Brosio's name had initially been put forward, that he lacked sufficient stature and would be withdrawn as a contender. But then the Italian government felt obliged to maintain his candidacy, since the French continued to promote him.[38] The Italians, while wishing to avoid embarrassing their American friends, also wanted to maintain good relations with de Gaulle and in any event would have liked to see an Italian as secretary-general.

The French, however, acted from different motives, and their objection to Stikker's politics may very well have been secondary. NATO, after all, was a transatlantic organization, and Stikker's sympathies should have been far more acceptable there than in the EEC Commission, a position for which, as was pointed out, he had also been nominated. De Gaulle appeared to be using the vacant position of secretary-general— which he had helped to bring about by thwarting Spaak's designs—as a means to further his own national policy. Brosio fit conveniently into de Gaulle's plans, because he did not at this time possess the same rank and international stature as had earlier candidates. De Gaulle's effort to diminish the office of secretary-general coincided with his overall strategy to downgrade the organization as a whole. Officially, the French stressed Stikker's halfhearted Europeanism, but they generally refrained from public denunciations because of the wide admiration he commanded.[39]

Technically, the French could hold up confirmation indefinitely because any appointment required unanimous approval. Alberico Casardi, the deputy secretary-general, assumed the chair in the Council pending a decision on the replacement for Spaak, who meanwhile slipped quietly out to rejoin his party. In Paris, suspicions over French motives grew. The United States resented France's attempt to use the vacancy as a means to pressure for changes in the political organization of Western security—changes that could be effected only after extensive discussions among the allies.[40] As the deadlock continued into March, positions hardened and governments became irritated. Unofficially, the British suggested as a compromise that another Englishman would perhaps be acceptable to the French. Lord Gladwyn, former ambassador to France, and Peter Thorneycroft, British minister of aviation, were mentioned as possibilities, as was Greek foreign minister Evanghelos Averoff.[41]

British diplomacy during this period reflected a sensitivity to Continental doubts about its dedication to Europe. The British also desired to keep their relations with France on a most cordial basis, as they were on the verge of applying for membership in the EEC. Meanwhile the United States, through its permanent representative, W. Randolph Burgess, was working hard behind the scenes on behalf of Stikker and was pressuring the British to halt their mediation efforts and come out unequivocally for the Dutch candidate.[42] The continued uncooperativeness of the French, coupled with the American efforts, led the British government to abandon the idea of finding someone agreeable to both sides and to throw their full support behind Stikker. The Italians, fearing the consequences of a prolonged split with themselves caught in the middle, soon thereafter informed the Quai d'Orsay that they had decided to withdraw Brosio's name from consideration. Completely isolated and left without a candidate, the French accepted Stikker. They could have proposed yet another candidate, but that would have constituted an unusually hostile action toward the Netherlands.

There was, however, one consolation for de Gaulle: it was assumed that Stikker's health would not allow him to stay in office for longer than two years. Even though it was not anticipated that he would approach governments in the direct manner or with the fervor of his predecessor, it was speculated that the demands of the job were likely to be more than he could endure over an extended period.[43] Also, it was highly probable that General Norstad would not remain much longer; his ties to the former Republican administration were too close. The Kennedy administration had promised a thorough reassessment of United States foreign policy, which would, of course, include a careful look at the Norstad plan to make NATO a fourth nuclear power. Once the United States had decided on its policy, it was assumed that the field would be surveyed for replacements for these two key positions. If Spaak's departure, which came unexpectedly, had produced problems, the reasoning was that the next one should not.[44]

Although Stikker won the approval of the Kennedy administration for the very practical reason that he was the best choice for the short term, this did not imply an American commitment either to him or to his policies. The decision to support Stikker was made, like many decisions, on the basis of a wait-and-see attitude. The reappointment of Norstad, who was highly popular and influential with Western Europeans, was made in the same spirit. The choice of people on a more permanent basis could only be made after full consultation with America's allies and after careful consideration of those persons who could best carry out any desired shifts in policy. At the beginning of his term President Kennedy did not want to upset the Western European governments' confidence in the United States, already somewhat uncertain about this relatively unknown (and new) president.

In Stikker, however, the Kennedy administration was fortunate to have found a skilled practitioner of the art of the possible. As mentioned earlier, Stikker wanted to be secretary-general and would probably have been asked sooner had it not been for the circumstances prevailing in NATO circles at the time of Spaak's selection.[45] Stikker had not been required to campaign for the office, but nevertheless he wanted to make quite sure that he would not be a rejected candidate.[46]

Stikker's reputation for pragmatism was crucial to the United States in its decision to support him for the secretary-generalship. Few surprises and no grandiose schemes would be forthcoming during his tenure. Also, as a committed Atlanticist and firm anticommunist, Stikker was definitely sympathetic to the American view of NATO. His first premise was that in present and foreseeable circumstances, the states of Western Europe could not hope to defend themselves outside the Atlantic alliance and without the nuclear sword of the United States.[47] Only North America and Western Europe in partnership, he felt, could maintain the West's freedom and prosperity. An integrated defense community, in turn, could provide the most effective implementation of this partnership. A neutralist Western Europe would invite conflict and was incapable of playing the part of a third force, or arbiter, between the United States and the Soviet Union.[48] Furthermore, NATO constituted the foundation of Western unity, a unity which Stikker felt must not be impaired, because division would favor the communist bloc. Logically, then, any solely Western European security organization must be of secondary importance, and "nothing must be done to devalue NATO."[49] NATO was the cement that held the Atlantic area together, and the dissolution or weakening of this alliance would endanger the entire West. Finally, Stikker believed that wider cooperation should be developed within the Atlantic area, looking toward the creation of an Atlantic community.

The United States thus came to be quite satisfied to have Stikker as NATO's third secretary-general. For Stikker, progress was achieved through a daily process of accommodation and compromise by which a body of practice reflecting the alliance's multiplicity of interests would emerge.[50] Stikker's careful and dispassionate assessments of costs and benefits reflected his commercial career. While he was, on occasion, described as unimaginative, it would be inaccurate to label him dogmatic; he was, as already pointed out, pragmatic. For example, because it appeared useful for NATO to use the OEEC's economic studies, Stikker arranged a procedure acceptable to the neutrals of the latter organization for NATO to obtain access to the OEEC's statistical data.[51]

Administration under Stikker

It was generally anticipated that Stikker's appointment would signal a return to Lord Ismay's leadership style of solid administration and behind-the-scenes conciliation.[52] In the former area, Stikker fulfilled all expectations. He regularly worked a fourteen-hour day, seven days a week, poring over piles of documents and background material.[53] The written word was his preferred mode of communication.[54] Methodical in approach, he researched all aspects of a problem before coming to a decision.[55] On the other hand, there were those who considered him the most talented of the secretaries-general.[56] Opinions as to Stikker's managerial abilities seemed to depend on one's politics: supporters of the Anglo-American concept of the Atlantic alliance were more likely to view his working methods as measured and thoughtful, while backers of the French challenge tended to see them as vacuous and obstructive.[57] Stikker paid great attention to detail and insisted that procedures be followed.

The question of Stikker's health, which had been a factor in his appointment as secretary-general, remained in the forefront throughout his incumbency. For the first year and one-half, he was able to work long hours, as he had done before his heart attack in 1959. Toward the end of September 1962, however, Stikker was hospitalized with what turned out to be cancer of the intestine.[58] The malignancy was successfully removed at Walter Reed Hospital in Washington, but it was three months before he could return to his desk. Although he was provided with communication facilities and a secretary, and was consulted at vital junctures, Stikker was effectively excluded from participating in NATO's affairs during several of the most crucial weeks that the West had experienced since the end of the war. October 1962 saw the Cuban missile crisis unfold, and December witnessed the Nassau Agreement between President Kennedy and Prime Minister Macmillan. This latter event was to become the primary justification for de Gaulle's veto of British membership in the Common Market in January 1963.

Because much of the secretary-general's influence derives from his prerogative to deal directly with governments through personal intervention on behalf of the common interests of the alliance, and from his ability to function as the West's spokesman, Stikker's illness prevented him from fulfilling two of his most important roles. Never completely recovering his strength, Stikker became ill again following the ministerial meeting in the spring of 1963. After several more weeks in the hospital, he returned to Paris uncertain about his capacity to carry on.[59] His physical condition continued to affect his performance for the remainder of his term, including limiting his social activities as secretary-general.[60] He chose to live at the Hotel George V, while the Villa Said was turned over to Alberico Casardi, the deputy secretary-general, and Casardi's successor, both of whom inherited some of the secretary-general's social responsibilities along with his residence. Stikker was not a naturally gregarious man; his warmth was most evident in small groups of close colleagues. In this respect he was indeed a great change from the voluble Spaak.[61]

This, coupled with the fact that he was not readily available to the press, contributed to his low-profile public image.[62] Still, Stikker enjoyed better relations with the press than did his more publicly temperamental predecessor. This was so, because he approached his press conferences with the same methodical care he brought to any task. Having been persuaded by the American delegation to engage more in public relations, Stikker gave press conferences that benefitted from the extensive preparations he made with his staff. When he did meet with newsmen, Stikker was careful to answer their questions fully.[63] In fact, he had more difficulty with his own press officer than with the press corps. All press releases required his personal approval, and he was not inclined to volunteer much information with which his press officer might respond to the numerous queries he normally had to handle on behalf of the secretary-general.[64]

Regarding his leadership of the Staff/Secretariat as a whole, Stikker fulfilled the expectations that had arisen at the time of his appointment. Like Ismay, Stikker fully used and relied on his personal staff, although he never enjoyed Ismay's popularity with them nor did he take them as much into his personal confidence. He did, however, try to look after his staff's welfare and to give the NATO Secretariat some functional coherence by curtailing the need for its members to turn to their delegations for assistance in obtaining better working conditions. When, for instance, the French blocked an increase in salaries, Stikker fought for the raise.[65] Stikker sought to balance the wishes of the delegations to have direct influence on the Staff/Secretariat's work, with the desire, mostly from the upper echelons of the Secretariat, for a politically neutral Staff/Secretariat. Even its official name, "The International Staff/Secretariat," reflected its ambiguous nature as both a nonpartisan international civil service and a multinational alliance-supporting staff.

A debate on recruitment procedures and the conditions of

service within the Staff/Secretariat had been going on within NATO prior to Stikker's arrival. One group held that the international staff should be drawn from national bureaucracies for short-term contracts of approximately two years. Another group argued that recruitment should be on a career basis. Lord Coleridge, who in effect controlled administrative affairs and who, like Lord Ismay, came from a long national tradition of impartial public service, supported the latter view, as did some of the smaller member states. The rationale behind this view was that good people could only be attracted to fill career openings. Also, in nontechnical areas, it was argued, people ought to acquire a broad international outlook, which was best cultivated if their fortunes were independent of national sanction. It was generally felt, for example, that the Political Division suffered from precisely the national parochialism that Coleridge desired to avoid.

Signor Casardi, with the strong backing of the big powers, took the opposite stand. He was convinced that the constant circulation of national bureaucrats into the Staff/Secretariat and back to their governments would advance NATO's interests among the member governments, where it ultimately counted. The majority of the delegations concurred with this opinion, as they saw fixed-term appointments as a means of safeguarding their interests in the organization. The issue was approaching resolution by the beginning of 1961, when Spaak chose to let the member states have their way. Stikker reluctantly accepted the dominant view soon after he became secretary-general. The Council subsequently endorsed the change to short-term contracts after a perfunctory discussion.[66]

Stikker retained many of the senior staff members. Lord Coleridge, who remained as executive secretary, benefitted considerably from the reversal in the working habits of the secretary-general brought about by the personal attention Stikker gave to administrative matters. Furthermore, Coleridge continued as secretary to the Council and its committees.[67] In sum, Stikker valued highly the presence of a capable and experienced British civil servant in the upper ranks of the Staff/Secretariat.[68]

Johnson Garrett, an American, stayed on as assistant

secretary-general for production and logistics, as did Robin Hooper of Great Britain as assistant secretary-general for political affairs. The Frenchman François-Didier Gregh remained in charge of the Economics and Finance Division. Understandably, Stikker wanted his own *chef de cabinet* to replace André Saint Mleux. The French ambassador, Pierre de Leusse, and Spaak both sent notes to the new secretary-general concerning possible choices.[69] But Stikker, who liked Americans, felt it was important to have one close to him and thus chose George Vest, a foreign service officer in the U.S. NATO delegation in Paris as his *chef de cabinet*. After Vest departed for Washington in 1963, another State Department officer, John Getz, took his place. Stikker's door was always open to his *chef de cabinet*, and Vest worked especially well with Stikker, often acting on his behalf with the permanent representatives and assistant secretaries-general, as a *chef de cabinet* must if he is to perform his job. He was one of the few people who enjoyed Stikker's complete confidence.[70]

A deficiency inherent in the office of the secretary-general, of which Stikker frequently complained, was the limited amount of information available to him. His major sources of information were newspapers (which Spaak had used predominantly); the permanent representatives, who passed along to him whatever they cared to; and the assistant secretary-general for political affairs (in this case Robin Hooper), who acted as a sort of extra set of eyes and ears. Most importantly, the secretary-general did not routinely receive the telegrams that normally convey the substance of diplomatic intercourse. A constant flow of information seemed to Stikker to be a prerequisite for the exercise of the office. He once complained about this to Secretary of State Dean Rusk and suggested that a personal representative of the secretary-general be authorized to sit with the Standing Group in Washington. This, Stikker argued, would give him the advantage of having a trusted aide well situated to monitor political developments in the capital of the alliance's leading member. There were, however, objections from all sides, and Stikker abandoned the idea.[71]

George Vest helped to mitigate this shortage of authoritative intelligence. As an officer of the United States government seconded to NATO—he was still paid by the Department of State—Vest had access to the cable traffic of the United States embassy in Paris. Early every morning before going to his NATO office at the Place Dauphine, he would examine the day's messages and then report relevant, unclassified material to the secretary-general. The British also began to send information through a similar channel, after Stikker repeatedly complained about the paucity of information available to him.[72]

When Stikker assumed office, the deputy secretary-general, Alberico Casardi, had been serving as acting secretary-general during the interregnum. Casardi had kept Stikker in the picture on decisions taken during the period when the French were holding up his appointment.[73] When Casardi left soon afterward to become Italian ambassador to Belgium, Stikker had the choice of three Italian diplomats to fill the post—two senior officers and one of relatively lower rank. Stikker picked the latter candidate, Don Guido Colonna di Paliano, partly because he had known him at the OEEC.[74] It is worth taking note of Colonna, for although extraordinarily discreet and tactful, he quickly established himself as an influence with the permanent representatives and proved his worth when he served as acting secretary-general during those periods when Stikker was incapacitated. Warm, sophisticated and wise, he received high marks from his colleagues for his contributions at all times, but especially for his leadership of the Staff/Secretariat during Stikker's absences.[75] General Norstad also worked well with Colonna, and the military authorities in general respected him.[76]

Presiding over the December 1962 ministerial meeting with firm authority, Colonna displayed none of the inhibitions that might come from the temporary nature of his position.[77] But, on the other hand, Colonna did not take any undue initiatives; nor did he challenge the secretary-general. In 1964, Colonna's earlier, and entirely creditable, performance made him the leading candidate in Paris to succeed Stikker.[78] However, when the official search for a secretary-general began, the Italian government was not prepared to put him forward as a candidate because of his unpopularity with the left wing of the ruling coalition in Rome.[79] Instead, Colonna was appointed a commissioner of the European Community.[80]

On political matters, the secretary-general consulted Robin Hooper and Hooper's German deputy, Joachim Jaenicke.[81] Hooper was the key man in the secretary-general's external communications, jointly shaping Stikker's image and NATO's, through an active supervision of the press office.[82] Hooper, along with Vest, Coleridge, Paul van Campen, François-Didier Gregh, and Gregh's deputy David Bendall, contributed to the secretary-general's speeches, which Stikker found needed little alteration.[83] Gregh was the only Frenchman to have an important administrative role during Stikker's tenure. In general, Stikker did not enjoy working with the French, because he felt they were constantly raising objections and creating tensions. But Gregh, who maintained good relationships with the Quai d'Orsay, was able to retain Stikker's confidence.[84] Unfortunately, his nationality made his position conditional in the eyes of the Americans, who, for example, objected to his inclusion in the discussions on the proposed NATO multilateral nuclear force (MLF). Stikker was unhappy about this but yet was unwilling to oppose the United States on the matter.[85]

On one occasion in 1962, when the director of information, John McGowan of the United States, was recalled to Washington, Stikker did refuse American advice. The United States NATO delegation insistently pressed its candidate and declined to present any alternative when Stikker asked for one, so Stikker turned them down in favor of a West German, Count Adelmann, who thus became one of the first of his countrymen to occupy a major executive position in the Staff/Secretariat.[86]

On economic and defense questions, Stikker relied heavily on Gregh for the data necessary for effective position papers. This reliance, in turn, led to the growth of the economic and financial directorate. As primary advisors on defense, Gregh and his British deputy, David Bendall, whom Gregh had requested, had the responsibility for the triennial review, which had been adopted in 1961 to replace the inadequate annual review process.[87] Bendall shouldered more and more of the burden from 1963 on, as the United States made it increasingly difficult for Gregh to operate in the area of defense policy. Gregh, who had reached the height of his influence at NATO in the late 1950s and early 1960s when Spaak delegated many administrative functions to him, thus ran afoul of the Franco-American dispute. His expertise and bureaucratic facility did not go unnoticed or unused by Stikker, but the secretary-general's desire to employ the assets of all the members of the Staff/Secretariat could not overcome the effects of the strained relations between the two powers. Even though Gregh was not a Gaullist, American nervousness with Gregh's expanded role in the secretariat was only intensified by the increasing tempo of Gaullist nationalism in the mid-1960s.

Furthermore, Gregh's managerial skills had earned him the respect of the British; and if there existed a strain between himself and Coleridge, it was that of creative tension. However, when the French and British quarreled over British membership in the EEC, Gregh suffered on two fronts. He lost whatever standing he had with the Gaullists because of his good working relations with the British, who in turn shied away from dealing with him because of the coolness and suspicion French Gaullism had engendered in NATO.[88]

Stikker himself was not immune from the negative side effects of France's political conflicts with her alliance partners. He had to contend with a hostile French attitude toward the Staff/Secretariat in general. French policy, which relegated international organizations to a secondary importance in the conduct of international relations, specifically aimed at diminishing the status and functioning of NATO's bureaucracy. Besides the veto of a pay raise, the French government frequently failed to respond to requests from the Staff/Secretariat for cooperation and would hold up approval of high-ranking staff appointments for prolonged periods. General de Gaulle continued to slight the organization through his treatment of its secretary-general, refusing to even receive Stikker throughout his term. As the leader of NATO, Stikker quite naturally resisted but with only limited success.

The difficulties Gregh and Stikker encountered were, of course, symptoms of the powerful cross currents enveloping NATO and the Staff/Secretariat during this period. A respected secretary-general offered the best chance to mediate the influence of the delegations and their governments on the Staff/Secretariat, for he alone could approach the members directly and muster support for a nonpolitical international civil service. The ability of the secretary-general to stand above partisan conflict and to keep the ear of all involved was thus paramount in determining not only his own success or failure, but also the future of the organization. Unfortunately, in his relations with the member states and their representatives in Paris, Stikker was not able to maintain a strictly neutral attitude chiefly because of the Franco-American rift.

Relations with the Council

As chief executive officer of the Staff/Secretariat and chairman of the alliance's highest organ, the Council, the secretary-general is at the political center of the alliance. Stikker would be briefed by the heads of each department—thus carefully respecting the chain of command—before each Council meeting, which with his aides—Vest, Hooper, Colonna, van Campen, and Coleridge—he carefully coordinated and planned. He kept a record of the position of each member state on the major subjects before the Council. New topics were first explored by his staff before they were debated in the Council, where a full exchange of views was encouraged. Thus, before entering the Council chamber, Stikker was always fully prepared; even novel approaches to problems appeared well thought out in advance, in contrast to the spontaneous ideas with which Spaak sporadically peppered the permanent representatives. If anything, Stikker was criticized for placing too great an emphasis on detail and giving insufficient attention to the broader picture.[89]

With more than a hundred people present at each Council meeting, there was a real need for the chairman to control the list and order of speakers, to limit discussion, and to intervene to cut off debate when it began to go astray. On occasion, the secretary-general had also to initiate debate on the implications for the alliance of some event or series of events. Having once been a member of the club-like group of permanent representatives, Stikker seemed to make a special effort to disassociate himself from the group in order to achieve the standing necessary to chair the Council.[90] He nurtured a sense of personal authority that not only tended to reinforce his ability to carry out the functions of his office but also imbued him with a supreme sense of confidence. Stikker was not above challenging a permanent representative by asking, "Are you under instructions or is this your opinion?"[91] Such remonstrances, useful as they might have been, were not welcomed by his former Council colleagues.

It was not Stikker's habit to openly dominate Council meetings, but in practice he sometimes gave that appearance. He returned to the form of agenda introduced by Lord Ismay by reducing the number of long, general, politically oriented speeches and by introducing more strictly military topics. Believing the Council should take seriously its supervisory functions of NATO's military arm, Stikker encouraged the civilians to ask for explanations from SHAPE.[92] Although he stressed that unanimity was not necessary for Council action, in practice, he recognized that wisdom and the spirit of the alliance required that every effort be made to reach a consensus; and so formal motions and votes rarely occurred.[93] Consideration of an agenda item often ended with a summary conclusion by the secretary-general and with his *"pas d'objection?"* Unless there was vigorous exception to the prevailing opinion, the chairman would then proceed to introduce the next order of business.[94] Having covered many facets of a question with his staff prior to the meeting of the Council, Stikker unintentionally at times tended to assume that all had been considered. When this occurred, those permanent representatives who felt excluded from the decision-making process were tempted to oppose some decisions and thus to insist that the secretary-general take explicitly into account their interests in the policy-formulation stage. The result made for some pointed exchanges between the secretary-general and some of the permanent representatives.

The contrast between Spaak's and Stikker's style was striking. Stikker was cautious and reluctant to test his ideas spontaneously, while Spaak was only too happy to share his thoughts with others, even if they were not too well thought out. Curiously, their dissimilar behavior caused a similar reaction in many member states, i.e., considerable anxiety over what they might say. Because he would at times do things with a minimum of prior consultation with the permanent representatives, Stikker could at times prove disconcerting. For example, at a press conference in Oslo in September 1962, Stikker expressed a personal desire to see the United Kingdom, and the other states seeking membership in the Common Market, accepted into the community.[95] While the United States and British governments might have been happy to have his support, other states, and France in particular, were somewhat displeased at this public intrusion into the affairs of the EEC by the secretary-general of NATO.

The representatives had been accustomed to close informal contact with the secretary-general, having been able to see Ismay and Spaak on short notice; those from the smaller states found Stikker relatively inaccessible and thus had difficulty assessing his intentions.[96] To compensate for this lack of access to the secretary-general, several representatives, including André de Staercke and Thomas Finletter, began to meet informally to share views and information on the problems of the alliance. Four or five would meet over lunch, where it was not necessary to weigh their words carefully or to follow their instructions rigidly. These representatives would sometimes agree on a common attitude, which, after being cleared with their governments, could then be quickly adopted in the full Council. Stikker was invited to attend these sessions but refused, stating that he preferred the traditional procedure and that the representatives should be free to consult in any manner they wished. After six or seven months, when the fruitfulness of these gatherings became apparent, most of the other permanent representatives joined the small caucus. These informal meetings eventually generated their own protocol: they would be held weekly at a luncheon to be hosted by each representative in alphabetical rotation.[97] Thus diplomatic intercourse began to bypass the secretary-general, rather than centering on him, but this was not intended to be in opposition to him.

André de Staercke, the doyen of the NATO diplomatic corps, played an important role in Council diplomacy during this period. A truly skillful diplomat, de Staercke maintained cordial relations with all member states and persons throughout what became more than twenty years as Belgium's permanent representative at NATO. He had been a leader in forming the

informal luncheon meetings and when necessary had taken it
upon himself to convey the permanent representatives' deliberations to the secretary-general. But, knowing well the modes of
diplomatic speech and behavior, he did not try to press Stikker
and avoided any possible confrontation with him. The substance
and subtlety de Staercke brought to his position as doyen,
whether handling interambassadorial disputes or negotiating
claims of privilege with the host government, more than made
up for any pretentions to power he might have exhibited.

The recurring complaints that Stikker either ignored or
bickered with the permanent representatives stemmed in part
from a resentment of the secretary-general's close association
with the Americans.[98] Stikker was convinced that the secretary-
general must be well acquainted with the thinking of the American government, a sentiment which, as mentioned earlier,
motivated him to propose that he have a personal representative
in Washington. Accompanied by his American *chef de cabinet,*
Stikker made frequent visits to the United States, returning
every three months during his last two years in office. From his
first meeting with President Kennedy, less than two months
after his designation as secretary-general, Stikker got along well
with the young American leader, finding him charming, dis-
cerning, and in full grasp of the complexities of the world
situation.[99] During a stay, which averaged about four days, he
would see Secretary of State Dean Rusk and Secretary of
Defense Robert McNamara and would be updated on developments at the Pentagon and Treasury through special briefings.[100]
Thus, the favored status Stikker accorded the Americans was
reciprocated in their respectful attitude toward him.[101]

Relations with Member Governments

Despite his open and easy connection to Washington, Stikker
did not enjoy much more than a formal relationship with the
American permanent representative, Thomas K. Finletter.[102]
Finletter, a New York liberal Democrat and leader of the reform movement, was known for his pungent and unsentimental
judgments.[103] Although he served on the president-elect's
defense establishment task force and was later appointed to

NATO, Finletter never gained a prominent voice in the Kennedy administration. He had been a latecomer to the Kennedy entourage, having supported Adlai Stevenson for the Democratic presidential nomination until the convention. Furthermore, having been secretary of the Air Force under President Truman, he opposed the limited war doctrine that was to be adopted as American policy in the early 1960s. A generation older than the typical New Frontiersman, Finletter nevertheless was recognized as possessing a tenacity of purpose and clarity of mind that made it unwise to take him lightly.[104] Stikker, however, preferred to work through his vigorous American *chef de cabinet* over the permanent representative to get a reading on thinking in Washington.[105]

In his desire to keep the channels to Washington clear, Stikker was inclined to see issues in terms defined by the United States. It appeared to many of his European colleagues that he would too quickly endorse American policy,[106] that he would too enthusiastically rally to its initiatives.[107] His frequent rejections of Gaullist-inspired proposals seemed too unconditional for the secretary-general of an organization depending heavily on international cooperation, and thus any chance that might have existed for him to mediate the Franco-American dispute was foreclosed.[108] Rightly or wrongly, some Europeans felt that Stikker tended to neglect the European point of view and thus was unable to create an independent NATO consensus.

Furthermore, his contested appointment as secretary-general was an inauspicious start with the French. As already mentioned, de Gaulle and Stikker personally had little regard for one another and disagreed with each other's policies.[109] De Gaulle's "Europe of States" from the Atlantic to the Urals, free of American influence, was unacceptable to Stikker, the devoted Atlanticist. Nevertheless, Stikker acknowledged the contribution de Gaulle had made to the West in reestablishing order and vitality to France. Considering the organization and strength of the French Communist party, the turmoil that had arisen in 1958 had given rise to fears of permanent damage to allied security. Only a man of great courage and unquestioned accomplishment could have succeeded in restoring stability to France. But Stikker judged de Gaulle's leadership as flawed by personalism and a pretension to grandeur. "My own feeling," wrote Stikker, "is that we of the Atlantic world owe, just as to Roosevelt and Churchill, a lasting debt of gratitude to de Gaulle for what he did in 1940 and 1958." However, he added that "under de Gaulle France has become, I believe, our weakest link. And I also believe that it is for just that reason that the leadership of Europe, which de Gaulle regards as France's mission and consonant with French grandeur, will, as it did when the EDC collapsed, elude France for the second time."[110] Because Dutch government policy favored the progressive development of institutionalized international cooperation, there may have been doubt as to whether de Gaulle would have approved the designation of any Dutch national as NATO secretary-general. On the other hand, however, the disaffected attitude that France adopted toward NATO raised questions as to whether any secretary-general would have made much of a difference.[111]

In spite of the inherent antagonism, Stikker made a genuine effort to maintain a working relationship with France. He carefully observed protocol vis-à-vis the French government, for he clearly understood that de Gaulle placed more than ordinary significance on the symbols of nationhood.[112] But the treatment Stikker received at the hands of the French government consistently fell far short of that accorded him by other governments. His petition to pay his respects to de Gaulle as the newly installed secretary-general of NATO went unanswered for three months. It was only after the intervention of his friend, Chancellor Konrad Adenauer, that he was eventually received. The ensuing interview lasted twenty-five minutes. They never spoke again, as de Gaulle chose to ignore Stikker even to the point of not responding to his request to make the usual farewell courtesy call on his retirement.[113] Stikker had no illusions as to his acceptability at the Elysée Palace but considered it his duty to find a formula to allow a unified NATO to continue and to minimize its internal conflicts.[114]

Stikker met with Prime Minister Michel Debré once and Prime Minister Georges Pompidou twice and had only one brief, private conversation with Foreign Minister Maurice Couve de Murville. There was thus some justification for his assessment of French diplomacy as petty. Only with Minister of Defense Pierre Messmer did Stikker have any sustained contact and rapport; they talked confidentially several times.[115]

Stikker's virtual ostracism from the highest levels of the French government was also an indication of the direction of French policy toward NATO: uncooperative and unflexible. Throughout much of 1961 the secretary-general volunteered to give the French permanent representative an official report after returning from official visits to Bonn, London, or Washington, as he did to the doyen and other key representatives.[116] The French never accepted Stikker's offer, and so he ceased extending it. And conversely, in the more than three years Stikker served as secretary-general, he read a French political report only once or twice.[117]

The French delegation, Stikker felt, refused to take part in substantial portions of Council and ministerial meetings, failed to exchange information or contribute to policy discussions. Stikker's list of the positions of NATO member states on major issues showed France with five times more disagreements with the consensus than any other member.[118] The individualism that characterized French foreign policy and the intensity of its nationalism seemed to Stikker to be contradictory to the spirit of the Atlantic alliance.

Having learned at firsthand of French displeasure with NATO and of the fruitlessness of efforts to rectify the situation through direct contact with French political authorities, Stikker resolved to carry on without confronting them. The severe limitation on what could be accomplished with goodwill, patience, and imperturbability made it prudent for Stikker to alter his earlier direct approach. Information could be, and was, obtained indirectly. His relations with the French became coldly courteous.[119] His tolerance was further strained by what appeared to him as France's willful destruction of the alliance's solidarity in unnecessary attacks on the United States. To Stikker, the times required mutual esteem and trust, not recrimination. Although publicly the secretary-general might refrain from direct criticism of the French, privately he would evince a sympathy for the United States. And, he was not above obliquely referring to the "disturbing influence of some."[120]

Inevitably, after repeated private clashes, the hostility between French leaders and the secretary-general came into the open.[121]

Surprisingly, in the face of these tensions, Stikker and François Seydoux, the French ambassador to NATO from 1962 to 1964, remained on good terms.[122] In what was invariably a receptive and congenial atmosphere, Seydoux would frequently confer with Stikker in the latter's office.[123] The explanation behind this paradox lay in a phenomenon peculiar to the Gaullist period: there existed two distinct levels of French diplomacy— state-to-state and person-to-person. The harshness of the official denunciation of the American hegemony presented a dilemma for French diplomats, who, given the still great community of interests shared by the two Western powers, had the unenviable task of complying with the governmental policy of the moment without compromising fundamental national interests. Perhaps appreciating the need for a margin of maneuver, the Quai d'Orsay allowed its NATO representatives a wider-than-usual latitude. Thus, even though cool official relations might impede intercourse at the highest level, the professional diplomats at the working level seldom let this interfere with their normal functions.[124]

Seydoux's predecessor, Pierre de Leusse, a career diplomat who had chosen to serve with the Free French during the Second World War, operated as independently of the Foreign Ministry as could be expected of a Gaullist in Paris.[125] Seydoux, who probably was a moderate Gaullist, also believed in the value of not publicly offending one's allies while defending his government's policy. Dean Acheson, sent to NATO as President Kennedy's envoy during the tense days of the Cuban missile crisis, addressed the Council at Seydoux's first appearance there. The latter gave the United States France's full support and subsequently never reflected the negative attitude toward NATO that his superiors at times demonstrated.[126] Seydoux utilized the leeway allowed him to cement ties within the NATO diplomatic community, specifically with the American permanent representative, Thomas Finletter, and the West German representative, Wilhelm Grewe.[127]

The British, who preferred a secretary-general with a low profile, were happy enough with Stikker. The older hands knew and trusted him.[128] Perhaps the Briton closest to Stikker was Robin Hooper, who was a great help to him in gaining the cooperation of the United Kingdom's delegation in Paris and in keeping Stikker up-to-date on London's attitude regarding NATO questions.

As long as Konrad Adenauer was chancellor—and even afterwards, for Adenauer had considerable influence with his handpicked successor, Ludwig Erhard—there was no doubt about Stikker's access to the West German government. Stikker's strong rebuff of Khrushchev's endeavor to undermine the allied position in Berlin, as well as his argument for a firm stand backed by military force including nuclear weapons if necessary, won him a warm reception with the government of the Federal Republic.[129] Stikker maintained an extended dialogue with Bonn from his earliest days in office, the Bundesrepublik receiving one of his first official visits after becoming secretary-general.[130] Adenauer trusted Stikker to consider West German interests sympathetically. For example, when at the ministerial meeting of December 1962 U.S. Secretary of Defense Robert McNamara made a statement alluding to the need for substantial increases in Western European conventional arms as the answer to potential aggression by the Soviet Union, the West Germans were deeply disturbed by the potential implications of this attitude for the stationing of American troops in Europe. Adenauer asked Stikker to come to Bonn, even though Stikker was still recuperating from illness and had been unable to attend the December meeting. The old chancellor clearly had confidence that Stikker would listen to him and convey his astonishment over this sudden shift taken by the United States without consulting him.[131]

Stikker had a checkered record with the other member states. While he was in office, the Italians did not figure prominently in NATO affairs, concentrating their energies on a turbulent domestic political scene that experienced another shock as the country acclimated itself to its first Center-Left coalition. With the Belgians, who were traditionally close to the French, Stikker carried little influence. André de Staercke was sometimes concerned about the secretary-general's somewhat distant manner and by his apparent occasional neglect of the smaller states.[132] Other member states shared de Staercke's feelings in varying degrees.

Although he did not always see eye-to-eye with Dutch Foreign Minister Joseph Luns, Stikker remained close to its NATO delegation. His colleague and former deputy permanent representative, Johan de Ranitz, was able to keep Stikker posted on diplomatic currents until de Ranitz went to Brussels in 1962. Stikker's successor as Dutch representative to NATO, Hendrik Boon, who had risen in the Dutch foreign service under Stikker's patronage, maintained the constant Dutch presence with the secretary-general.[133]

NATO Diplomacy

As each secretary-general had to deal with various phases of the problems surrounding Cyprus, the different methods they employed offer an illuminating comparison of their styles. When Greece, Turkey, and the United Kingdom reached a series of agreements in London and Zurich in August 1960 that granted Cyprus its independence, that troubled island appeared to have attained a degree of stability. At the Ministerial Council of December 1963, Stikker's inquiry to the Turkish and Greek foreign ministers elicited assurances that Cyprus was causing no trouble and relations between them had never been better.[134] These were optimistic assessments, for the constitutional arrangements of Cyprus had been eroding for more than a year. Only ten days after the Council meeting, civil war erupted when President Archbishop Makarios signified his intention to put into effect amendments to the constitutional accords that had been rejected by the Turkish government. War once more threatened to break out between Greece and Turkey over the island republic, which itself was not a NATO member or protected territory although it hosted strategic British military installations.

As the new year opened, there was no break in the crisis. In January 1964 a conference in London failed to resolve the dispute, and an Anglo-American plan to place an international force on Cyprus drawn from NATO member states in order to separate the two ethnic communities was refused by Makarios.

Stikker, who as Dutch foreign minister had opposed the expansion of NATO to the eastern Mediterranean, dispatched notes to the interested governments.[135] But until late April, when the Turkish government indicated it would likely bring the Cyprus question before the forthcoming ministerial meeting, Stikker confined his diplomatic activities to Paris. The one exception was a scheduled visit to Washington in early February, when Cyprus was among the topics he discussed with President Johnson. Stikker voiced his distress over the situation but noted that the alliance was not directly involved, because the island was not a member. He also noted that he did not believe the parties were on a collision course.[136] These public sentiments appeared strange in view of the dangerous trend of events and his privately declared concern over the high risk of war.[137] They may have reflected the secretary-general's desire to follow the American lead in minimizing his role in this volatile situation or his own desire to avoid being publicly out front if he could help it.

In fact, late one Sunday evening, hardly more than a week before Stikker's trip to the United States, American Representative Finletter and United Kingdom Representative Evelyn Shuckburgh, themselves recently apprised by their respective governments of preparations that signaled the imminent outbreak of fighting between Greece and Turkey, had disclosed the content of these reports to Stikker. He replied that on the basis of the report of the Committee of Three on Nonmilitary Cooperation, the secretary-general had the right and duty to intervene to help settle intermember disputes, but he was reluctant to act without more concrete proof.[138] Would the representatives supply him with the telegrams containing the necessary information? They declined to furnish him with the dispatches as the documents were classified. Stikker then called the SACEUR, General Lyman Lemnitzer, to see if SHAPE could confirm the intelligence.[139] Lemnitzer flew to Ankara and Athens where he was able to verify the seriousness of the situation. Turkish troops were massing and naval vessels were cruising off the coast of Cyprus. Greek special units had been ordered to stand by and air, naval, and army units had been sent out on combined maneuvers. An appeal from Stikker to exercise restraint and to suspend plans to intervene in Cyprus was heeded by Turkish Premier Ismet Inönü, thus temporarily averting hostilities, as both countries halted provocative military movements.[140]

February and March saw the United Nations grope toward the formation of a truce supervisory operation, while intercommunal fighting flared intermittently. Stikker conferred on the matter with UN Secretary-General U Thant while the latter was in Paris.[141] Finally, at the end of April, in preparation for the forthcoming ministerial meeting, Stikker traveled to the area, arriving in Ankara on 27 April. On the next day he left for Athens, where the Greeks undercut his mission by leaking their conversations with him to the press, because they did not want to regionalize the conflict by allowing NATO to participate directly, preferring instead the world forum provided by the United Nations.[142] Publicly Stikker again adopted the stance that there would be no hostilities between NATO members: "The word 'war' does not exist between Turkey and Greece."[143] The Ministerial Council, however, engaged in a bitter debate on the question of Cyprus. In conclusion, the Council decided to reaffirm its confidence in the United Nations mediator and instructed Secretary-General Stikker to follow the situation closely and to consult with the Council when he deemed it appropriate. It was a neat package: support for the effort of the United Nations to placate the Greeks and recognition of NATO's interest to satisfy the Turks.[144]

In June, under the Council's mandate, Stikker made a second trip to Ankara and Athens in an attempt to get the parties together to talk the problem over. He strongly denied any suggestion that he was acting as a mediator: "I am a watch-dog trying to diminish tensions between Greece and Turkey," was his description of the assignment.[145] The Greek government, which was committed to seeking a solution through the United Nations, balked at receiving him. However, the unexpected arrival of the U.S. undersecretary of state, George Ball, from Geneva ensured that the Greeks would at least listen. After a long conversation over dinner at the American ambassador's residence, Stikker and Ball departed the next day for Ankara, where they advocated face-to-face discussions, but without positive results.[146] Stikker's original skepticism about the value of the mission—given the tenuous standing of the secretary-general for handling a problem outside the jurisdiction of NATO—had been increased by the uncooperative stance taken by the Greeks. After having fulfilled the Council's request, Stikker threw up his hands and declared: "There is no chance for me to take any active role from this moment onwards."[147] He was content to keep abreast of the affair from his Paris office. It was not his style to interpose himself between disputing parties nor to render unsolicited advice, because he did not want to run the risk of offending unnecessarily a member of the alliance. The contrast between Stikker's cautious methods and those of his predecessor—direct, bold, and public—is striking. Stikker's conception of the secretary-generalship did not allow him to attempt to formulate an independent policy.

Another illustration of Stikker's style as secretary-general can be seen in his approach to proposals for the strengthening of the institutional framework of the Atlantic community. The unexpected success of the European Economic Community gave new impetus to the notion of creating common institutions among the industrialized, democratic states of Western Europe and North America.[148] The application of the United Kingdom and some of its EFTA partners for membership in the EEC gave rise to increased hopes for a United States of Europe. After considerable speculation, the British government submitted its application in August 1961, and formal negotiations began in January 1962. That same January, President Kennedy introduced in Congress a trade expansion bill, which he explained was designed to encourage a more tightly knit community of the Western states through reciprocal agreements to lower trade barriers. The purpose of the program was not only economic but also political, military, and cultural: it sought to strengthen the solidarity of the West.[140]

The response to these events was positive. At the beginning of 1962, private delegations from the fifteen NATO member states met in Paris to draft a statement of common principles. The conference was a manifestation of the expansion of the Atlantic movement, which had developed a network of associations in all the member states enjoying substantial elite support.

The Paris conference was attended by a former prime minister, several former ministers and cabinet officers, legislators, generals, and business and civic leaders. It adopted a seven-point Declaration of Atlantic Unity calling for: (1) an intergovernmental commission to draw up a charter for an Atlantic community; (2) a high council to act by a weighted majority on matters of mutual concern; (3) the transformation of the NATO parliamentarians conference into a consultative Atlantic assembly; (4) the establishment of an Atlantic high court of justice; and (5) other measures for the development of an Atlantic community. In November, the annual conference of NATO parliamentarians endorsed the Declaration of Paris and set up a subcommittee to study plans for greater Atlantic unity including the conversion of the existing conference into an Atlantic assembly on the lines recommended in the declaration.[150]

Immediately following the conference, the British government raised several practical difficulties involved in the implementation of the goals of the Paris declaration.[151] And the American government preferred a partnership based on collaboration between equals—a United States of Europe to balance the United States of America. Kennedy's Atlantic community rested on what became known as the twin pillar or dumbbell theory of cooperation.[152] Finally, de Gaulle vetoed Britain's bid to enter the Common Market.

Stikker was not identified among the proponents of an Atlantic community consisting of strong institutions. Due to illness, he had been absent from the 1962 session of the parliamentary conference, but at its meeting the next year, the secretary-general opposed what he labeled an "ingenious scheme to improve the working of NATO."[153] Specifically, Stikker felt the move to set up a consultative parliamentary assembly within the machinery of a wider Atlantic community a mistake. He preferred the informal conference, arguing that "as long as NATO remains an alliance of sovereign states, power rests with national governments." And states, in turn, are most effectively influenced through their legislative and bureaucratic institutions.[154]

As discussed in the previous chapter, one of the major reasons behind Spaak's energetic advocacy of an Atlantic community of broad political and economic functions lay in his assessment that the East-West struggle would be decided in the Third World. Stikker similarly perceived the need for the West to participate in advancing the economic and social development of the lesser-developed states.[155] So important was this task to him that he devoted the last years of his life in public service to the economic problems of the new states. However, Stikker never supported any of the plans to involve NATO as such in the Third World.

Military Affairs

Stikker probably mastered the politics of defense better than any other secretary-general. Even before he assumed the leadership of the alliance, Stikker championed the integration of national defense policies.[156] For example, he advocated the targeting of nuclear weapons on the basis of an alliance policy rather than on national strategy, which at that point was one step further than the United States was prepared to go.[157] He placed more emphasis on military than on political problems, one result of which was that Stikker found favor with the military staff who saw in him a secretary-general who genuinely understood their needs.[158] A demonstration of Stikker's emphasis on things military can be seen in his admonishments to member governments to maintain their defense forces at the highest level possible.[159] Throughout his term, he repeatedly cautioned against any relaxation of vigilance and strength, despite the beginnings of the Sino-Soviet rift and the first signs of détente, of which he was dubious.[160] These sentiments struck a sympathetic chord in most military circles. NATO's military leaders concurred fully in the secretary-general's judgment that accommodation with the socialist bloc could be achieved only if the West proceeded from a resolute and unified position.

Yet in spite of the basically friendly relations between Stikker and the military arm of NATO, there existed an element of discord because some members of the military staff resented what they saw as the secretary-general's intrusion into their domain. This represented both a bureaucratic protective reaction and a multinational manifestation of the familiar civil-military tension within governments. Stikker emphatically asserted the right of civilians to ask for explanations and receive answers from the military. Perhaps it was Stikker's forceful manner the military authorities objected to, but in any event problems arose at times over Stikker's attempts to exercise a measure of control over them.[161] The appearance in the early 1960s of a pronounced civil-military dichotomy in NATO can also be accounted for by its concurrent emergence in Washington, where the McNamara "whiz kids" were asserting their authority.[162]

Stikker might have found himself in a difficult position had he not enjoyed a close personal relationship with the SACEUR, General Lauris Norstad.[163] Young and energetic, Norstad sought to project SACEUR onto the international political stage, and European members of NATO, who stood to benefit from this exposure, gladly assisted him. Norstad possessed an appreciation for the nuances of power that enabled him to accumulate political influence unmatched by any other SACEUR, with the exception of General Eisenhower.[164] For example, West German Chancellor Adenauer sought Norstad's assurances before tying his government's military policy to NATO's integrated command structure.[165] In that ultimate test of his status on the Continent, Norstad was able to claim the respect of General de Gaulle; even the French leader admitted that Norstad was "un bon soldat."[166]

Norstad and Stikker were both professional and personal acquaintances. Before Stikker became secretary-general, they had spent many hours together discussing the problems of NATO and the West and working out hypothetical solutions. After Stikker assumed office, he and Norstad continued to collaborate on a number of projects. But of the two, Norstad was more likely to capture headlines. Stikker was not displeased with this, preferring a behind-the-scenes role. Stikker in particular supported Norstad's approach to the so-called "dilemma of the two hats" that arises from the SACEUR's dual position, first as the commander of United States' forces in Europe owing allegiance to the president as his commander in chief, and secondly as the supreme allied commander in Europe responsible to the multinational North Atlantic Council. Norstad held that the commitment of an officer of one member state to the common good was the major positive binding force of the alliance: an officer should, therefore, place his pledge on the public record. Norstad believed that if the United States were ever to hint that the SACEUR must choose between his country and the alliance, then no American should be permitted to hold the office. He stressed these views to American cabinet officials and in the White House. Eisenhower, Ridgway, Gruenther, and Norstad had all had the allies' trust, in part because their government recognized their dual responsibility. Presidents Truman and Eisenhower believed that their SACEURs were progressing generally in the right direction, and they did not interfere unduly in the affairs of SHAPE. Eisenhower, for example, listened to Norstad's recommendation that American forces be retained at their current levels when the question of their reduction was first introduced in the Pentagon.[167]

Stikker, too, depended on Norstad's counsel on a variety of NATO issues. The fact that Stikker seldom strayed from American policy gave rise to the suspicion that Norstad's influence extended into the Council.[168] The constant communication between the SACEUR and the secretary-general was construed in some quarters as a sort of minor conspiracy, which was precisely what the French feared.[169] Yet for the military organization of NATO, this close relation with the secretary-general was a constructive relationship.

As supreme allied commander, Norstad became almost too successful, too closely identified with Europe where he had been stationed for more than a decade. In March 1960 he announced the formation of a NATO task force to be equipped with both conventional and nuclear armaments. The United States, Great Britain, and France—West Germany agreeing in December—had tacitly agreed to the integration of a batallion from each country into a "fire brigade."[170] An American Congressional uproar quickly short-circuited any hopes for the transfer of the custody of nuclear arms and thus rendered the proposal's principal raison d'être moot.[171] Norstad continued to argue for a NATO nuclear force, revealing that it had been under consideration by the American government for some time. He wanted NATO to possess "a force balanced against the requirement to meet any act of aggression at any level up

to the condition of a general war."[172] The ability to defend
Western Europe against a large-scale attack, Norstad pointed
out, depended on the use of nuclear weapons, and thus there
was a growing desire for a broader sharing of the control of
these weapons. A search for a fair solution to the problem of
sharing and control was thus of vital concern to all members
of the alliance, although admittedly it was a complex and delicate political problem.

Norstad's cogent articulation of this popular sentiment in
Western Europe was not well received by the incoming Democratic administration. President Kennedy's appointment of
Robert S. McNamara as secretary of defense strengthened civilian
managerial direction of the defense establishment. A new generation of technicians—systems analysts, planners, and accountants—
invaded the Pentagon where they attempted to put into effect
"cost-efficient" defense programs. The thrust of their efforts
was to diminish the policymaking role of the professional
military staff. Although located in the suburbs of Paris, SHAPE
did not escape the effects of this bureaucratic conflict; it was
in fact a major target because of its responsibility for formulating NATO military policy. Specifically, the secretary of defense
was intent on supplanting the SACEUR in dealing with the
West Germans on the question of nuclear sharing. Differences
of opinion held by Norstad and McNamara made a certain
amount of tension between them unavoidable.[173]

Thus there was never much doubt concerning Kennedy's
determination to replace this independent-minded SACEUR.[174]
The White House did indeed act with reasonable dispatch,
forcing Norstad's resignation in the summer of 1962 (effective
November 1962) in order to appoint Chairman of the Joint
Chiefs of Staff General Lyman L. Lemnitzer as SACEUR and
to install General Maxwell D. Taylor as the new chairman of
the Joint Chiefs.[175] Kennedy had been anxious to bring Taylor
into the highest military post in the government in order to
bring about a "flexible response" doctrine in place of "massive retaliation."[176] The North Atlantic Council accepted
Norstad's resignation with deep regret and paid tribute to his
services to the alliance. Stikker felt a deep personal loss at the
departure of his friend.[177]

General Lemnitzer was officially nominated to be the SACEUR in July 1962, and after the French cabinet approved him, he was unanimously endorsed by the full Council on 25 July 1962.[178] Two days earlier, President de Gaulle had interviewed Lemnitzer—the only head of state to do so.[179] Upon hearing Lemnitzer's name, de Gaulle had reportedly remarked, "Je ne le connais pas."[180] This, however, was not surprising given the low visibility of Lemnitzer's military career. The British knew Lemnitzer from his service as Montgomery's deputy in the Mediterranean during the Second World War.[181] The Germans had no objections to Lemnitzer, but then few had, for he had built a reputation as a dedicated, modest soldier.

A 1920 graduate of West Point, seven years before Norstad, Lemnitzer had successfully handled several important staff assignments and diplomatic missions before commanding a division in Korea, which helped to qualify him as Army vice-chief of staff (under Taylor), chief of staff, and finally chairman of the Joint Chiefs.[182] However, the solid, unglamorous Lemnitzer did not fit in well with the more urbane New Frontiersmen of the Kennedy administration. Furthermore, after the Bay of Pigs fiasco, Kennedy wanted to replace him with someone closer to his own ideas and methods. In fact, Lemnitzer was unable to leave Washington until 1 January 1963 because of the events of the Cuban missile crisis. The Council accordingly postponed Norstad's retirement for two months.

As SACEUR, Lemnitzer performed well even if not as dramatically as his predecessor. His name appeared less frequently in the press than had that of his predecessor, and he willingly followed directions from the Pentagon while keeping the secretary-general informed.[183] In his own unobtrusive manner, Lemnitzer established himself in his new role, careful not to alienate anyone by taking an extreme or rigid position. His speeches accentuated the positive aspects of the alliance, while cautioning against hasty optimism regarding an East-West rapprochement, the opening round of which was celebrated with the signing of the Nuclear Test Ban (NTB) Treaty in the summer of 1963.[184] Lemnitzer's term did mark a definite change in the role of SACEUR, which henceforth accepted a policy framework fashioned by others. Consequently, without

Norstad, Stikker turned more and more directly to Washington for guidance.[185]

Berlin dominated 1961. Soviet Premier Khrushchev's ultimatum tactics were met with a substantial response. Tens of thousands of East Germans fled to the West. The Pankow regime erected a wall dividing the city of Berlin, and Soviet and American tanks faced each other across the boundary. The communists disrupted allied access to the isolated city, and in August 1961 the Soviet Union resumed nuclear testing, breaking a two-and-one-half year moratorium. President Kennedy reacted swiftly by increasing draft calls and reinforcing NATO units on the Continent. Russian saber rattling went on through the fall, and although the Soviet ultimatum was dropped, the early months of 1962 brought little relaxation of tensions. In this atmosphere of confrontation, Western European nervousness over the defense policy shift to flexible response in the United States was temporarily suspended. But the United States government had not abandoned the aim of revising its strategic doctrine.

Settled in office and with a firm grasp on the levers of power tested by a series of crises, the Kennedy administration began to assert its view on strategy in 1962. In a major policy address, agreed on by the Departments of Defense and State as well as the White House, Secretary of Defense McNamara outlined the new policy of flexible response at the University of Michigan's commencement exercises on 16 June 1962. NATO, he said, was strong only as long as it maintained a unified and massive nuclear deterrent force, subject to central control, which the United States alone was capable of providing. Because national nuclear forces were vulnerable and ineffective, the United States was convinced that the strategy of deterrence magnified the importance of planning, concentration of executive authority, and central direction. The United States expected that its allies would undertake to strengthen their nonnuclear capabilities in order that a decision to employ nuclear weapons would not be forced on NATO simply because there were no other ways to cope with particular situations of threat.[186]

The United States, therefore, put a high priority on persuading its Western European partners to contribute to the common defense.[187] There was also an economic reason for pressing this strategy: a large European contribution to NATO defense would ease the pressure on the U.S. balance of payments. The French opposed the new strategy in the strongest terms, contending that it relegated Western Europe to the status of a permanent dependency: Western Europe would be a supplier of men but would lack a voice in the decisions essential for its own defense. And from a purely domestic political perspective, large increases in Western European conventional forces were unpopular and unlikely.

Stikker stood somewhere in the middle during this controversy. He rejected the demands of SHAPE, for he understood the political realities in the member states.[188] Yet he believed that the original approval of the documents incorporating the doctrine of massive retaliation had been rather vague and subject to a number of qualifications, with the result that in fact the agreed line of policy fell somewhere between a strict trip wire strategy and one of flexible response.[189]

After some prompting from McNamara, and feeling himself that it was important to have an agreed NATO doctrine on nuclear strategy, Stikker organized a series of small meetings of the permanent representatives early in 1962, with one assistant each in attendance to discuss how to reconcile NATO strategy and resources.[190] Whether or not the United States was capable of planning independently, the Western European states could only make their plans against the background of an overall view of military requirements and national contributions.

The papers for what was named the "Stikker exercise" came from his own office. Norstad, already on his way out, made little contribution.[191] General Mel Colburn served as the liaison from the NATO military staff to Stikker's office, and David Bendall represented the civilian side.[192] Some progress was made and Stikker credited much of that to his private discussions with the French defense minister, Pierre Messmer.[193] The consensus of the group was for a greater participation of the Council in the making and execution of NATO military policy, as these decisions were political and should not be based solely on calculations of military efficiency. The group also discussed what voting procedures the Council should employ in an emergency. As unanimity, majority, and qualified majority voting all presented difficulties, however, no agreement was reached.[194]

The "Stikker exercise" led, at the Athens ministerial meeting in May of 1962, to the adoption of guidelines (called the "Athens guidelines") that broadly specified the circumstances in which NATO might have recourse to nuclear weapons in self-defense and the extent to which political consultation would be possible in various threatening situations. In addition, the United States and the United Kingdom gave assurances as to the availability of their strategic nuclear forces for NATO defense, and the ministers decided to institute improved procedures for the exchange of information concerning the role of nuclear weapons in NATO. France was the only member state not to accept the Athens guidelines.[195]

When Stikker became secretary-general, he had tolerated the diminishing French military contribution to NATO, but only for a short time. In 1962 he deplored the fact that, following the settlement of the Algerian conflict, the repatriated French troops were never reassigned to NATO. Stikker also became angered over the withdrawal of the French fleet from Toulon to Brest, as he felt it seriously weakened the allied position in the Mediterranean. Finally, he accused France of reneging on its previous agreement to participate in the integrated defense arrangements and thereby earned the open enmity of General de Gaulle.[196] His illness in the fall of 1962 marked the end of any influence he might have had with the French; events overwhelmed his personal capacity to deal with them. The Nassau Agreement confirmed de Gaulle in his decision to develop an independent nuclear force, and Stikker could but stand by silently as French naval units earmarked for the Atlantic and English Channel commands were withdrawn in late 1963, followed by the departure of French naval officers from the North Atlantic staff commands in April 1964.[197] By the time he retired, there remained only about half-a-dozen French submarines attached to NATO naval units, two French divisions in Germany, and three air wings participating in alliance commands.[198] France had thus unilaterally carried out its stated desire to reform the structure of military cooperation in NATO toward greater national responsibility, a process that started under Stikker's predecessor and culminated after the inauguration of his successor. French policy truly distressed Stikker, for he believed that it endangered the very existence of NATO and therefore the security of the West.[199]

The meeting of President Kennedy and Prime Minister Harold Macmillan at Nassau in December 1962 can thus be pinpointed as a turning point in the subsequent development of NATO's defense policy. The weeks before their meeting were full of signals of things to come. At the parliamentarians conference in November, Under Secretary of State George Ball announced the willingness of the United States to cooperate with other NATO member states in a multilateral nuclear missile force to be coordinated with the existing deterrent forces of NATO. He further stressed the need for Western Europe to shoulder a more equitable share of the burden of Western defense by building up its conventional forces.[200] Secretary of Defense McNamara, in a visit to his British counterpart Peter Thorneycroft, disclosed the disappointing tests of the Skybolt missile, which was to have occupied the central place in the United Kingdom's deterrent force from 1965 on. At the ministerial meeting in Paris in early December, Rusk and McNamara further previewed the American defense program. At Nassau, Kennedy obtained Macmillan's acceptance of the cancellation of the Skybolt in return for a promise to provide the United Kingdom with Polaris missiles without warheads on a continuing basis. The submarines were to be built by Britain and would be made available, along with an American contingent of at least equal size, to a NATO multilateral force (MLF). President Kennedy, in a letter to de Gaulle, offered to supply France with Polaris missiles on the same terms as the United Kingdom, but the French president flatly refused the offer.[201]

The MLF was a new and provocative element in the NATO defense debate. Integration in NATO had not previously meant the actual pooling of men and equipment from different member states; in this respect only the headquarters of NATO commands were internationally staffed. MLF was a purely American idea stemming from a speech by President Kennedy in May 1961, which was followed up by subsequent staff work within the American government spearheaded by Gerard C. Smith.[202] The proposal was to arm naval vessels with Polaris intermediate range ballistic missiles manned by crews of mixed nationality. The costs, ownership, and manufacture would be shared, but the United States would retain a veto over the decision to fire the missiles.[203]

For Stikker, an ardent believer in integration, MLF posed a dilemma: while it represented an extension of the logic of integration, there were many political and practical ramifications to the plan. Ever since the idea of a NATO nuclear force had become a serious topic of discussion, Stikker regarded it as both feasible—perhaps by delegating a subcommittee of the Council to implement it—and necessary as a sign of Western Europe's revived stature.[204] Stikker felt that the uncertainty surrounding the American commitment to Europe was in large part behind the French—and British—national nuclear programs.[205] The uncertainty had arisen with the development of a long-range Soviet missile force capable of devastating North America, and which Eisenhower had first tried to allay at the heads-of-government conference in 1957. According to Gaullist theory, the capacity to defend one's borders from any enemy and by any means— which in the modern era meant nuclear weapons—was the cardinal requirement of a sovereign state. Stikker objected to the French nuclear program on the grounds that it was a wasteful, unnecessary duplication, and that the logic behind it tempted other countries to institute similar programs—a thinly veiled reference to West Germany.[206] The Stikker exercise and the Athens guidelines, mentioned above, were initial attempts to prevent nuclear proliferation by giving substance to the pronouncements of the United States to broaden control arrangements for the use of its nuclear arsenal.[207]

Stikker favored the principle of sharing that the MLF gave expression to, because it gave a greater say to Europe in Western defense. Simultaneously, however, he was unenthusiastic because it represented no basic change in the American control over the deterrent.[208] Some NATO member governments appeared ready to approve the proposal at the Ministerial Council meeting scheduled for May 1963, but France wanted no part of it. Throughout a busy winter and into spring, Stikker attempted to strike a positive note, as consultations on the MLF and nuclear sharing progressed. These consultations included a special American explanatory mission to European capitals headed by Ambassador Livingston Merchant and an April session of the Permanent Council in Paris that included the foreign ministers of France, Italy, West Germany, the United States, and the United Kingdom.[209]

At its ministerial meeting in Ottawa in May 1963, the Council reached a number of conclusions regarding NATO's nuclear forces. On the basis of the permanent representatives' study of the Nassau proposals, the United Kingdom agreed to assign its strategic bomber force and three Polaris submarines to the SACEUR. It was also agreed that NATO officers take a more active part in the nuclear affairs of SHAPE and that fuller coordination of operational planning would occur between SHAPE and the U.S. Strategic Air Command Headquarters in Omaha, Nebraska. Accordingly, a deputy to the SACEUR for nuclear affairs was established. In August, Lieutenant General Florent V. P. van Rolleghem, formerly inspector-general of the Belgian Air Force, was chosen for the post of nuclear deputy. The staff position was created to serve as a focal point for all nuclear activities within SHAPE and for nuclear planning action throughout the European command. Within a year, more than a thousand officers from the European command were taking part in nuclear planning and related activities in NATO.[210] (The position of nuclear deputy was discontinued in September 1968 after a far-reaching restructuring of the NATO military organization.) The Council also approved measures to reinforce and regroup the alliance's nuclear strike force available for the defense of Europe. France, however, remained ominously quiet.

Permanent Representative Finletter of the United States was a most forceful proponent of MLF. Stikker, being more tentative, became uneasy with Finletter's "hard sell," and began to doubt Finletter's understanding of the MLF's military merits.[211] Stikker continued to vacillate on the question of MLF as long as it had the support of the United States. He did, however, decline to participate in the working group set up in October 1963 to elaborate plans for the MLF on the pretext that he would need Gregh to serve with him as his assistant on the working group, knowing full well that the Frenchman would be barred from the group in spite of his membership in the secretariat.[212] The working group, which was composed of the United States, Italy, West Germany, the Netherlands, Greece, Turkey, the United Kingdom, and Belgium, arranged to keep the secretary-general informed, but in practice there was little contact between it and Stikker or the secretariat. Consequently, when Finletter later pressed Stikker to talk with President Kennedy about the MLF, the secretary-general was unable to do so intelligently. But when the MLF proposals were finally abandoned, Stikker was in a good position to dismiss it as an overly publicized American idea.[213]

To demonstrate the effectiveness of the strategy of flexible response, the United States flew an entire armored division to Europe in about sixty-three hours in the fall of 1963. Coming on the heels of an article by former President Eisenhower urging the withdrawal of United States troops from the Continent and an address by Deputy Defense Secretary Roswell Gilpatrick hinting at reductions in defense expenditures, the operation aroused concern in Western Europe about American intentions. The West Germans in particular were alarmed, because it was on their soil that the bulk of U.S. troops were stationed. The suspicion was raised that this successful airlift operation would be used to justify the reduction of the U.S. forces in Europe. Assurances were given by Finletter in Paris, and by Rusk and Kennedy in Washington, that no such action was being contemplated.[214] But the demonstration of the American intercontinental airlift capability was not lost on its European allies. Greater cooperation with the new American defense policy, including support for the MLF, and increased contributions to NATO's conventional forces were frequently seen as the quid pro quo for the continued American presence on the continent.

There could be no doubt that pressure was being applied on Bonn to accept the MLF. West Germany, after all, was its primary raison d'être, since an important part of the complex purposes behind the MLF was not only to put to rest fears of a U.S. withdrawal, but also to dispose of the need for West Germany to seek its security unilaterally through the creation of its own nuclear force.[215] MLF was certainly aimed at diverting

the Germans from following the French example in construct-
ing a national nuclear strike force.[216]

Progress on MLF was achieved in 1963-1964 despite the
lack of enthusiasm from Europe. The NATO parliamentarians
conference in November 1963 split over MLF and so decided
to forego a discussion in order to avoid a fractious debate. The
NATO Working Group reduced itself to four to carry through
on the project. The Greek-Turkish feud over Cyprus removed
these member states from the group; the Belgians hesitated to
proceed in the face of unwavering French hostility; and the
British, always less than eager, also withdrew. Lord Mountbatten and many military figures regarded MLF as nonsense,
but the Foreign Office had initially gone along for political
reasons, as a buttress to the Anglo-American "special relationship."[217] The remaining four included the United States, West
Germany, Italy, and the Netherlands. In early 1964, Finletter
was confident that a detailed agreement could be signed by the
end of the year. In the spring, an experiment using a United
States destroyer was begun to test the feasibility of "mixed-
manned" crews. But there occurred a remarkable coincidence
in the fall of 1963, when the heads of government of the United
States, the United Kingdom, and West Germany were all replaced. Ludwig Erhard succeeded the retiring Adenauer in
October. Later the same month Macmillan stepped aside, hand-
ing a shaky government to Sir Alec Douglas-Home, and in
November the tragic assassination of John Kennedy catapulted
Lyndon B. Johnson into the presidency. The NATO ministerial
meeting in December was predictably uneventful. Although
each of the three new leaders was of the same political party
as his predecessor, the controversial nature of the MLF led to
speculation that it would be dropped; but this proved not to
be the case.[218] Finletter, however, confirming his reputation as
a tough bureaucratic fighter, joined with a circle of state department officials gathered around Livingston Merchant who had
resolved to keep MLF alive. In April 1964 they managed to
obtain the support of President Johnson.[219] When Stikker
retired at the end of July 1964, the fate of MLF was thus still
undecided, but he had managed not to offend anyone during
the course of the MLF debate.

In October the British elected a Labor government, and in November Prime Minister Harold Wilson proposed a broader strategic force, an Atlantic Nuclear Force (ANF), to supersede the MLF. The chief characteristic of the ANF was the absence of the "mixed-manned" crews, the integrative element that so distinguished the American plan. Having lost British support, the MLF was soon completely finished. Its demise was confirmed in the joint communiqué released at the conclusion of Prime Minister Wilson's visit to President Johnson in December 1964.

Leaving aside the nuclear debate, it was under Stikker that the work leading to a major reform of the military organization of NATO was begun. As previously pointed out, he knew the military organization well and got along with its leaders—Norstad, Lemnitzer, and the chairman of the Military Committee in Permanent Session, West German General Adolf Heusinger. Stikker had, in fact, defended Heusinger's appointment from attacks on his wartime service in Hitler's army.[220] In contrast to Stikker's previous and occasionally frustrating attempts to obtain information from the military, Heusinger provided him with full explanations, including charts and graphs.[221] But the problem of civilian control over the military in NATO did nevertheless continue to bother Stikker. The secretary-general was not the commander in chief in NATO, and he could not compel its planning bodies, the Military Committee and the Standing Group, to keep him advised of their proceedings. While the Council and Staff/Secretariat provided all possible cooperation to the military, the Standing Group and Military Committee nonetheless refused to reciprocate by permitting the presence of civil authorities at their meetings or to make records and working papers available. The result, Stikker concluded, was duplication of effort, waste, and inefficiency.[222]

The Standing Group was particularly guilty of ignoring the secretary-general. On one occasion, Stikker arrived in Washington annoyed because the Military Committee had dispatched messages to the permanent representatives more quickly than the Standing Group had delivered them to the secretary-general. The result was that, in the middle of a Council session, Stikker had discovered that he did not have the same preparation as the other members.[223] This had come about because the representatives of some member states to the Military Committee were also defense advisers to their permanent representatives, and the secretary-general was the only Council member without a defense adviser.[224] Stikker surmised, as mentioned previously, that a personal representative on the Standing Group would solve this discrepancy, but the idea was not well received. Rather, it was decided that the chairman of the Military Committee would notify the secretary-general of developments.[225]

General Lemnitzer concurred in Stikker's criticism of the Standing Group's attitude and performance. The three members—the United States, the United Kingdom, and France—either wrangled or spent so much time protecting themselves against every possible eventuality that little got resolved.[226] The paralysis of the Standing Group, which coincided with the U.S. shift to the doctrine of flexible response, caused it to be bypassed by the rest of the organization.[227] Stikker once berated the Standing Group to General Jean Houssay, the French representative to the group who retorted while removing his tunic that maybe Stikker would like to become a general.[228] Because it was known that Stikker had little regard for the Standing Group, the SACEUR and also the SACLANT (U.S. Admiral Robert Dennison) sent him plans during periods when the Standing Group was immobilized.[229] Finally, Stikker became convinced that the Standing Group should be abolished, because it made no sense to have the center of NATO's civil affairs on one side of the Atlantic and the center of military planning on the other.[230] He also felt that the Standing Group unnecessarily emphasized the national component of NATO. But reform of the Standing Group was a question that had to be considered within the wider context of alliance strategy and planning procedures, which Stikker felt needed revitalization.

Aside from political questions of nuclear command and control, the economic resurgence of Western Europe and the consequent proposals for greater sharing in the defense programs of the alliance—as well as the complexity, cost, and long lead times required for the development of sophisticated weapons systems—made imperative a more systematic budgetary decision process in NATO than the traditional confrontation sessions of national representatives who debated the distribution of the defense burden among themselves. Consequently, in July 1963 Stikker advanced a proposal to implement the Ottawa decisions by creating under his authority a planning group to study strategy, force requirements, and resources, to be drawn from the NATO Secretariat and the representatives on the Military Committee. France, objecting to the right of international experts to inquire into national forces, blocked the proposal. Several smaller changes were, however, accepted the following year. The Committee of Defense Research Directors was established, and the Council also approved an American initiative for sharing nuclear information and widening the area of consultation on nuclear affairs. Additionally, effective 1 July 1964, the members of the planning staff to the Standing Group were required to serve in an international capacity. Secretary of Defense McNamara, with Stikker's backing, was in large measure responsible for securing these changes.

In late 1963, Stikker, who had been warned by his doctors to slow down, apprised his colleagues that he would be forced to step down soon.[231] In April 1964 he formally informed the Council of his intention to relinquish his functions as secretary-general during the summer; he would have done so earlier had it not been for the uncertain situation following the assassination of President Kennedy. Tossed by events and affected by his own physical condition throughout his forty months in office, Stikker nonetheless had worked hard to make the alliance come to grips with the most important questions that he foresaw might impair its solidarity. If circumstances had been kinder, he might have been rewarded with greater success.

Notes

1. Dirk U. Stikker, *Men of Responsibility: A Memoir* (New York, 1965), pp. 20-21.

2. Ibid., p. 8.

3. Ibid., p. 6.

4. Ibid., p. 8.

5. Ibid., pp. 10-17; and *New York Times,* 11 February 1961.

6. Stikker, *Men of Responsibility,* pp. 22-28.

7. Ibid., pp. 9-10.

8. Ibid., chapter II.

9. *New York Times,* 11 February 1961.

10. Stikker, *Men of Responsibility,* pp. 283-286; and *New York Times,* 5 April 1948.

11. Dean Acheson listed Stikker among "the distinguished and able European six." The others were Ernest Bevin, Paul-Henri Spaak, Robert Schuman, Carlo Sforza, and Joseph Bech. Acheson, *Present at the Creation,* p. 417.

12. Stikker describes Adenauer as "my very good friend" and dates his friendship with the German chancellor from their first meeting in Bonn in 1949. Stikker, *Men of Responsibility,* p. 173.

13. See Spaak's account of one of these visits as reported in Spaak, *Combats,* 2:203-11.

14. Stikker, *Men of Responsibility,* p. 306.

15. *New York Times,* 11 February 1961.

16. Stikker, *Men of Responsibility,* p. 173.

17. Ibid., p. 325.

18. See Jordan, *Staff/Secretariat,* pp. 34-37.

19. S (1).

20. 21 (1).

21. Stikker, *Men of Responsibility,* pp. 227-48.

22. Stikker chose the following quotation of de Tocqueville's to begin his memoirs: "They insist on trying to make me a party man, and that I am not." Stikker, *Men of Responsibility,* p. xiii.

23. Ibid., pp. 256-57.

24. Ibid., pp. 250-55, 259, 275. His wife was also bothered by the extensive social obligations of a minister and pressed him to resign.

25. Ibid., p. 275. Except he disliked the smog, which gave him bronchitis and sinusitis.

26. Ibid., pp. 262-63.

27. 6 (9) and 3 (4).

28. 6 (9).

29. Stikker, *Men of Responsibility,* p. 324.

30. Quoted in ibid., p. 262. Spaak's memoirs contain no reference to this judgment.

31. Ibid., p. 276.

32. *Christian Science Monitor,* 2 February 1961.

33. See *Financial Times,* 1 February 1961.

34. *New York Times,* 11 February 1961.

35. *Le Monde,* 7 February 1961.

36. *New York Times,* 3 February 1961.

37. 1 (1).

38. C. L. Sulzberger, *New York Times,* 4 March 1961.

39. *New York Herald Tribune* (European edition), 17 March 1961.

40. *Daily Telegraph,* 8 March 1961.

41. *Sunday Times* (London), 12 March 1961.

42. 3 (4) and 23 (2).

43. *Times* (London), 12 April 1961.

44. C. L. Sulzberger, *New York Times,* 4 March 1961.

45. 31 (2).

46. 23 (2). Stikker said that "the post of Secretary-General was not one for which any man should put himself forward as a candidate." Stikker, *Men of Responsibility,* p. 335.

47. Stikker, *Men of Responsibility,* pp. 328-35.

48. *New York Herald Tribune,* 23 October 1963.

49. *Financial Times,* 25 January 1963.

50. Although Stikker was sincerely convinced that peace and freedom depended on the development of international law and the limitation of national sovereignty, this idealism never impinged on his pragmatism. Stikker, *Men of Responsibility,* pp. 287-89.

51. Stikker, *Men of Responsibility,* p. 307.

52. 33 (1).

53. 3 (4).

54. 24 (2).

55. S (1); 33 (1). Virtually nothing escaped his eyes; even the internal security of the headquarters was a "major concern." Stikker, *Men of Responsibility,* p. 339.

56. 3 (4).

57. 13 (1); 31 (1).

58. *New York Times,* 27 September and 9 October 1962.

59. Stikker, *Men of Responsibility,* pp. 343-44, 350, 378-80, 406.

60. 24 (2).

61. 8 (1). A reserved, distinguished figure, he stood well over six feet.

62. 30 (2).

63. 6 (9); 6 (5).

64. 30 (1).

65. Dirk U. Stikker, "The Role of the Secretary General of NATO," in *The Western Alliance: Its Status and Progress,* ed. Edgar S. Furniss, Jr. (Columbus, Ohio, 1965), p. 17.

66. 6 (8).

67. S (2).

68. One NATO official complained that the Americans tended to talk only to one another and write long memoranda, while the French worked

in nuances that were not always understood by others. 19 (2).

69. S (6).

70. 6 (8); S (3).

71. S (1).

72. Ibid.

73. Stikker, *Men of Responsibility*, p. 335.

74. S (3).

75. S (5); 33 (4).

76. 39 (5); 12 (2).

77. Inside NATO it was widely assumed that an Italian would take over from Stikker who was viewed as a transitional figure. It has been suggested that Colonna may well have been influenced by this attitude in his forthright direction of the organization. 33 (4).

78. 12 (1); 24 (2); 9 (2).

79. 6 (7). He later served on the board of directors of Fiat and Exxon.

80. 24 (2).

81. 33 (4) and 30 (1).

82. 30 (1).

83. 33 (2-3) and 31 (2). Van Campen, a Dutchman, had written a book on Dutch foreign policy and had been shifted to NATO's Political Division by Stikker. S (1).

84. S (3).

85. S (3).

86. 30 (1).

87. 23 (2); S (4).

88. 19 (2). It must be remembered that this was the period of the first French "veto" of British membership in the Common Market.

89. Dirk U. Stikker, "Effect of Political Factors on the Future Strength of NATO," *Atlantic Community Quarterly* 6 (Fall 1968):331; 6 (1); S (3); 6 (1); 3 (2); 23 (3); 1 (1).

90. 24 (2).

91. 6 (10).

92. 32 (1).

93. In his memoir Stikker denies that a rule of unanimity existed in the Council, except for the admission of new members as provided for in Article X of the treaty. Stikker, *Men of Responsibility*, pp. 291-93.

94. 3 (2). However, sometimes Stikker would refuse to make concessions once he had assumed a position and would end up arguing over trifles. 1 (1); 19 (1-2).

95. NATO, "Review of the Oslo Press," 11 September 1962.

96. 9 (1).

97. Ibid.

98. 31 (1); 6 (8); 1 (1).

99. S (1); *New York Herald Tribune,* 8 June 1961; Stikker, *Men of Responsibility,* pp. 374-75.

100. S (5-6); Stikker, "The Role of the Secretary General," p. 16.

101. During his illness and hospitalization in Washington, for instance, the United States provided him with the treatment befitting a head of state.

102. 9 (2) and 5 (1).

103. Arthur M. Schlesinger, Jr., *A Thousand Days: John F. Kennedy in the White House* (New York, 1965), p. 291 n2.

104. Ibid, p. 780.

105. 30 (1).

106. For example, see Stikker's remarks on the need for reform in NATO. *Times* (London), 30 June 1961.

107. A good example can be found in Stikker's speech endorsing the Nassau agreements, 22 May 1963 (NATO Information Service).

108. See, for example, *New York Herald Tribune,* 23 October 1963; 2 (1); 11 (1).

109. 2 (1); *Times* (London), 20 November 1964; and Stikker, "Effect of Political Factors," pp. 338-39.

110. Stikker, *Men of Responsibility,* pp. 352-57. Quotation from p. 352.

111. 40a (1) and 6 (7).

112. S (6).

113. Stikker, "The Role of the Secretary General," pp. 16, 18-21; Stikker, *Men of Responsibility,* pp. 357, 364.

114. 23 (3).

115. Stikker, *Men of Responsibility,* p. 363.

116. Depending on his schedule and the nature of his visit, Stikker would either meet personally with a representative or invite him to read and make notes from the report. S (5).

117. Stikker, "The Role of the Secretary General," pp. 17-18.

118. Stikker, "Effect of Political Factors," p. 331.

119. 6 (7).

120. *Times* (London), 9 March 1963.

121. 33 (1) and 19 (1).

122. To a lesser extent this was also true of Stikker and Pierre de Leusse, French representative 1959-1962 and also 1966-1967.

123. 40a (1).

124. 13 (1) and S (5).

125. 5 (5).

126. 40a (1).

127. Ibid.

128. Younger British politicians and Foreign Office people were less enthusiastic, partly because of their disenchantment with the Anglo-American agreement at Nassau on nuclear sharing, which was viewed as a face-saver for Prime Minister Macmillan after the Skybolt episode. (See p. 118, 147ff. for a description of the significance of this affair on NATO).

129. *New York Times*, 17 June 1961; *New York Herald Tribune*, 12 December 1961.

130. The date of the visit was 30 June 1961.

131. Stikker, *Men of Responsibility*, pp. 369-70; *Times* (London), 5 January 1963.

132. See, for example, Stikker's public chastisement of Belgium for its conscription policy. *New York Times*, 24 March 1962.

133. 1 (1); 23 (3); 19 (1).

134. Stikker, "The Role of the Secretary General," pp. 11-12.

135. Stikker, *Men of Responsibility*, p. 348.

136. *New York Times*, 6 February 1964; and *Times* (London), 4 February 1964.

137. Sulzberger, *Age of Mediocrity*, p. 63.

138. See chapter 2, part II, of the report (in Appendix 3).

139. S (3-4).

140. Stikker, *Men of Responsibility*, p. 348.

141. Ibid., pp. 348-49; and *New York Times*, 1 May 1964.

142. Stikker, *Men of Responsibility*, p. 349.

143. *Times* (London), 2 May 1964.

144. Ibid., 12 and 14 May 1964.

145. Ibid., 12 June 1964.

146. Ibid., 11 and 12 June 1964.

147. Ibid., 12 June 1964.

148. By January 1962 agreement on the Common Agricultural Policy had been reached within the EEC, and tariff reductions were proceeding ahead of schedule.

149. For Kennedy's message to Congress, see *Department of State Bulletin* 46 (12 February 1962):231-39.

150. *Atlantic Community News*, November 1962, pp. 1-3.

151. *Times* (London), 1 February 1962, p. 14. Lord Home pointed out (1) that for the last several months the NATO Council had shown a remarkable degree of unity, (2) that the NATO Council was already organized at the highest level, as prime ministers could participate, and (3) that economic cooperation might be more effectively built around the OECD than NATO, as the former enjoyed a wider membership.

152. See Livingston Hartley, "Atlantic Partnership—How?," *Orbis* 8 (Spring 1964):41-45.

153. Speech to NATO parliamentarians conference (NATO Information Service, Paris), November 1963, 4.

154. Ibid.

155. See, for example, his speeches to the ministerial meetings of May 1962 and May 1963 and the parliamentarians conference of November 1963 (NATO Information Service).

156. *Times* (London), 22 April 1961; and *New York Herald Tribune* (European edition), 8-9 April 1961.

157. Stikker, *Men of Responsibility,* p. 331. Interestingly, this alliance policy implied an ironclad nuclear guarantee of Europe, precisely what Gaullists were then asserting the United States would not provide.

158. 24 (2).

159. 23 (3). For example, see Stikker's address to the May 1962 ministerial meeting (NATO Information Service), p. 3.

160. See his speeches to the ministerial meeting, May 1963, to the parliamentarians conference, November 1963, and to the ministerial meeting, May 1964 (NATO Information Service), pp. 2-3.

161. 12 (2); 32 (1); 19 (1).

162. 12 (5).

163. 39 (5). See the previous chapter for further references to General Norstad.

164. Some of Norstad's political acumen may be glimpsed from his speech to the NATO parliamentarians conference of November 1960. In his address Norstad supported the creation of a NATO nuclear force. He observed that such a force would not be a substitute for independent (i.e., French) nuclear capabilities, but would partially satisfy the desires of others (i.e., West Germany) for greater participation in the control of nuclear arms. *New York Times,* 22 November 1960.

165. 12 (2).

166. Stikker, *Men of Responsibility,* p. 376. De Gaulle continued to value Norstad's advice even after the latter's departure from NATO in 1963. See Sulzberger, *An Age of Mediocrity,* p. 320.

167. 39 (4).

168. 1 (1).

169. 9 (2-3).

170. *Times* (London), 3 March 1960.

171. See Robert E. Osgood, *NATO: The Entangling Alliance* (Chicago, 1962), pp. 230-232.

172. *Le Monde,* 23 November 1960. Norstad's speech was widely reported. See also *New York Times,* 22 November 1960; and *Le Monde* 27/28 November 1960.

173. 12 (2). The administration was also displeased by Norstad's

opposition to General Clay's use of tanks during the 1961 Berlin crisis. 3 (5).

174. C. L. Sulzberger, for example, estimated Norstad would be replaced within eighteen months of Kennedy's inauguration. *New York Times,* 4 March 1961.

175. *Time Magazine,* 27 July 1962, p. 121; and *New York Times,* 21 July 1962.

176. See General Taylor's book, *Uncertain Trumpet,* for a scathing attack on the Eisenhower-Dulles policy of reliance on nuclear weapons (at the expense of conventional forces) for defending the West. See also Ward Just, *Military Men* (New York, 1970), pp. 135-38.

177. Stikker, *Men of Responsibility,* p. 344. As chance would have it, Stikker was ill and unable to attend Norstad's farewell dinner.

178. *New York Times,* 25 July 1962.

179. 21 (3).

180. *Time Magazine,* 27 July 1962.

181. 21 (3).

182. *Time Magazine,* 11 May 1959.

183. C-4; S (5); 21 (2).

184. For example, see his address to the Ninth Conference of NATO Parliamentarians, 4 November 1963 (NATO Press Service, Paris, 1963), pp. 29-34.

185. 12 (2); S (5).

186. McNamara's Ann Arbor speech is reported in the *Department of State Bulletin* 47 (9 July 1962):64-69; cf. Henry Kissinger, *The Troubled Partnership: A Reappraisal of the Atlantic Alliance* (New York, 1965), pp. 98-105.

187. 19 (1). See Secretary of the Army Elvis J. Stahr's address to the Seventh Conference of NATO Parliamentarians, as reported in the *New York Times,* 14 November 1961.

188. 19 (1).

189. Stikker, *Men of Responsibility,* p. 399; S (3).

190. 32 (1).

191. Ibid., (3).

192. Ibid., (2) and 6 (9).

193. Stikker, "Role of Secretary General," p. 27.

194. S (4).

195. Stikker, "Role of Secretary General," p. 15. It should be recalled that France had in the late 1950s withdrawn its Mediterranean fleet from NATO command and left the integrated air defense system. Both of these earlier actions had distressed Stikker. See Stikker, *Men of Responsibility,* pp. 328-29.

196. Stikker, "Effect of Political Factors," p. 333; 9 (2).

197. *New York Times,* 21-22 June 1963; ibid., 29 April 1964.

198. Ibid., 29 April 1963.

199. *Times* (London), 20 November 1964.

200. NATO, *Parliamentarians' Conference: Addresses by Speakers* (NATO Information Service), pp. 81-85.

201. An excellent discussion of the setting of the Nassau Conference and its effects may be found in Richard Neustadt, *Alliance Politics* (New York, 1970).

202. *Department of State Bulletin,* 44 (5 June 1961):834-43; and 23 (3). The Norstad plan to make NATO a fourth nuclear power may have influenced the United States to begin thinking seriously about how to involve the alliance in nuclear planning, but without sharing the "finger on the trigger."

203. Two good descriptions of the origins and rationale of the MLF may be found in Robert Osgood, *The Case for the MLF: A Critical Evaluation* (Washington, D.C., 1964); and Elizabeth Stabler, *The MLF: Background and Analysis of Pros and Cons* (Library of Congress, Unpublished, 1964).

204. *Times* (London), 22 April 1961; and *New York Times,* 22 April 1961.

205. Stikker, *Men of Responsibility,* p. 396. See Michael J. Brenner, "Strategic Interdependence and the Politics of Inertia: Paradoxes of European Defense Cooperation," *World Politics* 23 (July 1971):636-42, for a comparison of the British and French reasons for building a national nuclear force.

206. Stikker, *Men of Responsibility,* p. 396 ff.

207. For an intelligent discussion of the implications of national nuclear forces for the alliance, see Albert Wohlstetter, "Nuclear Sharing: NATO and the N+1 Country," *Foreign Affairs* 39 (April 1961).

208. 6 (9).

209. *New York Times,* 5 February and 24 April 1963; and *New York Herald Tribune,* 9 March and 24 April 1963.

210. *Times* (London), 23 May 1963.

211. S (3); 23 (3).

212. S (3). Gregh was at this time holding the dual posts of assistant secretary-general for economics and finance and deputy secretary-general for defense coordination.

213. S (3).

214. *New York Herald Tribune,* 17 October 1963.

215. 21 (2).

216. The Bavarian wing of the ruling Christian Democratic Party, led

by Defense Minister Franz Joseph Strauss, was identified with these desires. Publicly there was no evidence for this, but in the higher levels of international politics there were credible and persistent rumors that Strauss had approached the French for help in obtaining control of atomic weapons. In this light MLF could be viewed as a competitive response by the United States for influence with the Germans. (See Sulzberger, *Age of Mediocrity*, pp. 109-110).

217. 2 (2).

218. Sulzberger, *Age of Mediocrity*, p. 64.

219. Thomas K. Finletter, *Interim Report on the Search for a Substitute for Isolation* (New York, 1968), pp. 91-92.

220. *New York Times*, 26 January 1963.

221. S (3).

222. Stikker, *Men of Responsibility*, p. 385.

223. 10 (1).

224. 1 (1); S (1).

225. 10 (1).

226. Stikker, *Men of Responsibility*, p. 386.

227. 32 (2).

228. 19 (1).

229. 8 (1).

230. Stikker, *Men of Responsibility*, p. 387.

231. *New York Times*, 16 November 1963; *Sunday Times* (London), 8 December 1963.

4
Manlio Brosio: A Diplomat's Diplomat, 1964-1971

Introduction[1]

NATO's fourth secretary-general, Manlio Brosio, was born in Turin in 1897 in moderate circumstances as the son of a merchant. Even though quiet-mannered, Brosio's intelligence nonetheless manifested itself early in his life. He enrolled in the university in his home town but left in 1916 following his country's declaration of war. Brosio then entered the military school in Caserta and later served as an Alpine artillery officer with the Italian forces, receiving two decorations for his distinguished service. Brosio, like Spaak before him, felt the personal ravages of the First World War. Captured by the Austrians, he was held in a prisoner of war camp until 1918.

Following his release, Brosio returned to Turin where he resumed his studies. By 1920 he had received his law degree and had opened his own practice. Brosio's student days were also days of political activity. He strongly opposed the fascist movement then sweeping Italy and joined the antifascist group "Rivoluzione Liberale" where he served in the political section and collaborated in antifacist publications. He also became a member of the larger "Committee Against Fascism." Following the fascist capture of government under Benito Mussolini, Brosio was imprisoned several times for his political activities and in 1926 was banned from all participation in politics.

Brosio did not strictly abide by the terms of his political ostracism, as he retained contact with several leaders of the clandestine Italian opposition, notably the philosopher and historian Benedetto Croce and Luigi Einandi, an economist who would later become president of Italy. Yet Brosio could not openly participate in politics; therefore he filled the next seventeen years of his life with an active law practice that he supplemented through the contribution of articles to professional and academic journals.[2] It was also in this period of forced retirement that Brosio married his cousin, Clotilde, in 1936.

Profiting from the collapse of Mussolini's regime in 1943, he joined the secret Committee of National Liberation and thus participated directly in the Italian underground resistance to the German occupation. He also helped to revive the Italian Liberal Party that, like all opposition parties, had been disbanded under Mussolini. The allied liberation of Italy in 1944 brought with it the restoration of political liberty and civilian government. Brosio, having created for himself an important position in leading political circles, participated fully by this time in governmental activity.

From 1944 to 1946, Brosio served in the first three brief cabinets of the postwar era.[3] It was not as a minister, however, that Brosio earned his political reputation. Only once, as minister of defense, did he actually direct a ministry, and even then his primary responsibility was for border patrol. Brosio was appointed Italy's ambassador to the Soviet Union in 1947 and remained in that position until 1951. He personally conducted the negotiation of the Italian Peace Treaty and was largely responsible for such important achievements as the release of Italian prisoners of war, the settlement of Soviet reparations claims, and the establishment of normal diplomatic relations with the Soviet Union, which included a trade agreement between the two states. Brosio's skill as a negotiator did not go unnoticed, and he later earned high praise from his Western colleagues for his ability to negotiate with the Russians under pressure.[4]

Following his service in Moscow, Brosio was chosen in 1952 to represent Italy at the Court of St. James. Brosio thoroughly enjoyed the cultural and social life in London and made a number of friends within the London diplomatic community. Here again Brosio displayed his skill as a negotiator. With the same firmness and intelligence he displayed in Moscow, Brosio impressed Western diplomats with his conduct in the long and

Manlio Brosio, NATO secretary-general from 1964 to 1971. (Courtesy NATO Information Service)

intricate negotiations surrounding the status of Trieste and its eventual return to Italy. He was able to sign the final accord on behalf of his country before assuming his next post as ambassador to the United States in 1955.

It was during his stay in Washington that Brosio first received consideration as a candidate for the post of secretary-general of NATO. In 1961, the French supported Brosio as a

NATO headquarters, Brussels. Ministerial meeting, 2 December 1970. Kenneth Nash (left), NATO assistant secretary-general for defense planning and policy and Manlio Brosio, NATO secretary-general. (Courtesy NATO Information Service)

NATO headquarters, Brussels. Ministerial meeting, 2 December 1970. Manlio Brosio (left), NATO secretary-general and J. Luns, then foreign minister of the Netherlands. (Courtesy NATO Information Service)

manifestation of their dissatisfaction with Dirk Stikker. The Italians, however, caught in a cross-fire between the French and the Americans, who supported Stikker, withdrew Brosio's candidacy, thereby permitting Stikker to be unanimously approved. After having lost this "unforeseen race," Brosio arranged to have his assignment shifted to Paris, where he replaced the retiring Italian ambassador to France.[5] When in the early 1960s Italian domestic politics shifted to the left, Brosio realized that his chances of reentering a cabinet had largely faded. He therefore began to concentrate his efforts toward a single goal: to succeed Dirk Stikker as secretary-general of NATO. Through discreet actions in Paris, coupled with numerous trips to Rome and Milan, Brosio strove to make this goal a reality.[6]

In the last month of 1963, "in order to give ample time for the choice of my successor," Dirk Stikker notified the NATO Council of his decision to relinquish the position of secretary-general the following summer.[7] Upon receipt of this announcement, enquiries concerning persons qualified to fill NATO's highest post began to be circulated. By April 1964, one month before the new secretary-general would officially be selected by the Council, speculation had come to focus on four primary candidates. The first and one of the most obvious choices was Halvard Lange of Norway. Lange's name had been mentioned in connection with the secretary-generalship since the creation of the position. Lange could have had the post had he wanted it, but in April he let it be known that he did not wish to be considered a candidate.[8]

Also high on the list of contenders was Gaetano Martino, former Italian foreign minister, one of the 1956 "Three Wise Men" and president of the European Parliament since 1962. Martino's candidacy, however, was complicated by the presence of the Deputy Secretary-General Prince Colonna who had performed so well as acting secretary-general during Stikker's protracted illnesses. Many considered Colonna to be the logical successor to Stikker.

A fourth candidate to receive considerable attention was Sir Harold Caccia, permanent under secretary in the British Foreign Office. There were, however, objections raised as to the desirability and appropriateness of another Briton serving as secretary-general, especially from the French who had already voiced their suspicions about an Anglo-American domination of the alliance. Thus Sir Harold was passed over in favor of one of the other candidates. And with the withdrawal of Lange, the Italian cabinet found itself in the position of having to nominate the secretary-general—a task that it found difficult to accomplish.

Because he had once been nominated for the post, Brosio now began to be mentioned as a possible successor to Stikker. In his bid for the post of secretary-general, Brosio's tenure in Paris, where he had been "very much *persona grata* . . . while remaining a firm supporter of a developing Atlantic alliance," paid off handsomely.[9] Brosio was the one candidate who could receive unqualified endorsement from both the United States and France. By the end of April, Brosio's successful candidacy had virtually been assured.

On 13 May 1964, the ministerial meeting of the North Atlantic Council unanimously invited Manlio Brosio to assume NATO's highest civilian post. His accession to the position of secretary-general, however, was received with a certain ambivalence. In one breath the *New York Times* could hail Brosio's appointment as an "excellent choice" and acclaim him as one who "brings an impressive set of diplomatic credentials to a task that calls for high diplomatic skill," and in a second breath observe that "Mr. Brosio's appointment reflects a decline in the importance of the NATO Secretariat."[10]

The problem, as the *New York Times* went on to suggest, was that Brosio as an ambassador lacked the political stature of his predecessors. Lord Ismay had been the right-hand man to Sir Winston Churchill during the Second World War and had later held important diplomatic and ministerial posts in various postwar cabinets. Spaak and Stikker had both been foreign ministers and Spaak had served as prime minister of his country. And both Spaak and Stikker, though especially the former, had earned impressive reputations in the process of furthering the cause of Western European integration. Brosio, however, had been an executor rather than a formulator of policy—a representative of, rather than a holder of, power. Thus the *New York Times* was correct when it observed editorially that "the appointment of Mr. Brosio now substitutes a top-notch technician and mediator for a political officer in NATO's highest civilian post."[11] Furthermore, the withdrawal of French cooperation from the alliance had indeed reduced the importance and influence of the secretary-general and the Staff/Secretariat. Brosio's appointment, therefore, could be viewed as a de facto victory of the Gaullist conception of the alliance. Also, at sixty-seven, Brosio was the oldest secretary-general at the time of appointment. (Ismay was older by the time he retired.)

Yet in spite of the handicaps he faced, Brosio was well suited to the office he was to fill. Unlike Spaak and Stikker, Brosio had access to the French government and had earned its respect during his time in Paris. Brosio also made effective use of his seventeen years of ambassadorial service, which he coupled with his innate dedication and drive. An immensely hard worker, Brosio conscientiously kept himself current on all issues before him. As one aide expressed it: "When I tell him something that I've seen in the papers when he sits down at his desk at nine o'clock, he has already read it. And what's more, he tells me something more important on another page of the same paper that I haven't noticed."[12] By the time Brosio reached his office in the morning, he had already consumed several newspapers including *Pravda,* to which he subscribed. Before leaving home, he might have also played a set or two of tennis: he was in superb physical condition for a man his age, and he remained in the best of health.[13] His lifelong love for the game kept his tall frame lean.

Because of his wide forehead, closely cropped hair, and deep-set eyes, he was often described as ascetic and somewhat monkish. But Brosio's austere demeanor was belied by eyes that sparkled with life. He shared the characteristics often attributed to northern Italian countrymen: an uncomplicated and expressive demeanor coupled with a certain shyness and reserve. Brosio enjoyed discussion, which sometimes bordered on being discursive. Essentially a quiet figure, he could be friendly without being outgoing.

His schedule was always crowded, and he never seemed to falter in following it fully. In the United States, there were few Italian-American organizations that had not had the ambassador as their guest of honor at one time or another. In Paris, he visited the provinces more often than most ambassadors and ran a tight embassy, demanding precision and punctuality from his staff—qualities for which he could serve as a model. "He has never been late for anything, and no one who has ever been late for an appointment with the Ambassador has failed to be reminded of his errors," one staff member related.[14] But Brosio's manner of correcting the faults of others was not spiteful or rancorous, for he treated his staff with the same courtesy he extended to high-ranking officials. Brosio, ever sensitive to the nuances of words, insisted on precision in his written and spoken communication. He was subtle, though not devious. Possessing an acute and open mind, Brosio was quick to analyze a problem from many angles, and he wrote long memoranda clarifying the range and implications of the many possible courses of action that a problem suggested.[15] He devoted himself to his work, having no children and leading as quiet a social life as his position allowed.[16] Brosio's greatest recreation consisted in attending movies. When questioned at the beginning of his term about any hobbies he may have had, the new secretary-general replied, "I seek for excellence, patience and perseverance!"[17]

By nature a conservative, the details of his political beliefs cannot be clearly described, because they were revealed only as practical circumstances demanded. Something of a Machiavellian in the truest sense, Brosio did not act according to a theory or program and did not think a statesman had to be "good."[18] Publicly Brosio committed himself only to the most abstract notions—order, liberty, and democracy—but gave little in the way of hints as to how their contradictions should be eliminated.

His views on the problems of NATO were something of a mystery. He was certainly known to be a firm supporter of the Atlantic alliance, but the context of his support was unclear. In the spring of 1958, Brosio had somewhat favored a Gaullist interpretation of NATO's organization, but where he stood on such issues as military integration and the French nuclear deterrent was left purposely ambiguous. One possible benefit of this ambiguity, however, was the fact that in 1964 both France and the United States could support his candidacy for secretary-general.[19]

The state of the alliance in mid-1964 was succinctly described by a well-informed correspondent:

> The plain truth is that the urgent fear of war, NATO's most gripping cement, has dissipated. NATO has fewer troops in the field than two years ago. Its ground control system for aircraft lags so badly that two American planes were shot down, when they mistakenly strayed into Communist territory. Greece and Turkey totter on the brink of private war; English and Belgian contributions shrink; and the French sit-down strike continues.[20]

In the summer of 1964, NATO was under considerable pressure for political reorganization, especially from the French, and there were doubts about the ability of the organization to withstand its internal crisis. The challenge facing Brosio was perhaps greater than any faced by his predecessors, involving such intangibles as morale and calculations not only of the enemies' intentions, but of the allies' "reliability."

Brosio as an Administrator

Brosio took his position very seriously, convinced that a vigorous secretary-general was needed to sustain NATO as an entity distinct from its constituent members. It was up to the secretary-general, he felt, to articulate a view encompassing the interests of NATO as a whole.[21] Although Brosio was extremely cautious—excessively so according to some—his tenure of office saw an increase in the leadership provided by the secretary-general.[22] Brosio's style of leadership differed sharply from the methods employed by his predecessors. His relatively nonabrasive personality allowed him to function under the numerous circumscriptions that had chafed his predecessors. Brosio conceived of himself "serving the noblest of causes and defending, without hostility and with tolerance toward all peoples, the most flourishing and freedom-loving of civilizations."[23] These plain phrases, which he wrote himself, attested to his dedication. And that dedicated intelligence triggered a series of reactions within the Staff/Secretariat and with the member states that produced the energy to propel NATO forward.

Beginning early in the morning, when he arose to study German because he felt his knowledge was not good enough, until late in the evenings, when with a blanket around his legs he would sit with his personal staff reviewing the day's events, drafting speeches, and discussing any number of a wide variety of alliance questions, Brosio reputedly would read each and every NATO document sent to him.[24] He also wanted the secretary-general to be present at intergovernmental occasions whenever NATO's interests were involved. Toward this end, Brosio reversed Stikker's practice of declining social invitations. Although he did not ordinarily manufacture occasions, he did make full use of those that came his way to maintain NATO's presence and to give it a distinct political identity.[25] Brosio was sensible and well organized; he knew where to find what he needed and sometimes would telephone directly to the knowledgeable second man in a department for required information. He had an eye for detail, and yet he could back off and speculate on philosophical issues. Brosio was meticulous, whether dealing with administrative, political, or military matters.[26]

Under Brosio the decision-making process within the Staff/Secretariat was deliberate. He would request papers, would read them—remembering most of what was in them—and would listen to advice first from selected staff members and later from others such as the permanent representatives.[27] He would then mull the matter over before making a judgment. Brosio needed personal interaction and the stimulation generated by the opinions of others. It was once estimated that he required twenty-four hours before perceiving the best course to follow in a crisis.[28] Because he did not strictly follow a chain of command, perhaps too many people communicated directly with him.[29] He was, however, fully briefed. He firmly believed in abiding by protocol: for example, even if a third secretary represented his country at a dinner, he would be placed above the SACEUR.[30] In ways such as this, Brasio was always quite gracious.

Brosio was typical *homme de cabinet*—a man who worked in his study but whose influence extended everywhere. When he fought for his staff, it was done privately and certainly not for popularity, something that he neither sought nor cherished.

He performed better in small group situations, where he could talk privately with each person, than in larger bodies.[31] Those who worked closely with him came to think of him in terms of another century—a Renaissance man, an aristocrat imbued with a sense of noblesse oblige.[32] Though extremely conscientious about what needed to be done, Brosio did not make demands; he simply expected his directions to be followed.[33]

As might be expected, Brosio's conscientious methods applied to his conduct of press and public relations. Not a superficial person, he was concerned with substance, not image. The qualities he brought to the office of secretary-general— moderation, loyalty, thoroughness, and tolerance—were not entirely suited to the demands of twentieth-century journalism. He was not a propagandist; he felt that the press generally was neither useful nor potentially harmful in the diplomatic process. Most newsmen were uninterested in Brosio: he lacked flair, his desire for accuracy was too deeply rooted to be compromised for a colorful phrase, and his use of language was too judicious to make good copy.

Somewhat surprisingly, given the importance he attached to the office, Brosio did not seek personal publicity, even though he realized that his director of information could not command the media attention that he himself, as secretary-general, could. When questioned during an interview, he could say nothing in as many words as his interrogator required for his story. He was, however, always courteous. Not surprisingly, the press found it difficult to appreciate this individual. Even at his final dinner with the Foreign Press Association, Brosio was discreet. And, at his last ministerial meeting of the Council as secretary-general, he replied to a query as to what news had come out of the meeting with a characteristically dull yet profound answer: "In diplomacy novelty is a less desirable quality than patience."[34]

As might be expected, Brosio was responsible for his speeches, either writing them himself or rewriting drafts prepared by his staff in order to ensure that they reflected his thinking.[35] His speeches were clear, intelligent expositions that attempted to cover all aspects of whatever issue he was considering. In this connection, it should not be overlooked that Brosio (as with Stikker) worked in two languages—English and French—that were not native to him.

Brosio initiated few changes in the administrative staff. By the time of his official appointment in May, Deputy Secretary-General Colonna had departed, and Brosio was asked to accept James A. Roberts, the Canadian deputy minister for trade and commerce, as the deputy secretary-general, which he did.[36] Otherwise, Brosio sought to replace only one of the higher-ranking administrators—the *directeur de cabinet*—more for personal than political reasons. John Getz was removed from the directorship in favor of Fausto Bacchetti, a countryman and personal confidant of Brosio, who, in addition, had been on the Italian delegation to NATO and had good relations with the permanent representatives. Bacchetti, who remained throughout Brosio's term, served as the filter for people who wanted to see the secretary-general and whom Brosio wanted to see, thus making it difficult to penetrate the office but easy for Brosio to reach out. On the secretary-general's instructions, his *directeur de cabinet* was more likely to bar the door to a member of the secretariat than to someone from the delegations.[37] He was, therefore, only moderately accessible, depending on who wanted to see him. Brosio kept no secrets from Bacchetti and also relied on him for other than administrative tasks: Bacchetti was the initial sounding board for Brosio's ideas, he saw that all relevant material reached the secretary-general, and he would substitute for Brosio in dealing with the staff or delegations.

Lord Coleridge, meanwhile, continued to perform both in a secretariat and an administrative capacity. To Ismay, he had served as chief of staff and defense adviser. Under Spaak and Stikker, he had undertaken more direct responsibilities in military affairs and civil emergency planning. For Brosio, he managed crisis exercises and the communications and alert systems. And throughout, he was secretary to the Council, where he was responsible for preparing the agenda, briefing the chairman, and staffing its committees. As part of his duties on the Council, Coleridge chaired the Council Operations and Exercises Coordination Working Group, which developed and organized simulations played by the Council, the three major NATO commands, the Military Committee, and national capitals to test procedures for high-level decision making in a time of crisis. The Working Group was also called upon to give its advice on many aspects of the problems surrounding crisis prevention and management, which brought the subject of alert systems under scrutiny. With General Russell Milton, deputy chairman of the Military Committee, he cochaired the Working Group on the Alert System, for which the Staff/Secretariat and the international military staff provided joint staff work and submitted proposals for consideration.[38]

Another of Lord Coleridge's activities stemmed from his position as director of communications. The launching of the Early Bird communication satellite in 1965 brought long-range communication into a new era. With the advent of satellites came the promise of instantaneous communication to and from all members without reliance on secure ground corridors or favorable weather conditions. An example of the fragility of NATO communications can be seen in the fact that, because Turkey's communication lines went through Greece, when tensions rose between the Greeks and Turks, Ankara would be cut off from its NATO partners. Also, at the time of the Soviet invasion of Czechoslovakia in 1968, there was some difficulty in quickly contacting all the member governments.[39]

Once the United States, and especially Secretary of Defense McNamara, accepted the idea in 1966, the Council established the Senior Communications and Electronics Group (with Coleridge at its head) to plan and implement the NATO satellite communications system. NATO leased the satellites from the United States, since only the United States had the boosters to launch the satellites, and ran its own ground terminals, including training their operators. In addition, being secure and less susceptible to attack, the satellite system facilitated consultation between national capitals and NATO headquarters and between SHAPE and the various NATO commands. The major problems of the satellite system were financial, but paucity of cash was partially offset by the benefits derived from the dissemination of technical knowledge and skill among the members.[40] Coleridge supervised the program from its inception through the first satellite launching, for which he traveled to Cape Kennedy in March 1970. When the system became operational, plans were made to extend it directly to ships and lower military formations in the field. A second communications satellite (COMSAT) was put into orbit in January 1971.

In July 1970 Coleridge retired to his ancestral home in Devonshire and a chance to participate actively in the House of Lords. Following his departure, the duties of the executive secretary were redistributed. Air Marshall W. R. MacBrien took up those of the director of council operations and communications, and Coleridge's former deputy, Kurt Andreae, headed the secretariat with the title of executive secretary.[41]

The four assistant secretaries-general—Robin Hooper, Johnson Garrett, François-Didier Gregh, and William Allis (assistant secretary-general for scientific affairs)—all remained after Stikker's departure. The Political Division performed a coordination function for Brosio vis-à-vis the delegations by bringing their questions to the secretary-general's attention and by clearing his initiatives with them. As it was also charged with handling the multiplying contacts with the communist states brought on by détente, Brosio monitored the work of the division with special care. He personally reviewed every article to be published in the *NATO Review* and all the internal papers of the assistant secretary-general for political affairs before they were circulated. Joachim Jaenicke of West Germany, who replaced Robin Hooper in 1966, did not feel comfortable working under such close supervision; so Brosio was not unhappy when Jörg Kastl, also of West Germany, filled the position in 1969.[42]

François-Didier Gregh's last years in NATO as assistant secretary-general for economics and finance were difficult. It was a disappointing end to a career that had begun brilliantly. He had become *inspecteur des finances* at twenty-four—as compared to Maurice Couve de Murville who made it at twenty-five, and Valéry Giscard d'Estaing at twenty-eight—and *controlleur des finances* at twenty-five. He had also performed well at NATO, but as described earlier, by the time of Brosio's arrival he was becoming uncomfortable in his position. The fact that a Frenchman chaired committees on defense planning and policy and the annual-triennial reviews was construed by the Americans as an obstacle and an affront. When he was maneuvered out of these positions, he was left only with the Economic Committee, whose responsibilities were never great.[43] Arthur Hockaday of the United Kingdom, Gregh's deputy from February 1965 until the latter's departure, had gradually assumed Gregh's duties in the area of defense policy.[44] The French government could do nothing for him, even though it wanted him to stay.[45] Prospects for a high-level post for a Frenchman in NATO after Gregh were bleak. When he resigned in January 1967, he was appointed minister of state of Monaco, and the position of assistant secretary-general for economics and finance was abolished, with one for defense planning and policy established in its place.

Hockaday served briefly as acting assistant secretary-general for economics and finance until the change was ratified by the NATO ministers at their meeting in August 1967, when he became the new division's first chief. Since his arrival in NATO he had been chairman of the Defense Planning Working Group, which in 1967 became the Defense Review Committee. He also organized the international military staff and developed the procedures for the new civilian strategic planning groups—the Nuclear Defense Affairs Committee and the Nuclear Planning Group, and coordinated the role of the political and military personnel in the defense planning process.[46] In 1969, Kenneth Nash of the United Kingdom took over from Hockaday as assistant secretary-general for defense planning and policy. Johnson Garrett remained until 1966. He was succeeded for one year by John Beith of the United Kingdom. Another American, A. Tyler Port, became assistant secretary-general for defense support, which was the successor position to that held by Johnson and Beith.[47]

Another member of Brosio's inner circle was Paul van Campen, of the Political Affairs Division. Van Campen worked with Brosio throughout the crisis of the French withdrawal, but more importantly, he took an active role in the secretary-general's mediation efforts in the dispute between Turkey and Greece over Cyprus. He also made trips to Malta, London, and Rome during the sporadic negotiations on NATO's presence in Malta, continuing even after Brosio retired.

Relations with the Council

Brosio's stewardship was marred by the most traumatic occurrence in NATO's history: the withdrawal of France from the military organization, the expulsion of NATO military commands from French soil, and the subsequent removal of NATO headquarters to Belgium. Yet during this period, the Council of Permanent Representatives was remarkably restrained, much quieter in fact than it had been even during the relatively uncomplicated days of Lord Ismay. Much of the credit for this must be given to Brosio, who as secretary-general devoted an enormous amount of energy to the business of the Council; he produced scores of memoranda, background papers, draft recommendations, and revisions. For any topic, Brosio would have conceived of a number of reasonable alternatives and would have had papers prepared that incorporated all possibilities. Brosio's presence in the chairman's seat changed the complexion of Council meetings. He exercised far greater discipline than his predecessors, and yet this was not an authoritarian assertion—there was in fact a marked lack of assertiveness by the secretary-general—but rather represented the influence of his diplomatic method. Brosio would not force a solution; he knew when to remain silent. He felt the Council should reach a consensus on its own with only a slight (and often behind-the-scenes) push now and again from its chairman. Because of his contribution, he was called the sixteenth member of the Council, a sobriquet also enjoyed by Spaak and Stikker.

When presiding over the Council, Brosio would not tolerate harsh arguments or arguments ad hominem. He insisted that formal courtesies be observed, as a result of which Council members were extremely polite to one another. He also encouraged the representatives to participate actively in the debate and to take into account each other's statements. As chairman, Brosio emphasized his role as a servant to the Council and made it his firm policy not to favor any one member state, according equal attention to each.[48] He would not permit the Council to act unless all fifteen members were present. While this practice opened the door to obstruction by absence, it required each member to take its role seriously and through the emphasis on procedure, increased the secretary-general's power. In one of his first speeches as secretary-general, Brosio rejected Stikker's "doctrine of inflexibility." Brosio felt that when a group of states within the alliance wanted to adopt new forms of association, they should be allowed to do so even if others chose not to participate.⁴⁹

After the Council abandoned Paris, there was a further tendency to make its sessions into managed affairs. At first there was some apprehension that if the French became offended on any matter, they might leave the alliance altogether. To avoid this eventuality, members of the national delegations joined with the Staff/Secretariat in maintaining strictly proper relations with the French. Brosio was not immune to the effects of the French actions or the tensions they had caused within NATO ever since 1958. When it became clear the French would continue to adhere to the treaty, a quick process of normalization brought an anticlimactic end to the drama, as the Council returned to its business of communications projects and force levels studies.

Occasionally, when issues before the Council involved questions concerning constitutional or political principles of the alliance, Brosio would adopt a tough posture. For example, he was deeply skeptical of the Warsaw Pact's March 1969 proposal for a conference on European security and cooperation. By their proposal, the Soviets seemed to be offering improved East-West relations in return for a new and undefined system of European security. Brosio felt this proposed arrangement lacked substantive guarantees and therefore threatened all of Europe with Soviet political domination. In his understated, analytical style, Brosio inveighed against a conference on the terms proposed by the Warsaw Pact. He counseled rather for unhurried and fully considered preparation by the alliance of a unified negotiating stance that would receive the full support of all members and would contain a careful assessment of the procedures and substance of such a conference. He warned against "wishful thinking and unrealistic expectations. The Atlantic allies need to consult, to remain united, to agree on basic lines of a sensible position, and to stick to it. This requires time, firmness and patience."⁵⁰

In general, Brosio tried to keep the Council meetings constantly moving toward any one of a set of acceptable compromises that he had in mind. To avoid a clash he would sometimes be led to phrase a problem in convoluted terms. And, if the Council seemed to be completely on the wrong track, the item would be tabled for more private conversations; this technique seldom failed. Having estimated the furthest point at which agreement could be assured, Brosio skillfully managed men and information to preserve the spirit of cooperation and the appearance of unanimity. Thus, although he denied running the Council, there is some truth to the description.[51]

Brosio also handled a new or unanticipated subject with caution. When last-minute discussions would turn up an unforeseen problem, he was apt to defer consideration until it could be studied. He would then withhold presenting the subject until he had gathered the necessary background information, explored the various options, tested the sentiments of the permanent representatives, and sketched out preliminary areas of agreement.[52] This Brosio accomplished with the help of several aides, none of whom usually knew the full picture (except perhaps for Bacchetti who was as discreet as Brosio).[53] Only after this process was completed would he come back to the delegations and the Council.

Brosio, like his predecessors, depended on the media and the delegations for his information. The Americans, British, Italians, and, infrequently, the French, volunteered to show him their cables, but in contrast to Stikker, he did not regard them as essential to his work. The newspapers, rather, constituted his basic source of information. These he supplemented with information from the permanent representatives, who would keep him abreast of national positions and the rationale behind them. But such contacts reflected a particular point of view as opposed to the needs of the alliance as a whole, which Brosio felt he had to construct for himself.[54]

Brosio avoided public diplomacy wherein he would run the risk of arousing partisan interests. He would, therefore, never publicly oppose a member's foreign policy. For example, he resisted the attempts of the northern European member states to have the nature of the Greek regime that had been installed in the coup d'etat of April 1967 discussed in the Council. Brosio endorsed the sentiment of Michael Stewart, former foreign secretary of the United Kingdom in this regard: "If we, for lack of freedom in some of our member countries, allowed our security to be weakened, we might open the way to a much

more general and much broader loss of freedom in all countries."[55]

During the seven years of Brosio's stewardship, the Council
became more tightly knit, more club-like than ever before.
Comradeship crystallized around two institutions: the Council
sessions and the luncheons. Council sessions were highly formal,
due to Brosio's insistence of strict decorum, but the debate
was fruitful and generated a certain amount of mutual respect
among the representatives.[56] The luncheons, by contrast, were
a series of weekly, off-the-record gatherings of the permanent
representatives, stemming from the Stikker period, at which
a melange of dishes, languages, opinions, and quips were exchanged. As the practice continued, a set of rules evolved: no
one was allowed to quote anything said at a luncheon and no
substitute for a permanent representative was admitted. Brosio
asked to be invited, and when he was accepted, came alone.
Later he asked that the deputy secretary-general attend also to
keep continuity. Even later, it became practice to allow the
permanent representatives to send their chargés d'affaires if
they were away, in order that all states be represented.

The discussion at these gatherings was open and strictly
informal. A representative felt free to say what he thought, even
to the point of criticizing his own instructions, without fear of
repercussion. If the tenor of the conversation so indicated, a
representative might subsequently request a change of instructions. This unpressured situation permitted the development of
consensus among the representatives and a group loyalty to
that consensus. Brosio, by lending an objective view to the
proceedings, contributed to the growth of a distinct allegiance
to NATO.[57]

Brosio exploited the political potential of the organization
to its fullest by maintaining an extensive communications network that centered on his office. So successful was this communications system that one diplomat from a smaller member
state suggested that perhaps there was too much consultation.[58]
As a good example of his work, throughout the negotiations
between the Soviet Union and the United States on strategic
arms limitations, Brosio coordinated the parallel consultations
between the Americans and other allies.[59]

Relations with Member States and Especially
the United States and France

The element of personal leadership that the secretary-general contributed to NATO was important in solidifying the alliance. Brosio's natural constituency was the smaller members, but he also worked well with the larger states. As Brosio himself defined his role:

> I am the Secretary-General of an Alliance of fifteen states; . . . this is a more complicated task, directed not only to watching and facing our possible enemies, but also and perhaps mainly, to helping maintain the solidarity and the concurrent activity of countries differing in size and situation, as well as interests and character.[60]

Before the first year of his term had elapsed, Brosio visited all fifteen member states and conferred with their leaders, during which he displayed a marked ability for establishing a rapport.[61]

The most important, or at least the most significant, member of the alliance was still the United States. At the beginning of Brosio's tenure, following on from Dirk Stikker's period, American Permanent Representative Thomas Finletter was driving hard toward achieving the completion (by the end of 1965) of a detailed agreement on the MLF. Brosio, however, believed it unwise to proceed with this project, as it elicited too much opposition. In his deferential manner, the new secretary-general made his doubts known to the American government, its permanent representative, and to the public.[62]

It was, however, primarily a series of external events which buried the MLF. In the fall of 1964, the Labor Party under Harold Wilson had come to power in Britain. Nikita Khrushchev was toppled from power in the Soviet Union, to be replaced by Leonid Brezhnev as first secretary and Alexei Kosygin as premier. With these and other changes in government leadership, the moment was no longer propitious for MLF. Accordingly, the Johnson administration dropped all discussion of MLF, and NATO's proposed nuclear force was allowed to expire quietly. In the summer of 1963 Finletter, now over seventy years of age, submitted his resignation. Harlan Cleveland, assistant secretary of state for international organization affairs, was named to succeed him.[63]

Cleveland, forty-seven and a Democrat, came to NATO with extensive experience in international affairs. A graduate of Princeton University, he had also been a Rhodes Scholar at Oxford where Harold Wilson had been his tutor. Cleveland had served on the Board of Economic Warfare and with UNRRA in Italy and China; he also helped direct the Marshall Plan program, where in 1950 he invented the phrase "the revolution of rising expectations." During the Republican years, he had been a publisher of *The Reporter* magazine and then dean of the Maxwell School at Syracuse University.[64] Cleveland's intelligence and commitment to the construction of international institutions had been indispensable in the formulation of American policy toward the United Nations.

As a veteran bureaucrat and participant in his government's foreign affairs policymaking process, Cleveland used his talent to push the American delegation to NATO into a more active role in alliance decision making. For example, on more than one occasion, Cleveland would return to Washington from abroad in order to draft and clear an answer he desired to receive to one of his own cables.[65] While this incident is not typical, it does illustrate Cleveland's familiarity with foreign policy machinery and his willingness to bend it to his purpose. Cleveland's dynamism helped the American delegation to influence effectively the policy decisions of the American government and thus indirectly NATO. With the backing of Secretary of State Dean Rusk and Secretary of Defense Robert McNamara, Cleveland was more successful than most permanent representatives in personally contributing to NATO, especially in political affairs.[66] Rusk solidly supported Cleveland. McNamara's support was also strong, with the presence of Defense Adviser Timothy W. Stanley in the mission providing Cleveland with a direct access to the secretary of defense.[67] As a measure of the mission's political effectiveness in the Washington defense bureaucracy, according to the tally of one of its members it won ten, tied one, and lost three decisions appealed over the heads of the Joint Chiefs of Staff to the secretary.[68]

In Timothy Stanley and Philip W. Farley, Cleveland had two extremely able deputies. Farley, quiet and urbane, acted as a foil to Cleveland's own more aggressive personality. Stanley, on the other hand, a sharp, articulate defense specialist, educated the new permanent representative in the mysteries of the McNamara-era nuclear strategy and systems analysis. Stanley also prepared the American position on a variety of alliance matters: its responses to the Soviet naval buildup in the Mediterranean and to difficulties with Malta, and the formulation of a unified position on mutual and balanced force reductions.[69]

Although it is difficult to disentangle completely the respective contributions to the alliance made by Brosio and Cleveland, there is no doubt that the latter supplied leadership and ideas to help make this period a high point of political cooperation within NATO. More a politician than a diplomat, Cleveland actively pursued what he wanted. As an astute tactician, he quickly identified the influential players and the rules of the game. Cleveland was forthright—everyone knew where he stood and why—but he was also willing to compromise. This resulted in numerous initiatives emanating from the American delegation, which in turn imparted a sense of movement to the work of the Council. Partly this was simply the greater dissemination of information that was the natural result of a more forthcoming representative from the state possessing more information than any of the others.[70] He meant to involve the allies directly in policymaking, because he believed the costs involved in not consulting and, hence, in engaging in unilateral action—in terms of recrimination from allies and bad feelings— were high, as the Suez crises, the Bay of Pigs invasion, and other instances amply demonstrated. Then too, the habit of consultation could produce a sense of joint enterprise, even if there was not full agreement on all questions. Cleveland would hold meetings in his home to help enhance interpersonal relations. To accommodate everyone, he would at times speak French.[71] These personal actions reflected his larger concern for the unity of the alliance.

With the dedication of NATO's new headquarters in Brussels in October 1967, the Staff/Secretariat, the international military staff, the delegations, and the Military Committee were housed in a single structure. The Standing Group in Washington (which Stikker had never liked) was abolished. It was then never more than a short walk to see personally anyone connected with the organization.

Brosio and Cleveland both recognized that the participation of the United States was a prime requisite for any major alliance project. Brosio was thus delighted to have an activist American permanent representative, who, like himself, was constantly searching for solutions. Brosio would listen to, modify, and channel the best of Cleveland's ideas to test their reception by the other member states, taking up the favorable ones and gently ignoring the rest.[72] Cleveland, on the other hand, was most happy to have Brosio float his ideas, because it was better not to give the appearance of American domination of the alliance.[73] Furthermore, the secretary-general and the American representative would discuss regularly important items prior to Council sessions, but Brosio would not automatically follow Cleveland's lead at the meetings.[74]

However, Brosio cannot justly be accused of playing favorites. Although he supported American initiatives, he also responded to the ideas of the smaller member states. It is true that many of the papers that came before the Council were produced by the larger delegations—with the United States in the forefront—but Brosio recast them into an impartial form wherein they could serve as a framework for discussion among all the members. He understood and was willing to discuss the importance of a continued American presence in Europe, and to say plainly that the Atlantic alliance was not worth much without it. But as a European, Brosio attempted to temper the views of the North American member and to encourage the expression of an autonomous European point of view.[75] He saw it as his responsibility to encourage the centripetal forces of the alliance without offending the member governments. Except for a brief period in the late 1950s under Spaak's direction, the discussions in the Council had often been desultory and consultations rather random. During the Brosio years, however, there was a significant change for the better. Yet this could not have been achieved without the support of the United States.

Ironically, Brosio never developed an easy relationship with President Johnson or confidence in his leadership. The president showed an interest in NATO that heartened Brosio, but the secretary-general was concerned about Johnson's grasp of the political complexities of the alliance. In particular, Brosio was unsure about the president's intentions in his meetings with the Soviet Union. For example, believing it was wise to move slowly on détente, Brosio was delighted when Johnson's scheduled trip to Moscow in the fall of 1967 did not take place.[76]

The Nixon-Brosio relationship was completely different. President Nixon had written to Brosio before he took office, and within a month of the president's inauguration the secretary-general was in Washington. Brosio felt his talks with the new president were quite satisfying: their views on the Soviet Union and on the defense posture of the alliance were alike. Nixon showed himself to be a staunch supporter of NATO and its secretary-general and personally involved himself in the organization's affairs. He demonstrated his regard for Brosio by presenting him with the Medal of Freedom, America's highest civilian award. Brosio was only the ninth non-American to receive the decoration.[77]

Nixon's active interest in NATO served to undermine the role of the new American permanent representative, Robert F. Ellsworth. Before the president assumed office, he agreed to have Cleveland remain as representative until 1 May 1969. Ellsworth, a former Kansas congressman who had served as the national political director of Nixon's campaign, was appointed to succeed Cleveland in April. Since joining Nixon's entourage in 1967, Ellsworth had undertaken several missions abroad, had been appointed assistant to the president—the highest designation in the White House—and had prepared Nixon's February 1969 trip to Europe. He was known to share the president's belief that East and West should begin to move from confrontation toward conciliation. His appointment, therefore, was received in Europe as a reassurance that the allies would not be ignored in Washington's negotiations with Moscow.[78] When Ellsworth assumed his NATO post in June, he brought with him a small staff, led by Ralph Earle, the deputy assistant secretary of defense for international security affairs, who replaced Stanley as defense adviser. In contrast to Cleveland's dialogue with Washington, Ellsworth was inclined to accept his instructions without attempting to alter them. He was relatively unfamiliar with the ways of the bureaucracies in the State and Defense departments. Also, the trend toward the centralization of foreign policymaking in the White House in the Nixon-Kissinger era meant that much of the really important political staff work was being done in Washington.[79] The flow of initiatives that had come from the delegation under Cleveland declined, and American commitments or reassurances were no longer given without prior clearance from Washington. This resulted in a certain amount of confusion among NATO's other delegations and some embarrassment to the United States, as Brosio continued the practice of private American consultation at the mission level. Being thus removed from policymaking, Ellsworth resigned and left government service after less than two years at NATO.[80] For more than six months the position of American permanent representative remained vacant and was not filled until the last days of 1971. This was a blow more to Brosio's personal conduct of alliance affairs than to western policy because of Nixon's personal participation in the latter's formulation.

In addition to his contacts with the Americans, Brosio maintained open lines of communication to all the other delegations and most especially to the French.[81] In both the Elysée Palace and the Quai d'Orsay there existed a high regard for Brosio's abilities as a diplomat, and the secretary-general wanted to keep it that way. He was extremely careful never to annoy the French. For example, Brosio held a series of discussions on financial matters with the French permanent representative, and Foreign Minister Couve de Murville, in an endeavor to seek out their opinions and to engage them in the work of the alliance. Toward the same end, Brosio did his best to cooperate with those elements of the French government sympathetic to NATO.[82]

Pierre de Leusse, who had reoccupied the French seat on the Council of Permanent Representatives early in 1965, was never a rigid Gaullist. His politics were an interesting mixture of doctrine and common sense.[83] Roger Seydoux, French representative during 1967 and 1968, contributed greatly to the process of consultation in NATO, especially after Maurice Couve de Murville, who issued rigid instructions, left the Foreign Ministry in a switch of portfolios with Defense Minister Michel Debré in the wake of the upheavals of May 1968. In private, Roger Seydoux, the brother of François Seydoux who had served on the Council earlier, was apt to speak frankly.[84] He would not, however, disrupt Council meetings to request information on defense activities after France had withdrawn from the alliance's military organization.[85] Jacques Koscruisko-Morizet, Seydoux's successor, was an adroit diplomat but did not deviate from pronounced policy. François de Tricornot de Rose, who represented France for the last year and one-half of Brosio's term, returned to Seydoux's style: he would public-ly defend his government's position while privately conceding that there was another viewpoint. He even went one step further by later declaring himself an Atlanticist.[86] Maurice Couve de Murville, French foreign minister for all but about a year of Brosio's term (until 1974), maintained a distance from and an attitude of reserve toward NATO's diplomatic activity. Yet Couve de Murville's own role was limited as all major foreign policy decisions originated with de Gaulle.

Before becoming secretary-general, Brosio as Italian ambas-sador to Paris had had the opportunity to observe de Gaulle, whom he regarded as a noble leader, only from a distance. Dur-ing his tenure at NATO, however, Brosio had several interviews with the French president. These were strictly private affairs—no witnesses and no minutes. For the most part they were calm, courteous discussions. De Gaulle spoke about two-thirds of the time and Brosio the other third; yet the two leaders frankly exchanged points of view.[87] On those aspects of NATO of which de Gaulle was critical, especially the integrated defense arrangements, Brosio tried to show that their effects on France were quite moderate. The alliance's military organization, Brosio felt, did not merit the general's hostility, because it did not represent any danger to France's independence.[88]

De Gaulle refused to place his country in a position where France could be drawn into conflict without complete French concurrence. De Gaulle had expressed concern that French

participation in what he regarded as the American-dominated
NATO military system, which included installations on French
territory, involved the risk of having France drawn into a war
that it did not want.[89] In response, American Under Secretary
of State George Ball said in an interview in Paris that he was
"astounded to hear from certain quarters here that France's
participation in the integrated command could involve the
country in a war against its will."[90] Brosio contended that the
integration of defense forces was not a real restraint on the
French militarily, because it penetrated no further than the
staff level. Brosio was sufficiently Europeanist to believe that
a more equitable sharing in the leadership of NATO between
the United States and Western Europe was desirable. But rather
than antagonize de Gaulle through opposition to the general's
more unusual ideas, such as his concept of a Europe from the
Atlantic to the Urals, Brosio simply remained silent. Similarly,
knowing the general's firm intention to build a French nuclear
force, Brosio voiced no public objections.[91] Brosio did, however, present such arguments privately to the French delegation,
and publicly the secretary-general would refer obliquely to such
matters.[92] In all his efforts to reconcile France to NATO, the
secretary-general was a model of the tactful and discreet diplomat. In late 1965, Brosio still retained hopes that de Gaulle
would not provoke a new crisis and that the status quo within
the alliance would be maintained.[93] His hopes, however, were
soon disappointed.

In September 1965, on the same day Harlan Cleveland was
sworn in as American permanent representative to NATO,
de Gaulle gave one of his rare press conferences, in the course
of which he pledged to end "in 1969, by the latest, the subordination known as 'integration' which was provided for by
NATO."[94] Later, at Cleveland's induction ceremony, President
Johnson responded. NATO, the American president said, "is
bigger than any of its members. We must maintain its strength."[95]
Upon arriving in Paris, Cleveland called on French Permanent
Representative Pierre de Leusse to learn the meaning of de
Gaulle's provocative statements. Did the general intend to de-
nounce the treaty in 1969, as provided for in Article XIII, or
to withdraw just from NATO's military organization? Would

he then coordinate French armed forces with NATO's defense plans or sign bilateral treaties with its members? Cleveland wanted answers to these and other questions raised by de Gaulle's oracular phrases. But before Cleveland could begin the discussion, de Leusse cut him short: "I hope you won't ask me what the General meant," he said.[96] The problem was that de Leusse had no answers. In matters of high policy, there was no authoritative source of information besides de Gaulle himself.

By 1965 after the abrasive experience of the MLF proposal, all NATO efforts directed towards satisfying the French would prove futile. Even McNamara's proposal in June to set up a select committee of four or five defense ministers to consult extensively on nuclear planning for the alliance was rejected within a month.[97] To the American government this new proposal seemed entirely reasonable. To de Gaulle it was totally inadequate, for the American nuclear veto would not disappear. The general was fully decided on his course and his warning had been made clear: if NATO were not transformed to take account of his conceptions, France would not remain in the alliance. In the autumn of 1965, de Gaulle informed Charles Bohlen, American ambassador to France, that precise propositions governing France's continued association with NATO would be formulated within a year.[98]

Cleveland's views toward France were in substantial agreement with American government policy; he strongly felt France should not be permitted to delay alliance planning. He was also of the opinion that, in the event of French withdrawal from NATO, the alliance should be prepared to fight the Soviets without French help.

Secretary-General Brosio, on the other hand, did not adopt such a harsh line. He believed that in order for the alliance to perform its basic function of preventing war, modern conditions required that it have machinery that would enable NATO to plan, prepare, and stand ready to defend the North Atlantic area. The treaty was certainly a flexible enough instrument to accommodate the changes that had come about since 1949, the most important of which were the Soviet Union's acquisition of a nuclear arsenal and delivery vehicles and the subsequent consolidation of a balance of terror between the United States and the Soviet Union. If any modification in NATO structure were proposed as a response to these changes, the Council, Brosio felt, should fully and openly discuss them. He cited the defense ministers' meeting of June 1965, though without specifically mentioning the McNamara proposal, as a good example of the willingness of the allies to consider suggestions for change. If moderation, patience, and persistence were to be forthcoming, surely the alliance could meet the impressive challenge involved in formulating an adequate response to world events.[99] It was natural then, that Brosio should be disappointed with de Gaulle's refusal to examine the new American proposal. The secretary-general was even more unhappy with de Gaulle's desire to end French participation in the alliance's integrated military structure.[100]

At his first press conference after his reelection to a second term as president, de Gaulle reiterated his intention to break with the "obsolete forms" of NATO.[101] Two weeks later he sent handwritten messages to President Johnson, Prime Minister Wilson, West German Chancellor Erhard, and Italian President Saragat in which he detailed reasons for severing all French ties with NATO's military organization. He added, however, that unless in the coming three years events were to change the basic facts underlying East-West relations, France "would, in 1969 and beyond, be determined to fight on the side of her allies in the event one of them should be the object of an unprovoked aggression."[102] De Gaulle also referred to the infringement on French sovereignty by the presence of NATO's military organization. In reply, Johnson stated the American belief that something more than a firm commitment was "needed to achieve effective deterrence and maintain peace in the North Atlantic area."[103] Johnson, therefore, endorsed the alliance's collective efforts to assure its members' security and expressed bewilderment over de Gaulle's claim of NATO's infringement on French sovereignty.[104] The next day the French Foreign Ministry delivered memoranda to the other fourteen governments of the Atlantic alliance informing them of France's simultaneous decision to withdraw from the integrated commands and to have the headquarters of these commands removed from French territory.[105] It is worth noting that these communications were sent to the respective states' ambassadors to France and not to their permanent representatives to the NATO Council. The memoranda to Canada, the United States, and West Germany included a text referring to individual bilateral arrangements or agreements concluded to implement NATO military plans.

The United States, in an *aide-mémoire,* acknowledged the French message and requested details and clarification.[106] In a second *aide-mémoire,* of 29 March 1966, the French government set the dates for the implementation of its decisions and offered to discuss, either bilaterally or multilaterally, the many problems they entailed.[107] The termination of the assignment of French military personnel to allied commands was to be effective on 1 July 1966. This included two categories: (1) French military staff assigned to allied headquarters, and (2) French troops stationed in West Germany. This second note stated French readiness to discuss the status of its forces in West Germany with the Bonn government and did not exclude the possibility of continuing their presence on the basis of the Paris Convention of 1954.[108] Excepted were the French participants in the courses at the NATO Defense College, who would remain until the end of the current session, 23 July 1966. The allied commands in France were to complete their transfer by 1 April 1967, and the United States and Canada were asked to complete the evacuation of their various installations by the same date.[109]

The Crises with France and Its Effect on the Secretary-General and the Council

The reaction at NATO's headquarters at the Porte Dauphine to the French withdrawal was one of dismay; it was barely conceivable that de Gaulle would put such an abrupt end to so many agreements. There existed also a bit of confusion as to the appropriateness of a response by the North Atlantic Council. The Council, which had come to rely on Brosio's preparation and coordination of its operations, suddenly found itself adrift: the secretary-general was convinced that he and the Staff/Secretariat should not become involved in an affair between alliance members. Brosio perceived himself as the secretary-general of the whole organization, and as such it would not be appropriate for him to defend any one faction no matter how dominant. Brosio felt that if he were to exercise the function of the chairman of any of its bodies, every member state had a right to be present: none could be excluded.[110]

André de Staercke, still Belgian permanent representative and doyen of the NATO diplomatic corps, immediately stepped forward to fill the diplomatic gap left by Brosio's retreat to the sidelines. De Staercke offered to convene the fourteen NATO representatives and sit as chairman. The American representative approved, as he was quite happy to have someone else take the initiative and bear the criticism, if any should arise.[111] Thus, the fourteen, or *les quatorze* as they were known in Paris, meeting sometimes in de Staercke's apartment, went to work on a statement of their common commitment to NATO. In ten days of continuous consultations, starting with a British draft, they hammered out a simple declaration of their belief in the essentiality of NATO and its military organization to the security of their countries, and of their determination to continue in the joint enterprise.[112] This declaration was officially agreed to by the fourteen governments and was released simultaneously in each of their capitals. It was not, however, a NATO document.

On 16 March, Brosio accepted a strictly limited mandate from the full fifteen-member Council, which instructed him to conduct a study of the implications of the French withdrawal for the alliance. His staff quickly identified no fewer than fifty problems brought about by the withdrawal.[113] Because of the size of the task, the bulk of the work regarding the French action was handled directly among the fourteen delegations.[114] French Representative de Leusse was quick to see the practical advantages of such an arrangement, and he and the French Foreign Ministry joined with Cleveland and the American delegation to work out the details of the new French relationship to NATO.[115] This was an indication of the dominance of the Franco-American dialogue in these proceedings. In 1966 the United States had a network of more than twenty-five bases and over 750,000 tons of equipment on French territory. This was the result of five bilateral accords, which France denounced, as it did those with Canada, in its *aide-mémoire* of 10 March. Necessarily then, the United States alone faced a multitude of problems in complying with the French request, which included substantial financial claims against the French government for the expenses incurred in moving. Here especially, American domestic political factors influenced the bilateral negotiations and caused them to drag on.[116]

For example, Timothy Stanley headed the working group on the military problems of the transfer, which meant that either the American delegation in Paris or the government in Washington was responsible for preparing all papers.[117] The United Kingdom also made a noticeable contribution, while the West Germans preferred to keep a low profile. There was some grumbling among various officials about Brosio's neutrality because of the extra work this entailed.[118]

De Staercke energetically chaired meetings of the fourteen when they collectively considered the issues posed by the French withdrawal. Their discussions included such topics as the determination of liability for the termination of contracts with French firms and nationals, the cost of moving supplies and equipment, and reparations to NATO for the jointly financed permanent facilities—infrastructure, buildings, and other non-movable improvements. The fourteen continued their work until the early 1970s, when the crisis atmosphere finally subsided. Brosio, by his own choice, was excluded from a good part of the intense activity of *les quatorze.* Reports on their proceedings would be relayed informally to the secretary-general, however.

The central questions faced by the alliance concerned the possible removal of NATO's civilian headquarters and the transfer and reorganization of its military structure. The decisions affecting the military organization were relatively easier to make. The first casualty was the Standing Group, which, as discussed earlier, had not proved very effective. It was summarily abolished. The Military Committee moved to the alliance's European headquarters, thus ending the controversial division of the organization's political and military branches. The fourteen also agreed to give the Military Committee the planning functions previously assigned to the Standing Group and attached to it an international military staff for that purpose.[119] The foreign ministers ratified these decisions at a meeting the day before the regularly scheduled ministerial session of the Council in Brussels in June.[120] The implications of the French withdrawal constituted the main subject of the Ministerial

Council, although relations with the East, West German security, disarmament, and Cyprus were also reviewed.

The more difficult problems facing the fourteen involved the removal and the relocation of the new headquarters of the European Command (SHAPE). De Gaulle's letter and the French memoranda gave the impression that the status of NATO in Paris would be unaffected.[121] Yet when the fourteen assembled, it was one of the first questions to come under study.[122] Smaller member states like Greece, Portugal, and, most of all, Denmark wanted to encourage France to remain active in the alliance, partly to counterbalance the ever-growing strength of the other major continental power, the Federal Republic of Germany. To varying degrees, therefore, they favored staying in Paris.[123] Consultations were carried on among the other members to see whether or not a consensus could be obtained. The British definitely wanted to leave France, and there was some speculation that NATO would move back to its original headquarters in London.[124] The Belgians were hesitant to endanger their traditional amity with France, and the West Germans were reluctant to cool the Franco-German rapprochement.[125] The position of the American government was that as long as NATO could not be certain that France would support the allies in the event of hostilities, it would be unwise to run the risk of having its communication lines cut off in a crisis.

General Lemnitzer, as SACEUR, opened negotiations with General Charles Ailleret, French chief of staff, on future cooperation between NATO and France. But since no agreement was possible while de Gaulle remained in office, SHAPE prepared a set of contingency plans based on the assumption that the French would deny NATO its support in the event of war.[126] Due to the lack of unanimous opinion, the foreign ministers of the fourteen at their meeting in June deferred judgment on this question.[127] Brosio very discreetly backed those who resisted isolating France, but he never publicly expressed an opinion on this or most other matters that arose from France's break with the fourteen. The solid logic and political weight behind the Anglo-American position, coupled with signs that the French government would not adversely react to the removal of NATO from Paris, finally resulted in an unopposed decision to transfer the organization to Brussels.[128] Early in November, Brosio traveled to the Belgian capital to secure suitable facilities, thus closing the most hotly debated item among the fourteen.[129]

Brosio felt that it was important to restrict the French break to NATO's military arm in order to salvage the Council's usefulness in political consultation. Then later, when de Gaulle would be gone, defense cooperation could perhaps be reinstituted. It was understood all along that de Gaulle did not intend to sever completely France's relationship with the alliance. Brosio emphasized this fact, pointing to the confirming evidence of French public opinion in bolstering a conciliatory attitude among the fourteen.[130] The tense nature of the situation reinforced his instinct and inclination for patient, quiet, behind-the-scenes diplomacy. Therefore Brosio tried to suppress any tendency to dramatize the crisis.[131]

De Staercke certainly deserved the credit and recognition he received for courageously leading the fourteen. His had been a consistently strong voice in the Council to the point of appearing at times to rival the performance of the big powers. He had the first opportunity to speak because of the alphabetical rotation of the Council, and de Staercke used this advantage effectively.[132]

The scope of his role as doyen depended greatly on the character of the secretary-general and the degree to which the latter injected himself into the debates of the Council and intra-member affairs. Thus, de Staercke had played a role out of proportion to Belgium's influence otherwise, because he and his delegation acted as a bridge to France when the secretary-general felt he could not. This liaison, however, created some suspicion in the eyes of American, British, and Dutch diplomats (the Dutch especially were angry with the French for having recently blocked the evolution of the European Community). This "inter-national" approach to conducting Council business, however, proved to be less efficient than the usual multinational one, because fewer delegations put forward initiatives when they had to do so directly and on their own responsibility.[133] But when the French, after leaving the military organization, encouraged de Staercke to become permanent chairman of the fourteen, Brosio quickly reclaimed his seat. This became possible when the fourteen transformed themselves into the Defense Planning Committee (DPC) in order to direct the alliance's defense activities.

One of de Staercke's first and most difficult tasks centered on the transfer of SHAPE to Belgium.[134] In helping to arrange the move, the doyen dealt directly with General Lemnitzer. Both de Staercke and Lemnitzer maintained contact with the secretary-general, who had been asked by the Council to investigate possible sites. The general preference was for a site in the Benelux countries and Lemnitzer wanted one near Brussels, much as Rocquencourt was just to the west of Paris and across the road from Saint Cyr.[135] Lemnitzer's first choice was Wavre, which had an old airfield, but he would have been happy with any of a number of locations around the city—such as Waterloo to the south—that fulfilled his requirements for good communications, transportation facilities, and an adequate local labor force. Instead, Lemnitzer was taken to Beloeil, a chateau in the depressed southwestern region near the French border. When he asked about other possibilities, the Belgian general accompanying him said that this was all he was authorized to show him. Lemnitzer complained to the Belgian government and exchanged some tart words with de Staercke. The problem was that the Belgian government's invitation to SHAPE had by no means been unanimous. The socialists especially had voiced a strong opposition.[136]

De Staercke explained to the general that the presence of 4,000 foreign military personnel in the city—the size of the Brussels area is less than one-quarter that of Paris—might be inflammatory. Belgium was a small country that had experienced much destruction from foreign armies, and the distinction between a friendly protector and an occupation force might not be universally appreciated.[137] Thus, de Staercke argued, it was best for SHAPE to be located in the countryside. The Belgians had also chosen the southwest region for domestic political reasons. By placing SHAPE in that area they hoped to stimulate its economic development, which in turn would negate the internal opposition to SHAPE's presence. After pleading the Belgian case to NATO, de Staercke had the unpleasant task of turning around and making strong representations on behalf of NATO to the Belgian government to provide the materiel and financial resources for the construction of the SHAPE complex and support facilities.

Arguing poor communication facilities, Lemnitzer submitted a negative report to Brosio on the proposed site of Casteau, outside Mons.[138] De Staercke also informed Brosio of the impasse. Thus having become involved in the dispute, Brosio forwarded the SACEUR's recommendation to the Council where an intense discussion ensued as to the relative merits of the two positions.[139] After a round of spirited deliberations, Brosio requested the Belgian government to submit an alternate site, without being specific as he did not wish to interfere in the internal affairs of a member.[140] The Belgians, however, were not forthcoming, and de Staercke continued to argue his country's case for the site near Mons. De Staercke tried to buttress his case through a number of promises, such as that a motorway through the area would be completed soon. Finally, unwilling to upset the Belgian domestic scene, the Council approved Casteau as the site for SHAPE, and Lemnitzer reluctantly accepted the Council's decision.[141] Fortunately, there were no similar difficulties involved in the transfer of AFCENT (Allied Forces Central Europe) and the NATO Defense College. The Command went from Fontainbleau to Limburg province in the Netherlands, and the College was relocated in Rome.[142]

Lemnitzer, in completing the move of SHAPE to Belgium, showed a charitable political touch by writing to de Gaulle in early 1967 thanking him for the hospitality of the French people in receiving the personnel of SHAPE and asking for a departing interview to express his gratitude in person. De Gaulle kindly replied, voicing his high esteem for Lemnitzer and granting his request to call at the Elysee Palace.[143] At a ceremony at Les Invalides, President de Gaulle awarded Lemnitzer the insignia of a Knight, Grand Cross of the Legion of Honor, and entertained him at a formal luncheon. Two weeks later, with the lowering of the flags, SHAPE formally closed its headquarters at Rocquencourt/Louveciennes and severed all formal French ties with NATO's military organization.[144] The next day the flags were raised at Casteau.

The withdrawal of France from NATO's integrated defense

structure, in spite of all the energy it diverted from the alliance's primary tasks and the effect it had on the political unity of the alliance, nonetheless had some positive aspects. The abolition of the Standing Group and the transfer of the Military Committee to Europe consolidated the alliance's administrative machinery and improved the coordination of its military and political arms. The emergence of the fourteen and their functions furthered the rationalization of the military organization.

At the last ministerial meeting at the Porte Dauphine in December 1966, the Council agreed to have the fourteen, sitting as the Defense Planning Committee, carry on the direction of the military affairs of the alliance. The DPC had originally been established as part of the changes made at the ministerial meeting at Ottawa in May 1963, although it had not been effective since then. As a NATO committee, whether on the level of ministers or permanent representatives, the DPC now met under the chairmanship of the secretary-general.[145] France would not participate and acquiesced to the fact decisions could be made in its absence. The attitude of the French government on this point was a practical necessity for the operation of the DPC, because France could, as a member of NATO, exercise its right to sit on any of the organization's committees. In many lower-level NATO committees, no one paid attention to the fact that one member was not represented; it happened quite frequently in the case of the smaller member states. A country whose representative had failed to attend a meeting could always get the documentation and attend later sessions. Additionally, the agenda for meetings were normally available ahead of time for all to consult.[146] Many regarded this arrangement in the DPC, where France technically belonged, as the application to NATO of the "empty chair" doctrine of the United Nations Security Council.[147] In NATO, though, this procedure allowed France to enjoy the colloquial delights of having its cake and eating it too. Because France was cognizant of the business of the DPC, it could raise any topic it desired, even those on the agenda of the DPC, in the full Council. This, however, occurred infrequently: France was not directly involved in the decisions of the DPC.[148]

The DPC also added to the trend of civilian control over the military, because it received its guidelines from the defense ministers and passed its advice along to the Military Committee. And, as it was in permanent session, the DPC could continuously monitor and guide NATO's military arm along the lines set by the alliance's highest civilian authorities. After the French withdrawal, NATO's defense ministers regularly gathered to review and update the alliance's defense policy. Often these meetings were held immediately before the biannual ministerial meeting of the Council.

The French withdrawal not only produced changes in NATO's military structure but also led to adaptations in the political sphere. In response to the French action, the commitment of the United States to the alliance remained firm. American troops would be maintained in Europe and the American nuclear deterrent would continue to guarantee Western Europe's security.[149] At the same time, the attitude of the United States toward de Gaulle's invitation to leave France had been restrained: the Americans would leave quietly, efficiently, and ahead of time, though without formally accepting French deadlines. Instructions were issued that de Gaulle was to be treated with the utmost respect; no attacks on him by American officials would be tolerated. The French, as in their behavior toward the institutionalization of the DPC, also showed a desire to make accommodations with their allies in NATO.

At the ministerial meeting of 1966, both member states welcomed a proposal by Belgian Foreign Minister Pierre Harmel to chart the future course of the alliance in light of the changing international political environment. Officially, the ministers agreed "to undertake a broad analysis of international developments since the signing of the North Atlantic Treaty in 1949," in order "to determine the influence of such developments on the Alliance and to identify the tasks which lie before it in order to strengthen the Alliance as a factor for durable peace."[150] The United States and the other allies hoped that this exercise, later dubbed the Harmel Report, would serve as a means whereby France might be drawn back into the mainstream of the alliance. The French likewise desired an agreement on a set of political principles as a basis on which future common action by NATO might be prepared.

The work on these projects was begun in January 1967 under the terms of a ministerial resolution of 22 December 1966. Four specialized subgroups were established to handle particular areas: East-West relations, interallied relations, general defense policy, and relations with other countries. From the outset it was understood that high-ranking officials would participate in the study, and, accordingly, five rapporteurs drawn from outside NATO were selected to chair the subgroups. They were, respectively: Klaus Schütz, John H. Watson, Paul-Henri Spaak, Foy Kohler, and C. L. Patijn. Klaus Schütz was then an under secretary in the West German Ministry of Foreign Affairs. His cochairman, John Watson, was an assistant under secretary of state in the British Foreign Office. Paul-Henri Spaak had recently retired as Belgian foreign minister, and thus the former secretary-general was available to NATO. Foy Kohler was the United States deputy under secretary of state, and Professor Patijn, from the Netherlands, was a member of the Consultative Assembly of the Council of Europe. The secretary-general and the Staff/Secretariat were not assigned central roles in the preparation of the report, although Brosio kept himself abreast of the committees' progress. Brosio, or someone from his staff, attended the various drafting sessions and tried to help whenever possible, yet he expressed displeasure at this procedure, which bypassed the Staff/Secretariat.[151] In the summer of 1967, the subcommittees' preliminary reports were forwarded to the Military Committee for comments and then submitted to member governments. These reports, however, did not greatly influence the final report.

De Gaulle's trip to the Soviet Union in 1966 had revealed a new dimension in French foreign policy, and the failure of the French to contribute adequately during the drafting sessions led to uncertainty as to the future direction of French policy.[152] Much of the wording of the final draft was, therefore, prepared between Harlan Cleveland and Under Secretary of State for Political Affairs Eugene V. Rostow, on one hand, and Seydoux and senior French foreign ministry officials, like Couve de Murville, on the other.[153] As the deadline for the completion of the report approached, Brosio feared that the French might not agree with the draft and that two documents—one NATO and one French—would appear. During the consultation between the Americans and the French over wording and punctuation, the secretary-general and other representatives found themselves removed from the process. But eventually, everyone found the document acceptable, and the "Report on the Future Tasks of the Alliance" (or Harmel Report) was unanimously approved at the ministerial meeting of December 1967, the first to be held in the new headquarters near Brussels.[154]

The major aim of the report—to engage France in redefining the alliance's political assumptions—had been accomplished. In the tradition of the Report of the Committee of Three, the Harmel Report endorsed greater consultation among NATO's members. In contrast, however, this latter statement was much shorter and less sweeping. The report emphasized the continuing relevance of the alliance's twin political and military functions and stressed NATO's ability to adapt to changing conditions. Finally, the report defined two specific tasks for the alliance, one military and the other political. In the military realm, it noted the vital need to defend the exposed areas of the alliance, particularly the Mediterranean, where events like the Six-Day (Arab-Israeli) War of June 1967 had led to an expansion of Soviet activity. Politically, the report assigned top priority to the formulation of proposals for reducing tension between East and West. The keynotes of the report—defense and détente—have remained the main themes of the alliance well into the 1970s. The adoption of the Harmel Report also marked the disappearance of the possibility of a total French withdrawal from the organization, and afterwards Brosio was once more confident that NATO could proceed with its principal mission without debilitating internal dissension.

Relations with NATO's European Members

Aside from France, Brosio easily established and maintained friendly relations with the other member governments. He added to the cohesion of the alliance through his encouragement of free and frank discussions. In the Council, Brosio would never interrupt or fail to recognize a permanent representative and would invariably give each representative his undivided attention. Representatives from smaller member states were thus able to report that their particular interests were recognized.[155]

As the leader of the alliance, the secretary-general was supposed to be dedicated to serving and preserving its common interests. Thus, the smaller members depended on him to "remind" the big powers of their obligation to consult. When the American secretary of state or other high-ranking officials traveled to an important non-NATO country, the smaller allies wanted to know what transpired, and they wanted the secretary-general to be in the forefront of those urging the United States to share the substance of its diplomatic conversations. From the perspective of the small powers, Brosio performed well in this regard.

In spite of his role as mediator, Brosio did not always side with the smaller allies. For example, he did not sympathize with the difficulties Portugal encountered in fighting the liberation movements in its African colonies. Yet he did not join those who reproved the Portuguese government for its foreign and domestic policies. Criticism of the more traditional and less repressive Portuguese regime was restrained compared to the severe castigation that was directed at the authoritarian government in Greece that came to power in 1967. The northern Europeans were disturbed by the violation of political and human rights in Greece.[156] There was, in fact, some question as to whether or not the northern Europeans would come to the aid of the southern Europeans in the event of war. Under the purposely imprecise Article V of the North Atlantic Treaty, the parties agreed to take, individually and collectively, such action as they deemed necessary. These terms did not bind a member state to act against its better judgment, and this loophole was not going unnoticed.

The colonels' coup of April 1967 changed the internal political situation of NATO drastically. The Scandinavians worked with Greeks on polite terms, but they had a highly unfavorable view of the new regime in Athens. Brosio thought the subject of the internal policies of the Greek government should not be raised in the Council, which annoyed the Scandinavians for technically the secretary-general had no control over what a state could bring up for debate.[157] Brosio was aware of the reluctance of the northern Europeans to include Greece and Turkey in NATO, but he reasoned that the membership of France and Italy had set a precedent for the West's defense of the Mediterranean—a decision that was now irreversible.[158] In this, Brosio enjoyed the support from the rest of the alliance. The British position on Greece may be taken as representative. Britain considered it an error to confuse alliance and friendship; while it was proper to eject Greece from participating in the Council of Europe, Greece should, nonetheless, be treated as any other ally within NATO. Brosio, however, was emphatic about one aspect of the Greek junta: it had not seized power with the aid, connivance, or the support of NATO.[159]

As secretary-general, Brosio was careful not to become associated with, or alienated from, any member or group of members. His behavior during the crisis of the French withdrawal is a good example. Another example can be seen in the fact that he would not chair, or allow a member of the Staff/Secretariat to chair, any meetings of the Eurogroup. The Eurogroup was an informal caucus of ten of the European members—Iceland, France, and Portugal did not participate. It was formed in 1968, partly in response to trends within the United States favoring troop withdrawals from the Continent, and partly to increase the commitments of the Western European states to the alliance and to advertise the extent of this commitment.[160] Within the group, plans for a comprehensive European contribution to the common defense effort were discussed and approved. Although Brosio worked with the group and supported its goals, he did not formally involve himself with it, because on principle he did not want to antagonize member states who were not of the group.[161]

The British were major beneficiaries of France's lowered level of activity in the organization.[162] Furthermore, the British took advantage of the gap between the United States and the rest of NATO's members to reassert their role as conciliators, which the West Germans encouraged.[163] Within the Eurogroup, of which they were the most active members, the British developed a closer relationship with the West Germans. French policy had thus fostered an Anglo-German rapprochement in NATO, partly because the West Germans were alarmed at de Gaulle's flirtation with the Russians (the French *ost-politik*) and looked to the British as an alternative European partner.[164] The British role in NATO nevertheless remained limited because of an over-burdened economy that required the progressive reductions of their overseas commitments, including a cut of forces on the Continent.

During Brosio's term, the West German government took an increasingly active part in NATO. A constant and central concern of the alliance, West Germany in the later 1960s made the crucial transition from a cautious follower to an autonomous molder of Western policy. Here once again, French insistence on an independent course of action opened the way. France's deemphasis of its links with Germany and its policy of seeking areas of cooperation with the Soviet Union, allowed, if not required, Bonn to strike out on its own. The original conception of submerging the revival of West German armed forces in a broad Western defensive alliance had worked splendidly. An effective German military organization had been established within a multilateral structure, whose commands were integrated under American leadership. West Germany's relations with other Western European states were thus able to flourish because any fear was allayed of a resurgence of German nationalism leading to a renewed attempt at the military and political domination of Central Europe.[165] The comments of Danish Foreign Minister Per Haekkerup in May 1965 at the ministerial meeting of the Council in London typified the feeling on the Continent. Thanks to NATO, he said, relations between Denmark and West Germany were excellent. In his own remarks to the Council, Brosio chose to emphasize the difficult position of West Germany in the alliance.[166]

Earlier, in a speech to the German Atlantic Society, Brosio had shown a full awareness of the importance of the German problem to NATO. While noting that the Atlantic alliance offered West Germany a chance to exert its peaceful influence in the world, Brosio pointed out that every step toward the restoration of the Federal Republic's sovereign rights as an independent state had been strenuously opposed by the socialist bloc states. Still, he felt the amicable settlement of the question of German reunification and the final determination of the boundaries in

Central Europe remained an essential aim of the alliance.[167] Later, however, when France, by provoking a rift in the Common Market through its cultivation of relations with the Soviet Union and its departure from NATO's military organization, began to separate itself from the Western foreign policy consensus and specifically to neglect formerly close ties with West Germany, anxieties arose in Europe over the growth of West German power—power no longer restrained by a network of Europeanist policies anchored by France. Brosio was quick to perceive these fears and forthright in discounting them. Speaking of the alarms being spread in the press and in political circles of a too-powerful West Germany, he declared:

> First of all, I think it is better that we should worry about our weaknesses rather than our strength. Secondly, I am thoroughly convinced that we must trust present-day democratic Germany and that it could be disastrous for us if we do not manage to exorcise the ghost of the tragic past.[168]

West Germany was represented in Brussels by Wilhelm Grewe, one of the outstanding diplomats on the North Atlantic Council during this period. Grewe took a more prominent part in the Council's discussions than his predecessors. While he clearly advocated his government's policy, Grewe remained sensitive to the wider concerns of the alliance and was willing to compromise on that basis. Brosio's skillful promotion of a thorough debate on the German question was helpful to all. Representative Grewe and the West German government in general trusted Brosio, who was usually given advance knowledge of Germany's position in the Council. Grewe and Brosio were never politically far apart, and whatever differences they may have had can be most readily explained by the exigencies of the political roles they played.[169] In fact, their mutual friendship may be viewed as a significant contribution to allied unity throughout the crucial years of emerging East-West détente.[170]

Besides dealing with the business of the alliance that originated from the member states, Brosio had to contend with challenges to the cohesion of NATO from the periphery. Two nonmember states, both islands in the Mediterranean, confronted the secretary-general with serious difficulties that required his personal attention and action, as was the case for all three of his predecessors. The Council had never abandoned its concern for the effect of the dilemma of Cyprus on Greek-Turkish relations. Because of the ever-present threat to the integrity of the alliance of conflict in Cyprus, Brosio was quick to respond to any signs of danger. Less than two weeks after assuming office, Brosio dispatched a message to Turkish Prime Minister Inonu inquiring about the overflight of Cyprus by Turkish air force planes and placing his office at the disposition of the parties to aid in the settlement of any disputes that might arise. He also stressed that the unity of NATO should be given the highest priority in considering any possible action.[171] Ankara and Athens stood at the top of Brosio's list of capitals of member states to visit, and not for alphabetic reasons alone. The Council, in support of the secretary-general's efforts in the eastern Mediterranean, reaffirmed at the first ministerial meeting of his term the "watching-brief" that they had given to his predecessor.[172] And at the ministerial meeting of May 1965 Brosio was instrumental in bringing together the foreign ministers of Greece and Turkey, the first such meeting in sixteen months. Cyprus remained on the agenda of the Council and the secretary-general, but there were no flare-ups for a number of months.

In mid-November 1967, however, the killing of twenty-four Turkish Cypriots by the Greek Cypriot National Guard touched off a renewed threat of war between Greece and Turkey. The Turkish National Assembly authorized the government to dispatch armed forces "outside Turkey," and the prime minister declared that he would do everything in his power to halt the aggression against the Turkish Cypriot community. Demonstrations calling for war with Greece coincided with intense activity in the Turkish ports nearest Cyprus. The United States and the United Kingdom evacuated their nationals from Cyprus as United Nations Secretary-General U Thant appealed for peace and sent a personal representative to the area. On 22 November President Johnson announced that he was appointing Cyrus R. Vance as his special emissary to mediate the dispute, and the next day Vance arrived in Ankara to begin consultations.

All the while, Brosio had been conferring with the permanent representatives to obtain a reading of the situation and to counsel restraint on the part of Greece and Turkey. When the gravity of the crisis became clear, he informed the Council of his readiness to go to the Greek and Turkish capitals "to explore the possibilities of lowering tensions between the two Allied countries." The Council unanimously endorsed his initiative, and the Greek and Turkish representatives, both of whom had full confidence in Brosio, had no qualms about accepting his offer.[173] Accompanied by political adviser Paul van Campen, he immediately left for the eastern Mediterranean.

Even though Harlan Cleveland did his best to cooperate with Brosio, Washington seemed to have forgotten NATO in its calculations for solving the dispute by failing to consult with Brosio before deciding on the Vance mission. In its wish to remedy the situation, the United States appeared to have taken insufficient account of its complexities. Brosio was fearful that if NATO were ignored in this matter, the organization would suffer and the office of secretary-general would lose stature. Cleveland, also concerned about the strength of the organization, helped Brosio to inject an international dimension in the American mission. Part of the difficulty Brosio faced was that as secretary-general of NATO he was limited in what he could do—he had no formal diplomatic mandate on which to see Cypriot President Makarios, for instance, since Cyprus itself was not a NATO member state. Nor did he wish to appear to be interfering in the internal affairs of the member states involved in the dispute.[174]

Perhaps realizing the restrictions Brosio's presence might place on his freedom of maneuver, Vance was diffident. But after a meeting at which Brosio made a case for protecting the interests of the alliance, Vance's misgivings were dispelled and they worked together on the best of terms, coordinating their shuttle between capitals. When Vance flew to Nicosia to obtain Makarios' agreement to a tentative compromise, Brosio went to Athens and Ankara to reinforce and refine the American suggestions.[175] It was characteristic of Brosio's diplomatic style that it was only after all parties agreed to the plan that he was publicly heard to utter an optimistic word.[176] Vance probably could have accomplished the mission alone, although the role of NATO had made the settlement somewhat more palatable to the disputants.[177] Brosio had not exercised an independent role; rather he had leaned on the influence of the United States. Even though he did not want to take credit for the settlement, he would not deny his contribution because he wished to preserve the prestige of his office.[178]

Unlike Cyprus, problems with Malta did not appear until several years after it became independent in September 1964. Yet there were some obvious parallel elements in the two cases: both were Mediterranean islands, both were former colonies of the United Kingdom, and both were nonmembers of NATO. Initially NATO and Malta had a mutually beneficial relationship, because NATO maintained a base there for which it paid a rent. At the time Malta received its independence in September 1965, the Council declared itself ready to examine the problems that might be raised in that state's relations with NATO because of the altered circumstances. Several days later, the government of Malta confirmed that pending the outcome of discussions with NATO, the status of the NATO establishment on the island would continue to be governed by the laws, regulations, and practices that had applied prior to its independence. Malta wished NATO to remain, because it derived substantial benefits from hosting the NATO installations, which provided employment for approximately 20,000 persons. The government also desired to retain the security guarantee it had enjoyed as a colony of the United Kingdom.

In November 1965 a first-stage agreement between Malta and NATO was reached. The Council adopted a resolution in the form of a joint statement with the government of Malta in which the two parties reiterated their willingness to discuss all matters affecting their mutual relationship. The Maltese government reaffirmed that, subject to future decisions, the legal status of NATO installations would remain unchanged. The Council assured Malta that consultations within the framework of the alliance would be held whenever the territorial integrity or political independence of Malta were deemed to be threatened.[179] There was, however, no formal legal ratification of the NATO-Malta agreement, and discussions between the two continued sporadically. In June 1967, Naval Command South (NAVSOUTH) was established in Malta as a principal subordinate command under the commander in chief, Allied Forces Southern Europe.[180] And the United Kingdom maintained its substantial aid in partial payment for NATO's use of facilities on the island.

In August 1968, as concern with the strength of the Soviet naval presence in the Mediterranean grew, Brosio took a strong lead in formulating NATO's response.[181] An open-ended working group under his chairmanship was created to consult further with Malta, as envisaged in the Council resolution of 1965.[182] However, the group remained unsuccessful in its efforts to formalize the NATO-Malta relationship. In June 1971, when the Labor party led by Dom Mintoff won a slim majority in the parliamentary elections, the new government threatened to evict NATO and replace its presence with Soviet naval forces. The crisis was further heightened by the expulsion of Admiral Gino Birindelli, the NAVSOUTH commander, from the island.[183] Mintoff bargained firmly for a large increase in the payments made by Britain for NATO's privileges. He tried to use the Soviet concessions offered in exchange for naval rights in Malta as a lever to pry a quadrupled aid package from Britain. Lord Carrington, British secretary of state for defense, went to Valletta, the Maltese capital, with an offer of increased British aid supplemented by contributions from several member states. Brosio sent Assistant Secretary-General for Political Affairs Jörg Kastl and Paul van Campen, special adviser in the Political Division (whom he had also used in the Cyprus crisis), to protect NATO's interests in the negotiations. They in turn kept the secretary-general abreast of developments.[184] After two weeks of negotiations, a settlement was reached along the general lines of the British-NATO proposal.[185] Brosio had once more shown his preference to have NATO become directly and actively involved in a NATO-related crisis rather than let a settlement be reached among the involved states outside the framework of the organization.[186]

Brosio's Role in the Process of Détente

Even before the Harmel Report was formally adopted, the alliance began to turn away from its internal problems and to deal with external challenges. Having settled the question of France's place in the alliance, NATO, including its secretary-general, was able to concentrate its efforts on its principal mission of ensuring peace and security in Europe. In addition to a review of the Six-Day War in the Middle East and the erosion of Greek-Turkish relations over Cyprus, the Council devoted most of its attention in September 1967 to the questions of disarmament and European security. Brosio already had called for a sober consideration of the meaning of peaceful coexistence as advocated by the Soviet Union, and stressed the need for NATO to remain alert. He felt that although the political climate in Europe had improved, none of the fundamental issues that divided Europe had been settled.[187]

The alliance had, of course, been continually grappling with the interlocking problems of the division of Germany and the reduction of tensions in Europe. Since 1963 there had been talk of détente. But Brosio had misgivings about the supposed change in the nature of the Soviet political goals, and he was, therefore, shocked at the discussions of détente that were held at the initial ministerial meetings he chaired.[188] He believed that such discussions were decidedly premature. The intransigence of the Russians over the previous fifteen years toward settling the question of Germany and Berlin had perpetuated the uncertain and insecure political climate of Central Europe. In this context it is most interesting to contrast Brosio's statements about détente with the Soviet Union with those of other Western leaders. For example, Brosio's suspicions about Russian motives, which he voiced in June of 1967, are sharply at variance with President Johnson's speech earlier in the spring in which he had emphasized the common interest of the American and Russian peoples.[189] In the mid-1960s Brosio did his best to alert the West to the dangers of a precipitous rush into accommodation with the Soviet Union. His primary aim during this period, when various bilateral attempts to deal with the Russians were being made, was to safeguard the unity of the alliance. He feared the consequences of any diminution of Western strength.[190]

This does not imply that Brosio was unalterably opposed to détente; rather, he believed that there was a delicate balance between the alliance's defensive mission and the West's hopes for détente. Theoretically, détente and defense were compatible, but to upset the balance was to invite contradiction and disintegration. The French at this time were especially keen on establishing a friendly relationship with the East. In the summer of 1966, de Gaulle had spent eleven days in the Soviet Union, where he received a most enthusiastic welcome and signed a number of cooperation agreements in the economic, scientific, and cultural fields. Given these developments, Brosio saw his task as reducing strains within the alliance by containing differences. His intent was not to establish himself as the spokesman for the West, as Spaak had been wont to do; rather he judged that he could contribute most by articulating NATO's fundamental precepts. Conversely, he felt that to publicize or aggravate divisions would be seriously harmful.[191]

Brosio was able to make a contribution toward preserving the unity of the alliance during the negotiations for a nuclear nonproliferation treaty (NPT). In mid-1965, Lord Chalfont, the British representative to the Eighteen-Nation Disarmament Conference (ENDC) presented a plan to the Council for its consideration.[192] The ENDC was scheduled to reconvene in August 1965 in Geneva after an adjournment of more than a year. The problem facing NATO was that the Soviets would only agree to an NPT if strict provisions were accepted barring West Germany from the possession or control of nuclear forces in any form (which would include any arrangement like MLF). On the other hand, West Germany desired to obtain something more substantial than the promise of the United States to employ nuclear weapons in defense of West German security.[193] It was at this point that new arrangements to take the place of the MLF (to broaden the participation of NATO in strategic planning) were being evolved. Brosio feared that the NPT might drive a wedge between the members of the alliance and therefore sought to work out a formula that would be satisfactory to Bonn and the rest of the allies.[194] The sensitivity of these issues reinforced Brosio's natural prudence. The ensuing discussions on the British plan in the Council were conducted in strict secrecy, as were the later consultations conducted simultaneously with the negotiations in Geneva over the next year and one-half. One known fact about these proceedings in the Council is that they were used by the nonnuclear member states to stress the need for the inclusion of a provision in the NPT on the prohibition of the threat of use of nuclear weapons against nonnuclear states. As a result, when the United States and the Soviet Union agreed on a draft treaty in January 1968, its text was already familiar to those at NATO headquarters in Brussels.

Before the NPT had been approved, President Johnson proposed further talks with the Soviet Union on slowing the nuclear arms race.[195] In March 1967 Kosygin indicated to the United States that the Soviet Union was willing to "discuss means of limiting the arms race."[196] That same month, Harlan Cleveland promptly opened consultations in the Council on the question of whether or not the United States should build an antiballistic missile system (ABM) and its effect on Western security. These consultations continued as President Johnson attempted to widen the basis for détente through a series of meetings with Premier Kosygin at Glassboro, New Jersey, in June 1967. The United States used the Council as a forum to allay the fears of the Europeans that a deal would be struck with the Soviet Union without European participation. Brosio encouraged the United States to share with the Council the substance of its exchanges with the Soviet Union in order to reduce these fears.

The Russians appeared to respond positively to the West's search for détente. At a July 1966 meeting of the Warsaw Pact in Bucharest, the states of Eastern Europe declared themselves in favor of strengthening peace and security in Europe on the basis of respect for the principles of independence, national sovereignty, equality and noninterference in the internal affairs of other states. A year later twenty-four communist parties of Eastern and Western Europe gathered at Karlovy Vary, Czechoslovakia, and issued a detailed statement of their policy in Europe. This included recognition of the existence of two German states, notice of the inviolability of the borders of Central Europe, a call for withdrawal of all foreign troops and bases from Central Europe, and a call for the convening of a conference on European security and cooperation (CESC).

With the adoption of the Harmel Report in December 1967, the member states of NATO had begun preliminary talks among themselves (in the Committee of Political Advisers) to examine various alternatives for the reduction of forces in Europe.[197] At their June 1968 meeting in Reykjavik, Iceland, the ministers, while affirming the necessity of maintaining an effective military capability, elaborated guidelines for the permanent representatives to continue their discussions about mutual force reductions.[198] They also invited the Soviet Union and other Eastern European states to explore specific and practical steps in the arms control field. When the organization slowed its activities during the summer, it was with the understanding that, after President Johnson's scheduled trip to Moscow in the fall, hard bargaining with the socialist bloc would commence. Brosio likewise did his best to prepare for the upcoming negotiations before going on vacation in August.

The Soviet-led intervention in Czechoslovakia, beginning on 20 August 1968, changed NATO's carefully laid plans. Brosio immediately returned to Brussels where, on the following day, he chaired an emergency session of the Council. After prolonged discussion, the Council only decided to keep a close watch on events. General Lemnitzer, the SACEUR, flew back from Washington shortly afterwards to consult with Brosio.[199] The Council concluded that the intervention was a clear violation of the Charter of the United Nations and of international law, but it was careful not to exacerbate the situation. On 4 September, the Defense Planning Committee issued a statement affirming "the necessity of maintaining NATO's military capability and taking into account the implications of recent developments in Eastern Europe in the planning of national forces."[200]

Brosio, who never felt that the crisis in Czechoslovakia threatened NATO, was instrumental in avoiding a confrontation on the Czech border by helping persuade SHAPE to shift its scheduled military exercises from West Germany to England.[201] Still, he acknowledged with some relief that while not abandoning efforts for détente, the alliance would now place greater stress on defense.[202] In view of recent events, Brosio declared,

Moscow's policy of peaceful coexistence could no longer be accepted at face value, and improvements in NATO's defenses were therefore necessary.[203] Brosio's message was echoed by General Lemnitzer, who advocated an increase in Western military forces to match the Russian forces that had been moved west.[204]

In response to the Soviet occupation of Czechoslovakia, the Council undertook a series of studies which analyzed the implications of Soviet actions under the so-called Brezhnev Doctrine. This included a review of the technical side of crisis management, because there had been a distinct lack of information in NATO about the timing and extent of the intervention. Lord Coleridge directed this study, which eventually led to a reorganization of the crisis center.[205] The Council, while preparing these studies, decided to move up by a month the date of the normal year-end ministerial meeting.

The Soviet invasion of Czechoslovakia was, of course, the central topic of discussion at the November ministerial meeting. The ministers flatly rejected the Brezhnev Doctrine as contrary to international legal norms and a violation of the independence of states. They underlined the dangers of the Soviet contention of the right to intervene and the destabilizing potential caused by grave uncertainty as to the intentions of the Soviet Union that had been created by its use of force. Finally, while voicing regrets over the setbacks to further détente measures, as had been foreseen at their June meeting in Reykjavik, the ministers reaffirmed that NATO's ultimate objective was the establishment of secure and peaceful relations between East and West.[206] The Soviet Union's intervention produced one beneficial side effect for the alliance: it reduced the individual efforts by members to deal bilaterally with the Russians. When the allies returned to Brussels in 1969, consultations among them were much simplified.[207]

Early in 1969 the alliance celebrated its twentieth anniversary. At a ministerial meeting held in Washington, D.C., in April of that year, the members announced the indefinite continuation of the alliance. Secretary-General Brosio had been working toward that goal for a number of months. His attitude of studied neutrality throughout the crisis over the French withdrawal from the military organization had been taken in hopes of forestalling any thoughts France may have had of further separating itself from the alliance. When the crisis had passed, Brosio welcomed the Harmel Report for the renewed vigor it gave to NATO's activities and goals. He also repeatedly made it clear that the North Atlantic Treaty had no time limit. NATO, which had shown its ability to adapt to changing circumstances, therefore continued to have a vital role to play in the world.[208] The Washington meeting was thus something of a personal tribute to Brosio's ability to hold the organization together and to infuse it with new life during a period of stress and basic change in international relations.

At that same April meeting, the ministers instructed the permanent representatives to draw up a list of those issues that would best lend themselves to fruitful negotiations with the East.[209] In March, the Warsaw Pact states, in their most conciliatory statement to date, had once more called for a general European conference to discuss problems of security and cooperation.[210] President Nixon, in his remarks to the Council, observed that the time had come for conciliation to replace confrontation as the dominant mode in East-West relations. Henceforth, he declared, détente was to become the major theme of the alliance.

Regarding arms control and disarmament, the Council was effective in helping the United States prepare its position for the strategic arms limitations talks (SALT) it was to conduct with the Soviet Union.[211] In January 1969 Cleveland had already presented his colleagues on the Council the catalog of American objectives and principles for SALT. To insure maximum secrecy, these meetings were held in Brosio's private conference room. The European members of NATO were worried about the possibility of the two superpowers reaching a private agreement, and Brosio, with his inimitable gift for diplomatic understatement, voiced their concern: "The Council supported the general lines proposed by the United States, noting the importance of bearing in mind the interests of the alliance as a whole."[212]

During his visit to NATO headquarters in February 1969, President Nixon had promised full consultation with the allies prior to negotiations with the Soviet Union. After it became apparent in the summer of 1969 that SALT was in fact going to occur, intensive analysis got under way in the Council with all members having a chance to make their views known. The procedure was continued as the SALT talks progressed. The U.S. negotiator continued to brief the Council at informal sessions in Brosio's office, for which the secretariat under Brosio's direct supervision prepared some papers outlining the Council's position on certain aspects of the talks.[213] It should be kept in mind that although the Council and the secretary-general followed SALT closely through its conclusion in May 1972, the negotiations were a bilateral affair between the United States and the Soviet Union, carried on outside of NATO. There was no action required of the alliance and scant reference to SALT in its published record. Final communiqués of ministerial meetings were limited to welcoming the opening and resumption of the talks. Nevertheless, SALT was an important manifestation of the direction of East-West relations, an outstanding example of the nature of NATO's part in the evolution of détente, and a typical case of the method, in which Brosio played an integral part, employed by the alliance to further the trend.

Another breakthrough in East-West relations—the normalization of West Germany's relations with Eastern Europe—was handled in a similar manner. Before 1966, Bonn's policy had been one of isolation of East Germany and noncooperation with the other communist states. After 1966 the coalition government of Christian Democrats and Social Democrats (SPD) had sought a rapprochement with the East in little steps, such as improving economic and cultural relations. In spite of the abatement of cold war tensions that was occurring in the mid-1960s, the West German policy had not met with any notable success. When the SPD came to power in a coalition with the Free Democrats in October 1969—with Willy Brandt becoming chancellor and Walter Scheel foreign minister—a significant change occurred in the Federal Republic's foreign policy. The new government adopted an *ostpolitik,* or Eastern policy, which accepted the existing situation in Central Europe. That is, it was willing to recognize the existence of the East German communist state, to honor frontiers of the region, and to normalize its relations with the states of Eastern Europe.[214]

The Brandt government opened negotiations with the USSR in December 1969, with Poland in February 1970, and with East Germany in March 1970. In August and December, the Bonn government signed treaties with the Soviet Union and Poland, respectively, recognizing the inviolability of the present frontiers in Eastern Europe and agreeing to conduct its relations with these states exclusively by peaceful means. The intra-German negotiations, which concerned more numerous and complex issues, continued on until December 1972. The improved international atmosphere engendered by Bonn's *ostpolitik* was also partly responsible for the start of talks on Berlin among the four powers responsible for the divided city.

Although the *ostpolitik* was basically a national policy manifested in a series of bilateral demarches, the fundamental change it brought to East-West relations was of transcendent importance to the alliance. Permanent Representative Grewe consistently consulted with the secretary-general and the Council throughout the sensitive negotiations. Brosio had not been surprised at the direct approach of West Germany to the East, having foreseen it as an inevitable development of détente.[215] He was, in fact, quite satisfied with the manner in which Bonn was conducting the negotiations and the results it was producing. He was reassured by statements of the leaders of the Federal Republic that the opening of relations with the East would not in any way weaken their solidarity with the West and specifically their commitments to the alliance. Brosio did, however, caution against drawing premature optimistic conclusions. Rather, he emphasized again that ardent vigilance and firm but moderate action were required more than ever.[216]

The Council had been engaged in intensive analysis of the potentialities of détente for some time before exchanges began with the socialist bloc states. President Nixon had given impetus to these activities in his personal appearances in the Council during his visit to Brussels in February 1970 and at the ministerial meeting in Washington in April.[217] As mentioned earlier, in their several meetings at the time, Brosio and Nixon had established a firm rapport, and Brosio had come away with an impression of having obtained a good understanding of the president's thinking. Nixon conveyed a good grasp of the issues and an enlightened but realistic policy towards the East, which Brosio found to be in large measure in accord with his own views. Encouraged by the essential agreement of views between himself and the president, Brosio was less opaque in his position on the issues facing the alliance in this period. Without being assertive, Brosio spoke more forthrightly, and his speeches took on a more definite posture. Although this did not necessarily give him a decisive part in setting Western policy, it did enhance his contribution to the maintainance of cohesion in the alliance and in conveying the rationale of Western policy.

The Warsaw Pact states revived their proposal for a pan-European conference on security and cooperation in March 1969, at the time of the first meeting since the invasion of Czechoslovakia. A conciliatory communiqué issued at the close of the postponed meeting contained no criticisms of American foreign policy or of West German "revanchism," but it did omit mentioning the participation of the North American members of NATO in such a conference.[218]

In May 1969 the Finnish government sent a note to all European governments, the United States, and Canada offering to act as a host for a conference on European security.[219] Brosio remained skeptical of the East's proposal for a number of reasons. For one, the Soviet Union appeared to want to bar the United States and Canada from taking part. More basic, he was concerned that a conference would undermine NATO without replacing it with a system of security that protected the legitimate interests of the states of Western Europe.[220] His fears were confirmed in September when the Canadian government announced its intention to reduce its forces in Europe. In the United States, the resubmission of Senator Mansfield's amendment to cut substantially American forces in Europe represented further indication of the trend. Brosio strongly warned that the alliance should not be abandoned in favor of an uncritical acceptance of a status quo guaranteed by the Soviet Union. To prevent the Russians from dominating Europe, Brosio believed NATO must not weaken its resolve or unity.

Pleased with the support for a conference on European security, the foreign ministers of the Warsaw Treaty Organization, meeting in Prague in October, proposed that it take place in the first half of 1970.[221] The next week the Council held a session attended by ministers and senior officials of member states to review the list of issues for possible negotiation with the East. The Council concluded that the recent Prague statement of the Warsaw Pact gave no new evidence that the socialist bloc states were ready for serious talks on the fundamental problems dividing Europe. The permanent representatives were therefore instructed to continue their studies, which, Brosio pointed out, should not interfere with the maintenance of a strong defensive posture.[222] The Council had thus again chosen to take the cautious path favored by Brosio.

On 28 November 1969, West Germany signed the nonproliferation treaty and two weeks later began talks with the Soviet Union on the renunciation of force in their mutual relations. At a meeting in Moscow in December, the socialist bloc repeated its proposal for a conference on European security. At the NATO ministerial meeting in Brussels later the same month, the allies examined the studies of the permanent representatives on issues for negotiation with the East. Brosio had played a key role in defining a consensus between the United States and the European members on recommended negotiation strategy. The ministers then made explicit the position of NATO in a framework for East-West détente. First, they were receptive to the idea of a conference on European security, but stressed that careful advance preparation and prospects of concrete results were essential prerequisites. As Brosio put it: "We want to show good will, but we do not want to be hurried into a dangerous, risky, and possibly unsuccessful conference or negotiation."[223] Second, recalling the Reykjavik signal and the lack of results so far forthcoming from it, the ministers expressed their interest in MBFR negotiations and requested the permanent representatives to submit a report on models for mutual force reductions as soon as possible. Third, the attitude of the Soviet Union in the negotiations on Germany and Berlin was another area that would show whether the Russians were sincere in their avowal of fostering a relaxed political climate in Europe. Finally, the ministers adopted a declaration laying out their negotiating position on the major issues of East-West relations: i.e., arms control and disarmament, Germany and Berlin, and economic, technical, and cultural exchanges.[224]

1970 saw important developments in the settlement of the problems over Germany. As pointed out above, Bonn's *ost-politik* had achieved success with the Soviet Union and Poland. The four-power negotiations on Berlin started in March. The Federal Republic agreed to hold off ratification of its treaties with the East until the Berlin talks had been satisfactorily completed. This left NATO to concentrate on the question of mutual and balanced force reductions. In May the ministers approved principles for negotiations on MBFR drawn up by the permanent representatives and invited the socialist bloc states to hold exploratory talks on such force reductions. There was, however, no positive diplomatic response on MBFR from the Soviet Union for more than a year. There was therefore a pause in the expansion of détente, as talks on Berlin also progressed slowly.

In June 1970 some movement in the East's position occurred at a meeting of the Warsaw Pact in Budapest: the early convening of a conference on European security with the participation of the United States and Canada was proposed.[225] Brosio nevertheless continued to advise against hasty answers or the unconditional acceptance of the proposal: "Negotiation consists in a mutual exchange of conditions which require examination and reduction to a common denominator."[226] NATO's reply would therefore be, as always, moderate, considered, and constructive. Brosio subjected the Budapest resolution to a scrupulous analysis, indicating its ambiguities and assumptions, as he did to all such proposals. Running throughout his critique was a consistent rejection of the notion of the imminent dissolution of blocs. As long as the security of Europe required it, the Western European–North American alliance must remain strong.[227]

At their meeting in December 1970, the NATO ministers took stock of the developments of the preceding months and explicitly tied their willingness to enter into contacts with the Eastern European governments to the satisfactory conclusion of the talks on Berlin.[228] When the socialist bloc states assailed the West's linking of the Berlin talks with a conference on

European security, Brosio defended the connection in no uncertain terms: "The link between Berlin and European security is not an artificial condition intended to delay or avoid a conference, but is an extremely limited and moderate reflection of the obvious connections between European security and the German problem."[229]

Hopes for an agreement on Berlin by early 1971 did not materialize, nor was there much progress toward opening negotiations on mutual and balanced force reductions. It was at this time of stagnation in détente that Brosio made known his decision to retire as secretary-general before the end of the year. He informed the Council early enough so that his successor could be appointed at the ministerial meeting in the spring.

Relationship with the Military

When Brosio became secretary-general, General Lyman L. Lemnitzer was SACEUR. When he stepped down, General Andrew J. Goodpaster became the supreme allied commander. Although the two men had contrasting styles, Brosio got along with both quite well.

Lemnitzer was a more traditional army officer, conceiving his role in strictly military terms. In his eyes, the SACEUR's authority rested on his military expertise, and Lemnitzer was inclined to exert a jurisdiction on that basis.[230] His reports to the Council on force levels were often given in the imperative mood. Lemnitzer never shrank from confronting the Council when he was convinced it was neglecting the alliance's military needs. Brosio, who on the contrary liked to avoid confrontations, approached Lemnitzer indirectly through his deputy, General Theodore Parker, who was known to be aware of the large politico-strategic aspects of the Council's work. In this manner, Brosio had some success making Lemnitzer aware of the necessity of considering the domestic political constraints of Council members, in particular those of its European members.[231]

Lemnitzer consciously tried to preserve the aura and protect the prerogatives of his position. The SACEUR, as the symbol of the American guarantee to the allies, was for Lemnitzer the most important post in NATO. But because the American permanent representative outranked the SACEUR according to protocol, Lemnitzer's sensitivity to the status of his position could sometimes create a problem in coordination and precluded a close relationship with Secretary-General Brosio.[232] Paradoxically, however, Lemnitzer found it very easy to work with the secretary-general, in part because he had no pretense of engaging in the political aspects of the alliance.[233] Not only did he define his role in utterly apolitical terms, he also did not put much stock in public relations, nor did he like to make speeches.[234] He was willing to leave this task to the secretary-general, thus eliminating a major area of potential conflict between the two, and an area that had caused some problems for his predecessor, General Norstad.[235]

General Lemnitzer was very effective when dealing in the substance of military affairs—troop support, deployment and movements, weapons systems and fire power, etc.[236] Give him a strategy and he would develop the battle plans. He was a professional soldier and uncomfortable with the demands of politics. When, during SHAPE's transfer from Paris to Belgium, Lemnitzer was the object of conflicting pressures from American congressmen and French generals, from NATO Council members and secretariat officials, from the press and the administration in Washington, he was tempted to be resentful of the political authorities for having created the situation. His aim was to complete the enormous job of moving with dignity and as expeditiously as possible, and in this, he and Brosio saw eye to eye.[237] For weeks lines of trucks carrying tons of equipment filed out of France, but there remained the problems of what to do with permanent installations and what arrangements would be made with the French military authorities. Then a new agreement on the status of SHAPE and its personnel had to be negotiated with the Belgian government. As the SACEUR, Lemnitzer handled all these questions with aplomb and efficiency.

Lemnitzer's strictly military definition of his role had a dampening effect on the input that the SACEUR had traditionally had on policy matters. From Eisenhower through Norstad, the SACEUR had been deeply involved in deciding

NATO's strategy. People like Timothy Stanley at the U.S. delegation and Robert Einthoven at the Pentagon in Washington, who were perceived as amateurs by the career military men in SHAPE, were instrumental in bringing the McNamara-era business-derived management and cost-effectiveness techniques to military planning, and Lemnitzer at times experienced difficulty in competing with their expanding influence.[238]

The shake-up of NATO's military organization as a result of its withdrawal from France further eroded the SACEUR's influence on strategic policy. Lemnitzer approved of the abolition of the Standing Group, which had never had much to do with SHAPE and which proved to be slow and of little help when it did.[239] The American NATO delegation also largely ignored the Standing Group. Thus, NATO itself did not benefit from having the group in Washington. Even though the Pentagon officials provided hospitality for it, there was a minimum of contact between the two, Pentagon officials preferring to have the Standing Group insulated from internal Defense Department affairs. The Joint Chiefs of Staff, after several frustrating experiences with the group, had begun to work directly with SHAPE.[240] The abolition of the Standing Group was thus welcomed by all, because it affected none.

SHAPE raised no objection to the transfer of the Military Committee to Brussels, although there was slight resistance to it in British military circles. Having the Military Committee in Washington enabled the British to keep a large military mission there and thus ensured a palpable Western European presence at the Pentagon, which they regarded as overly insular.[241] Once in Brussels, the Military Committee would become just another level in the NATO bureaucratic complex, while losing day-to-day acquaintance with the personalities and policy debates at the center of the alliance's most powerful member government. The British did not press their case very hard, realizing that the other member states, especially West Germany and the Netherlands, were strongly in favor of moving the military policymaking organs to Europe. Once the transfer was accomplished, Lemnitzer saw the advantage of proximity that the SACEUR had enjoyed in Paris vanish.

The installation of the Military Committee in the same

building in Brussels as the civilian authorities changed considerably the relationship of the SACEUR to the committee and the North Atlantic Council. The position of chairman of the Military Committee was strengthened relative to the SACEUR. The Council and the secretary-general dealt with Lemnitzer only on operational affairs, while the chairman was brought into discussions on the coordination of military and political affairs.[242] For example, when the crisis management alert system was reformed in the wake of the Czechoslovak crisis, representatives from the Military Committee and its staff worked with those from the Council and Staff/Secretariat.[243] The fact that some of the representatives to the Military Committee, mostly from the smaller member states, also acted as defense advisers to their permanent representatives to the Council further strengthened the Council–Military Committee link, which inevitably affected the Council-SACEUR relationship. The link should not be overemphasized, however. The traditional military-civilian dichotomy persisted even after the consolidation of all of NATO's military and civilian functions in Brussels.

Intragovernmental differences, such as those that occurred between ministries of defense and foreign affairs, could not help but be reflected in NATO. The British permanent representative at this time, for instance, refused to show his telegrams from London to his counterpart on the Military Committee. The American representative on the Military Committee, General Burton E. Spivey, Jr., would sometimes get different instructions than did Timothy Stanley, the military adviser to Mr. Cleveland.[244] If the practice of having representatives to the Military Committee serve as defense advisers to the Council representatives had been universally adopted, greater coherence between NATO's civilian and military staffs could have been achieved. But that required coordination among ministries in the member states' capitals, which was not always forthcoming.[245]

Belgian General Baron Charles P. de Cumont, who was chairman of the Military Committee during the period of restructuring from 1964-1968, was accustomed to observing the work of the Council and the Staff/Secretariat from afar and left NATO before he fully adapted to the new organizational patterns. But he was helpful in establishing a procedure for French

participation in the Military Committee. France, when it withdrew from NATO's integrated commands in 1966, also ceased
to participate in the military policy organs of the alliance.
Although not wishing to maintain membership on the Military
Committee or other military bodies, the French wanted to keep
informed of relevant deliberations. An arrangement was reached
whereby the French would send a military mission to sit on the
Military Committee without the prerogatives of membership.
The head of the French military mission was usually a colonel
and never a top-echelon general. The sessions of the Military
Committee were then split. The first part was devoted to broad
discussions of strategy and policy, which normally would be
referred to the full NATO Council later on. Part two encom-
passed more detailed questions of weapons systems, troop
deployment, contingency planning, and the like, which would
be reviewed by the Defense Planning Committee of *les quatorze.*[246]

Among the various committees and boards concerned with
defense matters that had evolved in the general review of military policy starting with the Athens guidelines in 1962, the
Military Committee had some trouble in carving out a distinc-
tive role for itself. The DPC and its satellite committees, which
exercised control over all facets of defense policy, the SACEUR,
who was in charge of operational matters, and an expanded
Staff/Secretariat, whose effectiveness had been bolstered by
sophisticated analytical techniques, left limited room in which
the Military Committee could operate. A case in point was the
periodic review process. The Defense Review Committee (DRC),
a subsidiary body of the DPC, was created in 1963 at the
instigation of McNamara in part as a device to get around what
he regarded as the inefficient Standing Group-Military Committee apparatus in Washington and in part to establish a greater
civilian voice in the planning process.[247] The DRC was responsible for conducting a searching examination of the force proposals prepared by the NATO commands, after they had been
reviewed by the Military Committee. The DRC then reported
to the DPC, which reconciled the recommendations of the
DRC and the Military Committee. The insertion of a civilian
body between the Military Committee and the ministers was

a blow to the former's oversight function.

The competition for influence between the DRC and the Military Committee spilled over into a rivalry between their respective staffs, the civilian Staff/Secretariat and the International Military Staff (IMS). The Staff/Secretariat found that the IMS had difficulty working in a committee situation that lacked a hierarchical element.[248] Members of the IMS, on the other hand, believed that the Staff/Secretariat undermined the command structure. The IMS was also suspicious of the expertise of the DRC, as it was also of the NATO center for the civilian systems analysts.[249]

The SACEUR, too, had troubles with the new organization of the military planning function in NATO—in particular with the DPC committees that had responsibility for nuclear planning. When Secretary McNamara first made the proposal for a nuclear planning group, Lemnitzer was surprised because the proposal had been formulated in Washington without consulting him.[250] When the proposal was accepted, he was even more uneasy, because it excluded the SACEUR. Not only was the SACEUR to lose his predominant role in the formulation of alliance strategic policy, but he was also not to have a coequal role in the new procedure. Although Lemnitzer was successful in maintaining the dignity and symbolic place of his office, he was not able to retain the broad influence the SACEUR enjoyed during the earlier period of the alliance when NATO represented the bulwark of the West against what was perceived as a threatening communist menace.[251]

In addition to functional tensions between the SACEUR and the Military Committee on the one hand, and NATO's civilian defense structures on the other, there were more muted tensions between the SACEUR and the Military Committee. The dividing line between planning and operations was not always clear, and so now and again each would feel the other was intruding into his jurisdiction. These differences were not usually great, but the potential for conflict between the SACEUR and the chairman of the Military Committee was quite real and could have been serious depending on personalities.[252] The SACEUR had the advantage of high public visibility and of being able to formulate a cohesive policy. The chairman of the

Military Committee was saddled with the combined views of the chiefs of staff of fourteen member states. The result, as the product of many compromises in order to make it acceptable to all, was necessarily a watered down version of a strategic concept.

To facilitate communication among the various components of the NATO military organization and to minimize conflicts, Secretary-General Brosio on occasion invited the senior military and civilian officials—the chairman of the Military Committee, the SACEUR, the assistant secretary-general for defense planning and policy, and a few others—to lunch with him. These luncheons later became institutionalized into informal meetings without notes or agenda and served as an important coordinating medium on major issues.[253]

On 12 March 1969 the DPC unanimously agreed to release Lemnitzer from his duties as SACEUR to permit him to retire. He was going to be seventy in August. Effective 1 July, as mentioned earlier, Goodpaster took up the assignment as SACEUR. Goodpaster, fifty-four, was a West Point graduate and had earned a doctorate in politics at Princeton University. He had served with Generals Eisenhower and Gruenther in the early years of SHAPE, on the White House staff during the Eisenhower presidency and on the staff of the Joint Chiefs of Staff, and was deputy commander of American forces in Vietnam when he was appointed supreme commander in Europe. Tall, trim, grey-haired and spectacled, Goodpaster appeared to have a more reflective temperament that most generals. He was quick to recognize that the SACEUR's effectiveness depended on political factors and that to recapture the position the SACEUR held earlier would require from him adroit political talents.[254] Goodpaster could tolerate better than Lemnitzer the blurred edges of SHAPE's jurisdiction in the NATO organizational complex. Thus, conflicts involving the SACEUR's role faded. Also, as the Nixon administration in Washington seemed more willing to give the professional military officers more leeway in running the defense establishment, civil-military hostilities at the Pentagon diminished substantially.[255]

Like Lemnitzer, Goodpaster found Brosio easy to work with, and in many respects he shared the views of the secretary-general. In the period of growing détente, Goodpaster was frequently cautioning the member states to avoid disunity, to refrain from unilateral reductions in NATO's military strength, and not to expose themselves to political and military pressures. He exhorted the members to remedy deficiencies in NATO's forces and to reverse the trend of proportionately shrinking military budgets.[256]

Goodpaster did have to contend with a chairman of the Military Committee who was in a better position than his predecessors to enlarge his role. De Cumont's successor was Admiral Sir Nigel S. Henderson. Henderson, who had been the United Kingdom's representative to the Military Committee from 1965 to 1968, was thoroughly familiar with NATO and was ably assisted by his deputy, General Theodore Milton. Henderson took over some of the ceremonial functions previously performed by the SACEUR, because it was more convenient.[257] Lacking the authority that the SACEUR had as the commander of forces necessary for the defense of Europe, Henderson could not attain the public image that Goodpaster could, and Goodpaster was more concerned about his public role than had been Lemnitzer. But Henderson was the first chairman of the Military Committee to maintain a personal relationship with the secretary-general, even though Brosio did not allow that to interfere with his relationship with the SACEUR.[258] It brings to mind a curious fact, which is also a great tribute to Brosio's excellence as a diplomat: while his tenure saw the expansion of political control over military affairs, Brosio, the civilian leader of NATO, gained the nearly unanimous respect of the alliance's military officials.

Without doubt the most significant development in NATO's military organization occurred in the midst of the most difficult days of Brosio's term. After the MLF proposal was dropped in late 1964-early 1965 in the face of stiff opposition, the U.S. government searched for an alternative policy for sharing the nuclear responsibility. But such a policy, to be acceptable, would be subject to multiple and not completely consistent demands. It had to satisfy the Europeans and, above all, the West Germans' desire to participate in their own nuclear defense; it had to remain within the limits of American law and political feasibility; it had to avoid unduly antagonizing the Russians; and it had to win the approval or at least the tolerance of the French. The MLF had foundered because it had too many requirements to fulfill, both politically and militarily.

At a meeting of NATO defense ministers in the spring of 1965, American Secretary of Defense McNamara sponsored the creation of a select committee of four or five members to extend nuclear planning and consultation within the alliance. The proposal was received unusually well: the French and West Germans promised to study it.[259] Brosio found the proposal constructive, although characteristically he was less sanguine than others and discouraged exaggerated expectations. Realizing that the small member states would resent being excluded from a select committee consisting of only the larger members—the United States, the United Kingdom, France, West Germany, and possibly Italy—Brosio did not unreservedly endorse the McNamara proposal. He felt it needed a great deal of study and discussion, and the interests of all member states had to be taken into account.[260]

But it was not long before France informed the North Atlantic Council that it was not interested in the plan. De Gaulle wanted nothing to do with any procedure that implied subordination to the United States. The French made clear, however, that they had no objection if others wished to go ahead.[261] Without this express absence of French opposition, Brosio might very well have felt compelled to decline any further part in the proceedings.

For the next several months there was considerable diplomatic activity in Paris and between it and the capitals of member states concerning the McNamara proposal. Brosio actively supported the idea, because he agreed with its major premise that having learned the facts of nuclear life, member states would be in a better position to realize the consequences of decisions to use nuclear weapons. But he appended a subtle condition: "It is . . . equally in the interest of *all nations of the alliance* to have an opportunity to learn what the use of nuclear weapons in practice means."[262]

At a meeting of defense ministers in November, the Special Committee of Defense Ministers (the so-called McNamara committee) under the chairmanship of the secretary-general was formed to review ways of improving allied participation in nuclear policy and planning. A compromise had been reached whereby three working groups were established to deal with communications, data exchange, and nuclear planning. They would work under the guidance of a steering committee consisting of the permanent representatives of the states represented on the subgroups.[263] Each group would be composed of five members, one of whom would act as chairman. Brosio would not sit on any of the groups. The United States, the United Kingdom, West Germany, Canada, and Belgium were the members of the Intelligence and Data Exchange Group, which was chaired by J. P. Waterfield of the United Kingdom. The Communications Group was composed of the United States, the United Kingdom, Canada, Denmark, and the Netherlands, which supplied the chairman, General Willem de Toon. McNamara chaired the Nuclear Planning Group (NPG), which was made up of the United States, the United Kingdom, West Germany, Italy, and Turkey. These compromise arrangements, while managing to include all interested NATO member states, favored McNamara's conception, because the important questions of nuclear sharing would be considered within a select committee comprised only of defense ministers. As chairman of the overall exercise, Brosio was left with a formal position devoid initially of important influence.

The working groups met for the first time in February 1966, just as the French were totally withdrawing from NATO's military organization. While the Data Exchange and Communication Groups were finished with their work by May, the NPG continued to meet into the fall.[264] In Rome at the fourth meeting of the NPG, Brosio was present for the discussions that largely concerned organizational questions, as did the July meeting at headquarters in Paris of the full Special Committee of Defense Ministers.

McNamara's ideas had dominated the NPG. The American defense secretary felt it was imperative that national political authorities at the highest level be personally acquainted with the details of nuclear strategy. He had every desire to expose American nuclear planning to the top political leaders of the alliance in order to ensure that they would understand it, comment on it, and contribute suggestions to it. As chairman of the NPG, McNamara had established the procedural rules: no non-authorized person was allowed to talk with the ministers; there was to be no reading of papers, long briefings, or programmed discussion, as was normal in many intergovernmental meetings; and preparatory work was to be completed far in advance of a meeting in order that it could be transmitted to members who could read it before arrival (which was insisted on). This procedure resulted in intensive sessions among the government ministers on subjects of the highest concern to all.

McNamara was very happy with the results and wanted to preserve the structure for more permanent consultative arrangements. He had, however, come to recognize the importance of Brosio's support and the value of his participation in the small group.[265] By the aforementioned last meeting of the NPG in Rome, McNamara was willing to have Brosio chair both the large steering committee and the small working group (the NPG), but he still wanted to keep the group to five, because, he reasoned, the smaller it was, the more work it accomplished. Brosio again took the part of the smaller member states by arguing for a larger committee: it would be an unwise precedent to exclude a member state from any committee of the alliance (the original NPG was only a temporary body). A compromise was settled on in the fall: the small group would consist of seven members, four permanent—the United States, the United Kingdom, West Germany, and Italy—and three rotating, elected for eighteen-month terms. The steering committee, to be called the Nuclear Defense Affairs Committee (NDAC), would be open to all members, although France, Iceland, and Luxembourg decided not to participate. The recommendations of the McNamara committee, establishing the NDAC and the NPG and making them responsible to the DPC, were ratified at the ministerial meeting in December 1966.

The NPG met for the first time in April 1967 in Washington and has met approximately twice a year since then, under the chairmanship of the secretary-general. There had been a spirited rivalry for the three nonpermanent positions, which Canada, the Netherlands, and Turkey had won. The procedures of the temporary NPG were adopted, the United States again insisting that a special table be built for its meetings—this time eight-sided for the seven ministers and the chairman. The room was organized in such a way as to almost force the participation of the ministers in the discussions and to force the limitation of discussion to the ministers, that is, excluding them from relying on staff. At the original group, the SACEUR was not allowed to participate as a member but did participate in discussions of matters affecting SHAPE. The development of the NPG was aimed not in the direction of a group that would decide whether to push the nuclear button, but toward the establishment of a foundation of knowledge that allied political leaders would need to know in order to participate intelligently in consultations as to the conditions under which the president should "go nuclear" in their common interests. Hardware-based alternatives were dispensed with.

One of the first topics that nonnuclear member states chose to inject in this new forum for the discussion of nuclear strategy was tactical nuclear weapons. There was a general lack of satisfaction with the extent and adequacy of planning for using tactical nuclear weapons, which were supposed to play a major role in the defense of Europe. Brosio was one of those actively pushing for more thorough planning in this area. Another of the earlier concerns of the new defense machinery was to get agreement on a revised strategy for the alliance. After a major effort in the NPG, the NDAC, and the Military Committee, the DPC in December 1967 adopted a strategy based on the concept of a flexible and balanced range of responses—conventional and nuclear—to all levels or threats of aggression. The defense ministers at the same meeting adopted, for the first time, a five-year force plan covering the period 1968-1972. This ministerial meeting, which also saw the approval of the Harmel Report, indicated that the alliance still possessed viability; it marked the entrance of NATO into a new phase of its existence.

One of Brosio's last initiatives came in the military field. Taking a cue from President Nixon's speech to the Council in April 1969, Brosio took a personal role in guiding an in-depth examination of NATO's defense problems for the next decade, thus the name of the study—AD'70 or Allied Defense for the

1970s. He did his best to make AD'70 a NATO study in contrast to the Harmel Report, which he regarded as independently produced.[266] With the stress on the maintenance of adequate defensive strength, the AD'70 report reiterated that NATO's approach to security in the 1970s would be based on the twin concepts of defense and détente.

Although the timing of Brosio's retirement was not unexpected, it came about in quite unanticipated circumstances. In the course of 1970, it became known that Brosio planned to retire sometime in 1971. At the time, the Berlin talks were stalled (which froze Brandt's *ostpolitik*), no progress was being made in engaging the Soviets in negotiations for MBFR, and SALT was proceeding at an unencouragingly slow pace. In March 1971 Brezhnev without warning gave a positive response to the alliance's proposal for talks on MBFR, and made it clear by repeating it in May.[267] At their meeting in Lisbon in the spring, the NATO ministers promptly answered by stating their desire for intensive contacts with the East in order that they could move on to negotiations on MBFR as soon as possible. To facilitate the negotiations, the Council was instructed to prepare studies for a meeting of deputy foreign ministers or similar high officials to review the outcome of the exploratory contacts. Brosio, who regarded MBFR as a touchstone of détente, welcomed the decisions.

On 3 September 1970, the four powers responsible for Berlin signed an agreement defining the status of the city and guaranteeing access to it. A month later the NATO Council of Ministers consulted on the next steps to MBFR. The representatives of the governments of the alliance (except France) appointed Brosio in his personal capacity—since he was by then no longer secretary-general—to conduct exploratory talks with the Soviet Union and other interested governments on the subject of MBFR. He was scheduled to go to Moscow, but the Soviet Union later rescinded the invitation. Still, Brosio's stillborn mission represented an unmistakable sign of the confidence the members of the alliance had in him.

When Brosio had arrived at NATO, the alliance was floundering. He left it reformed and revitalized. After more than seven years at its helm, and nearly seventy-five years old, Brosio explained his wish to retire as a desire for a change and a chance to return to his native Italy, where he continued to contribute to the political life of his country with the same indefatigability and integrity with which he had served NATO.

Notes

1. Because Manlio Brosio has not written his memoirs, it has not been possible to benefit fully from his own description and insights into the events of his life prior to his assumption of the office of secretary-general of NATO. The biographical material in this section has been compiled from a variety of sources, including personal interviews. Two of the most succinct and easily available biographical sketches of NATO's fourth secretary-general may be found in the *New York Times,* 14 May 1964; and the *Times* (London), 14 May 1964.

2. Brosio, essentially a political man, felt severely constrained by his inability to participate in the political life of his country. Even after his retirement from NATO at the age of seventy-four, Brosio enthusiastically returned to Italian domestic politics, joining the Republican Party and serving as a senator of the Republic. 22 (1-2).

3. He was minister without portfolio in the Bonomi cabinet of 1944-1945, vice-president of the Council of Ministers in the Parri cabinet of 1945, and minister of defense in the first de Gasperi cabinet of 1945-1946.

4. *New York Times,* 14 May 1964.

5. *Le Monde,* 31 March 1961. See the previous chapter for a more detailed account of Dirk Stikker's candidacy for secretary-general.

6. Sulzberger, *Age of Mediocrity,* p. 57.

7. *Times* (London), 8 April 1964.

8. Ibid.; and *Sunday Telegraph,* 8 December 1963.

9. *Times* (London), 14 May 1964.

10. *New York Times,* 14 May 1964.

11. Ibid.

12. Ibid.

13. 33 (5).

14. *New York Times,* 14 May 1964.

15. 5 (2).

16. 18 (1).

17. 22 (1).

18. Sulzberger, *Age of Mediocrity,* p. 57.

19. The West German government was perhaps the only member of the alliance to express any reservations about Brosio as secretary-general; Brosio had offered little encouragement towards a resolution of the German unity-security dilemma. 2 (1-2).

20. C. L. Sulzberger, *New York Times,* 11 May 1964.

21. 6 (3). This conception of the office of secretary-general was well received by the smaller members of the alliance.

22. 13 (1); 19 (3); 6 (10); 6 (7).

23. Speech by the secretary-general before the Interallied Confederation of Reserve Officers (NATO Press Service), 22 July 1970.

24. 22 (1); 19 (1); 34 (1); 30 (1).

25. 11 (1); V (1); 33 (1).

26. 19 (1); 33 (4); 22 (1).

27. These often were Fausto Bacchetti, his *chef de cabinet,* Lord Coleridge, Arthur Hockaday, Paul Van Campen, Kenneth Hunt, and William Seim.

28. B (1), 33 (3), and 19 (1).

29. 6 (1).

30. 6 (10).

31. 30 (2).

32. Brosio was aristocratic by demeanor only, not by birth. He also could be cold and disdainful if he felt imposed upon.

33. 33 (4) and 22 (1-2).

34. 22 (1); 33 (5); B (1); 22 (2); 22 (1).

35. 38 (2-3); V (2).

36. *Times* (London), 14 May 1964.

37. 30 (1).

38. 6 (3); 6 (11).

39. 6 (4).

40. The French did not participate in the NATO communications network. C (1).

41. *NATO Letter* 18 (September 1970):25-26.

42. 5 (1); 30 (1); 33 (5); 30 (1-2).

43. 16 (1).

44. After the French pullout, Gregh had difficulty gaining access to certain NATO classified documents, which hampered at times his ability to function in this area. As an illustration of the high regard in which he was held by the permanent representatives, Gregh was given a silver bowl upon his retirement by the representatives. Traditionally, this is given only to departing permanent representatives. Only Lord Coleridge and General Norstad had been given the same honor.

45. 13 (1).

46. 16 (2-3); 16 (1).

47. The original title, assistant secretary-general for production, logistics, and infrastructure, was changed in 1967. See chart in Appendix 1, p. 272.

48. 18 (1); 18 (1-2); 27 (1).

49. Address to the NATO parliamentarians conference, 16 November 1964 (NATO Information Service, Paris), 4, 6-7. Brosio helped put the MLF to rest by advocating that fundamental changes in the alliance should be the result of frank discussion and unanimous consent.

50. Speech to the NATO Defense College, Rome, 14 February 1971 (NATO Information Service, Brussels).

51. 33 (1-2); 6 (1); 30 (2); V (2).

52. 6 (1); 33 (4); 6 (10).

53. V (2). Brosio's manner at times irritated his Anglo-Saxon staff members who were accustomed to more openness between the secretary-general and his staff. 19 (1) and 6 (1).

54. B (1).

55. Speech to the Atlantic Treaty Association, the Hague, 21 September 1970 (NATO Information Service, Brussels), 8; 4 (1); 18 (1). For a full discussion of the impact of the Greek coup, see p. 206ff.

56. 40 (1).

57. 37 (2); 9 (1-2); 6 (2); and V (3).

58. 9 (1).

59. V (3); 4 (10); and 33 (3).

60. Speech to the American Club of Paris, 22 February 1965 (NATO Information Service).

61. 33 (2).

62. See, for example, Brosio's speech to the NATO parliamentarians conference in November 1965 (NATO Information Service). See the previous chapter for a fuller discussion of the MLF.

63. *New York Times*, 2 July 1965.

64. Cf. Schlesinger, *A Thousand Days,* p. 427.

65. C (3).

66. 35 (2).

67. G (4). Partially to retain the confidence of his superiors, Cleveland conformed to the administration's policy on Vietnam. In NATO, Cleveland would conscientiously explain American actions, defend his country's policy, and solicit aid, in whatever form, from the other members of the alliance. See *Le Figaro,* 21 January 1966.

68. 37 (2).

69. 28 (2).

70. 5 (2).

71. 19 (3); 28 (2).

72. 20 (1).

73. C (2).

74. 35 (2); 30 (2); 30 (3); 19 (1); 19 (3).

75. 33 (1); 22 (1-2).

76. 20 (1).

77. *New York Times,* 30 September 1971.

78. *New York Times,* 12 April and 17 June 1969.

79. 20 (1). It was also rumored that Ellsworth had found it difficult to carve out a role for himself on a White House staff dominated increasingly on the interntional affairs side by an aggressive Dr. Kissinger.

80. *New York Times,* 15 January 1970; *New York Times,* 28 April and 14 May 1971; 28 (2); 6 (3).

81. 5 (1); 5 (2); 19 (3).

82. 20 (1).

83. B (2).

84. 9 (6). See the previous chapter for a discussion of Francois Seydoux's diplomacy at NATO.

85. B (3); 40 (1).

86. 9 (6).

87. B (2).

88. For an example of de Gaulle's concept of NATO and its deleterious effect on French sovereignty, see his Twelfth Press Conference, 9 September 1965, Ambassade de France, New York, Speeches and Press, no. 228, pp. 7-8.

89. Thirteenth Press Conference, 21 February 1966, Ambassade de France, New York, Speeches and Press, no. 239, pp. 8-9.

90. *Le Monde,* 1 April 1966.

91. B (2).

92. See, for example, Brosio's speech to the Association Française pour le Communanté-Atlantique (NATO Information Service, Paris), 27 January 1965, pp. 3-4.

93. Sulzberger, *Age of Mediocrity,* p. 214.

94. Twelfth Press Conference, p. 7.

95. *New York Times,* 10 September 1965.

96. C (3).

97. *Times* (London), 10 July 1965.

98. André Fontaine in *Le Monde,* 19 October 1965.

99. See Brosio's speech to the Anglo-American Press Association, 10 June 1965 (NATO Information Service, Paris), pp. 3-4.

100. Following de Gaulle's September 1965 press conference, Brosio delivered an address to the NATO parliamentarians conference in New York on 4 October 1965 in which he uncharacteristically revealed his critical attitude towards French policy.

101. Thirteenth Press Conference, p. 8.

102. De Gaulle's letter to President Johnson is printed in *NATO Letter* 14 (May 1966):22.

103. Ibid.

104. Johnson repeated his arguments in an address to the Foreign Service Institute, 25 March 1965, reprinted in the *Department of State Bulletin,* 11 April 1966, pp. 554-56.

105. Ambassade de France, New York, Service de presse et d'information, *French Affairs* no. 192 (April 1966):1-4. There were two commands stationed in France: SHAPE and AFCENT (Allied Forces Central Europe). *Le Monde,* 20 March 1965, for the United Kingdom's response.

107. Ambassade de France, *French Affairs* no. 192 (April 1966):5-8.

108. This Franco-German exchange may be found in the *NATO Letter* 14 (July/August 1966):24-85. See also Stein and Carreau, "Law and Peaceful Change," pp. 633-35, for details on the resolution of the status of French troops in West Germany.

109. An additional exchange of notes between the United States and France occurred before direct negotiations were begun. See *Department of State Bulletin* 54 (2 May 1966):609-701; and *Nato Letter* 14 (July/August 1966):24. See also the *New York Times,* 26 April 1966, for more on the start of face-to-face talks.

110. G (1). Brosio operated so cautiously that his position on major questions remained unclear even to some of the highest officials in Paris. 37 (2).

111. C (6).

112. *NATO Letter* 14 (May 1966):24.

113. Speech to the Royal Institute of International Relations, Brussels, 31 March 1966 (NATO Information Service).

114. France also conducted a series of bilateral negotiations with the other members regarding the ramifications of its action.

115. C (3); B (2).

116. 37 (2-3). For a lucid exposition of the substance of the Franco-American negotiations, see Stein and Carreau, "Law and Peaceful Change," pp. 622-25, 635-38.

117. 37 (2).

118. Ibid.

119. *New York Times,* 24 April 1966, p. 1. References to these arrangements have been made earlier in this chapter.

120. *New York Times,* 7, 9, and 15 June 1966.

121. Ibid., 10 March 1966.

122. Ibid., 15 March 1966.

123. Ibid., 30 March 1966; 37 (2). Compare the comments of Danish

Foreign Minister Per Haekerrup reported in *Le Monde*, 20 April 1966.

124. *New York Times*, 4 May 1966; and *Le Monde*, 4 May 1966.

125. *New York Times*, 1 June 1966.

126. Sulzberger, *Age of Mediocrity*, pp. 311, 320; and *New York Times*, 2 October 1966.

127. *New York Times*, 7 June 1966.

128. Ibid., 25-28 October 1966.

129. Ibid., 10 November 1966.

130. B (2).

131. See, for example, his speech to the Danish Atlantic Association in Copenhagen, 4 November 1965 (NATO Information Service).

132. C (3,6); B (3); 19 (3); B (2). At times his witty asides could be cutting and therefore annoying.

133. 19 (3); 8 (3); 37 (2).

134. *New York Times*, 15 March 1966.

135. Ibid., 7 and 11 June 1966.

136. *New York Times*, 5, 22 and 23 June 1966; 21 (3); 9 (4).

137. For example, the French word *hôte* can mean either host, guest, or occupier.

138. *New York Times*, 22 August 1966, p. 11.

139. Ibid., 27 August 1966, p. 3.

140. Ibid., 7 and 10 September 1966.

141. Ibid., 14-15 September 1966.

142. Ibid., 24 April and 12 October 1966. In the end de Staercke was more embarrassed than relieved, because his government did not fix up the headquarters site as promised.

143. *Times* (London), 9 February 1967.

144. Ibid., 17 and 31 March 1967.

145. *New York Times*, 8 December 1966.

146. C (4), B (2), and 18 (3).

147. Cleveland, de Leusse, and de Staercke all saw it in this light. B (2). Harlan Cleveland, *NATO: The Transatlantic Bargain* (New York, 1970), pp. 191-92.

148. One instance where it did occur was in reference to NATO's position on negotiations on mutual (and balanced) force reductions with the East. 18 (3).

149. See President Johnson's speech to the National Conference of Editorial Writers, 7 October 1966, *Department of State Bulletin*, 55 (24 October 1966):623.

150. *NATO: Facts and Figures*, p. 56.

151. See Brosio's speech to the Parliamentary Assembly of the WEU, 17 November 1970 (NATO Press Service, Brussels), p. 4; 9 (5); 38 (1).

152. B (3).

153. 40 (1) and 38 (1).

154. The full text of the Harmel Report may be found in Appendix 6, pp. 301-304.

155. 6 (10); 20 (1).

156. Ironically, the Dutch and the Scandinavians, not wishing to become involved in the perpetual antagonism between Greece and Turkey, had initially opposed their inclusion in the alliance. 18 (3).

157. 18 (1).

158. B (4).

159. See his speech to the Atlantic Treaty Association, The Hague, 21 September 1970 (NATO Press Service, Brussels), p. 7.

160. *New York Times,* 10 December 1974.

161. B (4).

162. 9 (6). For example, French-speaking diplomats were forced to ask for translations of documents and speeches, which had not been necessary before.

163. 2 (2) and 40 b(1).

164. B (4).

165. See Harold van B. Cleveland, *The Atlantic Idea and its European Rivals* (New York, 1966), pp. 34-35, for a lucid explanation of West Germany's special place in the alliance.

166. *Times* (London), 12 May 1965, p. 6; and *Die Welt,* 12 May 1965.

167. Address to the Deutsche Atlantische Gesellschaft, Bonn, 25 March 1965 (NATO Press Service, Paris), pp. 7-9, 12-14. Cf. Three-Power Declaration on Germany annexed to the final communiqué of the NATO ministerial meeting in London, in *NATO Letter* 13 (June 1965):28.

168. Address to the Royal Institute of International Relations, Brussels, 31 March 1966 (NATO Press Service, Paris), pp. 8-9.

169. 37 (2); C (5); B (3); 19 (1).

170. See Brosio's warm description of Ambassador Grewe in his address to the Deutsche Gesellschaff für Auswartige Politik, Bonn, 22 April 1971 (NATO Press Service, Brussels), p. 3.

171. *Times* (London), 11 August 1964.

172. *NATO Letter* 14 (January 1966):22.

173. *Times* (London), 25 November 1967; 20 (1).

174. See pp. 134ff. for Stikker's constraints in dealing with the Cyprus question.

175. *New York Times,* 27 and 29 November 1967.

176. Ibid., 30 November 1967.

177. B (4) and 33 (3).

178. 25 (1).

179. *Times* (London), 4 November 1965.

180. *NATO Letter* 15 (July-August 1967):ii.

181. 28 (2).

182. NATO Information Service, Brussels, 22 August 1968.

183. *New York Times,* 28 June 1971.

184. *Times* (London), 7 August 1971; and 5 (1).

185. 33 (3).

186. In December 1971, after Brosio had departed from NATO, Mintoff unilaterally abrogated the agreement with NATO, and NAVSOUTH was subsequently relocated to Naples, Italy.

187. Speech at the Opening Session of the ministerial meeting, Luxembourg, 14 June 1967 (NATO Press Service, Paris), p. 3.

188. B (2).

189. *Department of State Bulletin* 52 (21 June 1965):986-89.

190. See his Address at the European Luncheon Club, London, 25 February 1966 (NATO Information Service, Paris), pp. 9-10; and his speech to the Royal Institute of International Relations, Brussels (NATO Information Service, Paris), pp. 3-4.

191. B (2).

192. *Times* (London), 26 and 27 July 1965.

193. See the statements by West German Foreign Minister Gerhardt Schröder in the *Times* (London) 12 July and 28 August 1965.

194. See Brosio's speech to the Western European Union, Paris, 16 November 1965 (NATO Information Service, Brussels), p. 7.

195. See the President's Budget Message for Fiscal Year 1968 in January 1967, in *Documents in American Foreign Relations, 1967* (New York, 1968), p. 33.

196. *Department of State Bulletin* 56 (20 March 1967):445.

197. See p. 203ff for a discussion of the Harmel Report.

198. *NATO: Facts and Figures,* p. 368.

199. *New York Times,* 25 August 1968.

200. *Times* (London), 5 September 1968.

201. B (4).

202. *New York Times,* 15 October 1968.

203. Ibid., 12 November 1968.

204. Ibid., 13 November 1968.

205. See p. 177ff. for Coleridge's responsibilities in this area.

206. This communiqué may be found in *NATO: Facts and Figures,* pp. 369-71.

207. Harold van B. Cleveland, *The Atlantic Idea,* p. 26.

208. *Times* (London), 20 September and 18 October 1967.

209. *New York Times,* 12 April 1969. The ministers also instructed

the Council to pursue its studies in the field of disarmament and arms control including mutual (and balanced) force reductions.

210. *Le Monde,* 19 and 20 March 1969.

211. 18 (1).

212. Quoted in John Newhouse, *Cold Dawn: The Story of SALT* (New York, 1973), p. 139.

213. Ibid., p. 224; 18 (4).

214. For a lucid analysis of the *ostpolitik,* see John H. Herz, "Ostpolitik—Antecedents, Problems, Prospects," paper presented to the Northeast Political Science Association Meeting, Saratoga Springs, New York, 4-6 November 1971.

215. See his speech to the National Press Club, *Washington Post,* 19 November 1966.

216. Speech to the Atlantic Treaty Association, The Hague, 21 September 1970 (NATO Information Service, Brussels), pp. 11-12.

217. For the texts of Nixon's addresses to the Council in February and April, see *Documents on American Foreign Relations, 1969* (New York, 1970), pp. 144-48, 148-54.

218. *Times* (London), 18 March 1969, p. 1.

219. *New York Times,* 15 May 1969.

220. See his speech to the North Atlantic Assembly, *New York Times,* 19 October 1969.

221. *Times* (London), 1 November 1969; *Le Monde,* 3 November 1969.

222. *Times* (London), 6 November 1969; *Le Monde,* 7 November 1969.

223. *Times* (London), 6 December 1969.

224. *NATO: Facts and Figures,* pp. 374-76.

225. *Times* (London), 27 June 1970.

226. Address to the Inter-allied Confederation of Reserve Officers, Brussels, 22 July 1970 (NATO Information Service, Brussels), p. 4.

227. See, e.g., his speech to the Parliamentary Assembly of the Western European Union, Paris, 17 November 1970 (NATO Press Service, Brussels) pp. 8-9.

228. *NATO: Facts and Figures,* p. 382.

229. Speech to the NATO Defense College, Rome, 19 February 1971 (NATO Information Service, Brussels), p. 3.

230. C (5).

231. 19 (1).

232. C (5).

233. B (2).

234. B (1); 21 (2); 6 (3); V (4); B (1).

235. See p. 82ff for a discussion of General Norstad's style as SACEUR. Lemnitzer would even have let Brosio clear his speeches with the Council's authorization. 21 (3).

236. 6 (3); V (4).

237. 12 (4).

238. C (5,6).

239. 21 (1); 19 (2); 14 (1).

240. 14 (1); 19 (2).

241. 6 (3); 19 (2).

242. 6 (11).

243. 6 (2).

244. 6 (2,3).

245. 6 (11).

246. 14 (1,2).

247. 14 (1).

248. G (4).

249. 14 (1); 12 (5).

250. 11 (1).

251. 12 (2,3).

252. 6 (3).

253. 10 (1); 14 (1).

254. C (5,6); 37 (2); 12 (3).

255. 12 (5).

256. See his speeches to the North Atlantic Assembly, *New York Times,* 19 October 1969; and *New York Times,* 11 November 1970.

257. 12 (5).

258. 14 (2).

259. *Times* (London), 2 and 7 June 1965.

260. Speech to the Anglo-American Press Association, Paris, 10 June 1965 (NATO Information Service, Paris), p. 4; and speech to the NATO Parliamentarians Conference, New York, 4 October 1965 (NATO Information Service, Paris), pp. 11-13.

261. *Times* (London), 10 July 1965.

262. Speech to the Danish Atlantic Association, Copenhagen, 4 November 1965 (NATO Information Service, Paris), p. 7. Emphasis added.

263. *NATO Letter* 14 (January 1966):25.

264. *Times* (London), 28 April 1966.

265. Cleveland, *The Atlantic Idea,* p. 56.

266. Speech to the Parliamentary Assembly of the Western European Union, Paris, 17 November 1970 (NATO Information Service, Paris), pp. 4-5.

267. *New York Times,* 31 March and 15 May 1971.

Conclusion:
Can the Office Transcend
the Organization?

The Organization and Office in Perspective

The North Atlantic Treaty Organization is the offspring of two unlikely parents: fear and optimism. In 1947, the iron curtain, in Churchill's majestic phrase, was descending over Eastern Europe. Through the tactics of subversion, as in Rumania, and guerrilla warfare, as in Greece, the Soviet Union's sphere of influence and control crept westward. In 1948 Czechoslovakia fell to a communist coup and the Soviet Union imposed a blockade on the island city of Berlin. Two years later, the North Koreans launched their massive assault on the south. At the time, many thought this was the opening round of the Third World War and looked anxiously toward a nearly defenseless Europe. It was this fear of imminent war in 1950 that, in Averell Harriman's words, put the "O" in NATO.

Yet this was also a period of growth, innovation and optimism. The Brussels Treaty of 1948, which created the Western European Union, and the European Coal and Steel Community in 1951, presaged the much broader NATO and European Economic Community, respectively. These developments injected into Europe a renewed vitality and a new sense of direction. And the Marshall Plan of 1947, coupled with the Organization for European Economic Cooperation (OEEC), laid the foundation for increased economic cooperation between the United States and Europe. With the reorganization of NATO at the Lisbon Conference early in 1952, many political leaders felt the new organization would become the basis for a genuine partnership between the two continents, and they looked forward to the progressive emergence of an Atlantic community.

Into this wary yet dynamic milieu stepped NATO's first secretary-general, General Lord Ismay. To him fell much of the responsibility for the definition and development of the office, including the secretary-general's role above and beyond the purely administrative functions attached to the position. The ability of the office to transcend the organization was then an open question. Ismay, however, elected not to explore the political limits of his office, in advance of necessity. He chose, rather, to focus his attention on the construction of a Staff/Secretariat that was both competent and international. Ismay ran NATO in the best tradition of the British civil service he admired: he was a quiet, behind-the-scenes conciliator and coordinator. He saw it as his responsibility to build up the North Atlantic Council as the primary political entity of the alliance. Impetus for the formulation of policy was to be left to governments and their representatives. Yet Ismay's contributions to the office were not inconsiderable: he set a precedent for competent administration and gave the new office a sense of legitimacy that would become important in weathering the future storms of nationalism.

It was left to Ismay's successor, Paul-Henri Spaak, to test the political limits of the office. Spaak, the vibrant globalist, sought to create for the secretary-general an international diplomatic rank nearly equal to that of a head of state. To Spaak, NATO, like the EEC, must eventually transcend the nation-state; he viewed the alliance as not merely as association of states, but as a potential supranational entity unto itself. To permit NATO to fill this role, Spaak felt it essential that the secretary-general have frequent access to heads of state where he could mediate directly and defend alliance considerations personally with them. Always a man of action, Spaak did not hesitate to implement his ideas publicly. With NATO, it was Spaak the secretary-general, not the Council of Permanent Representatives, that dominated the organization. Spaak personally directed the Council, frequently prodding and chiding its members. When he felt it appropriate, Spaak would bypass the Council and appeal directly to member governments; as he had cajoled and bullied the states of Europe into the EEC at

Messina, so he hoped to push the NATO partners into a genuine and active Atlantic community, and the alliance into military and, eventually, political integration.

Yet if Spaak's tenure was the period of exploration and tentative expansion of the scope of the secretary-general's office, it was also a period of reaction and contraction. Spaak's dynamic postwar internationalism collided with the resurgence of European nationalism. And when the dust settled, it was clear that the older force had won. Charles de Gaulle, more than any other Western political figure, personified traditional nationalism and personally led its assault on NATO and the secretary-general. From the first, de Gaulle refused to deal directly with Spaak; to do so would have been a tacit admission of the secretary-general's international diplomatic standing the General wished explicitly to deny. Through his September 1957 memorandum de Gaulle proposed what was tantamount to the elimination of any hope of the secretary-general acting as an independent political figure and of NATO as an international organization. And while the General's "triumvirate," or directorate, proposal never materialized, it symbolized a conception that de Gaulle unceasingly sought to impose on the alliance. After struggling to preserve his notion of an emerging Atlantic community against de Gaulle's nationalist encroachments, Spaak resigned in disappointment.

Dirk Stikker, Spaak's successor, assumed office under the most difficult of circumstances: not only had France openly declared political war on his office and opposed his appointment, but he was forced while in office to contend with French obstructionism in the day-to-day military affairs of NATO and to mediate between France and the United States on the sensitive issue of nuclear sharing. In both areas, success was virtually impossible; de Gaulle would never abandon his quest for nationalist grandeur and political independence, and the United States would not—and legally and politically could not—relinquish control over its virtual nuclear monopoly. Stikker, a moderate Atlanticist, found an ally in the United States, but this only served to render France, and de Gaulle, more implacable. The strains within the alliance were too severe and the divisions too deep for one man or one office to bridge.

Stikker, suffering from recurrent physical disabilities, could only watch as France began to disengage itself from the NATO military command structure. It was during this period that the political limits of the office of secretary-general became apparent: he could neither stand as an independent political force against the wishes and actions of member states (and especially the larger members), nor impose his good offices on the parties to a dispute. He could only offer them. In addition, the Council, in the form of the permanent representatives, began to develop its own informal modes of consultation and policy formulation.

Manlio Brosio, perhaps better than his predecessors, understood the limitations of his office. During the upheaval caused by the French withdrawal from the integrated military command structure and the removal of NATO headquarters from Paris to Brussels, Brosio discreetly sought to preserve his office by deliberately refusing to become involved in any dispute that would make him appear to favor some members over others. For example, realizing that the moment called for calm and considered action rather than emotional reaction, Brosio minimized as best he could the effects of the French withdrawal. The Council, under the leadership of its doyen, assumed for a time primary responsibility for conducting alliance political relations with France. And perceiving his absence of political power vis-à-vis the larger members, Brosio emulated Ismay's style of quiet, unobtrusive diplomacy. He functioned as a coordinator, conciliator, and discreet initiator. He performed the role he had fulfilled for years as an ambassador. In this manner, by placing the alliance and the secretary-generalship as much as possible beyond partisan politics between the allies, Brosio succeeded in maintaining the integrity of his office. He had to be careful to preach caution without appearing obstructionist. But it is clear that this preservation was purchased at a price: the secretary-general could no longer presume to stand as the leader of a supranational body with a political life independent of its members.

The Boundaries of the Alliance and the Office

The ability of the secretary-general to assume a role that would transcend the organization depended on the progressive development of an Atlantic community. But when this community failed to materialize, the multinational diplomatic role of the secretary-general remained limited to the narrower and more purely European-related political/military aspects of NATO. Today little remains of the broad Atlantic community that Spaak so energetically sought to build on the foundation of Article II of the North Atlantic Treaty. Nonmilitary cooperation between the NATO partners has primarily been limited to economic issues, and until Britain's accession to the Treaty of Rome, was handled on a trilateral NATO-EEC-UK basis. The relations have since assumed the attitude of a bilateral dialogue between the EEC members (or alternatively the Eurogroup in NATO) and the United States and Canada. Most of the current nonmilitary problems facing the NATO members—energy, monetary policy, East-West trade—are being handled through other means. The OECD (which Spaak opposed as a threat to the NATO-centered Atlantic community), the IMF, GATT, the newly formed International Energy Agency, and even more traditional ad hoc multilateral negotiations such as those that produced the Smithsonian Agreements in 1971 have served as the mechanisms for consultation and economic problem solving across the Atlantic. The overall effect of this decentralization of institutionalized consultation and cooperation has been to restrict NATO to its narrow defense responsibilities and to deny the secretary-general a leading role in the nonmilitary affairs of the NATO member states.

Similarly, the geographical scope of the alliance limits the ability of the secretary-general to play an international role among powers who have extraregional or global concerns. NATO, by design and then by necessity, has become narrowly European and anticommunist. The inability of the secretary-general to play a major role in such extraregional though NATO-related disputes as Cyprus and Malta illustrates the geographical confines within which he must operate. Because defense for the United States constitutes a global and not simply a regional problem, the secretary-general has found himself serving as a proponent of European considerations to NATO's largest member. While this is an important function, it nonetheless compromises the secretary-general's freedom to adopt the global posture requisite for his functioning as an independent political personality. And conversely, the Western Europeans, especially the smaller members of NATO, do not wish to see the secretary-general abdicate this role as their spokesman to the United States in favor of an independent, all-NATO position, rather like a sixteenth member.

Because NATO is the child of the Cold War, the secretary-general, in order to justify his existence as well as that of the organization, has viewed détente with skepticism, since NATO's original purpose was to deter an attack by the Soviet Union on Western Europe. And when Spaak could not entice the NATO partners to expand allied activities to embrace other forms of political and economic cooperation, the alliance was forced to rely on its deterrent function as its primary raison d'être. This, in turn, by the mid-1950s required the continued perception of overt hostility and potential conflict between NATO and the Warsaw Pact. But the Suez crisis of 1956, which split the alliance and began the French "go it alone" policy, and the onset of détente following the Cuban missile crisis in the early 1960s robbed NATO of some of its purpose. In this sense, détente, rather than France, has emerged as the most persistent threat to NATO.

The Soviet repression of the liberalization movement in Czechoslovakia in 1968 quickly rejuvenated NATO, but the effect was only temporary. By 1971, with the success of the West German *ostpolitik* (that had followed the French version of *ostpolitik*) and the Soviet calls for a European security conference, détente once again became the major theme in East-West relations. Throughout this period, the secretary-general consistently expressed suspicion of détente and opposed the bloc-to-bloc negotiations for mutual and balanced force reductions (MBFR)—or more exactly, MFR, following the Russian insistence. While not successful in his opposition, it is significant that it was through NATO that the Western states prepared their joint positions for the MFR negotiations, and that this in turn permitted the secretary-general to participate in the formulation of Western policy. Yet the secretary-general's role was again not that of initiator; he primarily functioned in the more limited capacity of liaison between the Europeans and the United States. He did not speak for the alliance to the East bloc.

If détente remains the theme of the 1970s and 1980s—which appears the likely course unless events in the Middle East or Africa lead to renewed Soviet-American confrontation—there seems to be little opportunity for the secretary-general to play a role in the formation of a global nuclear or political strategy. He is not the leader of the noncommunist coalition of states. Any such grouping must eventually be expanded to include Japan, especially on economic questions. And the United States, through its series of regional treaties—the Rio Pact, SEATO, CENTO, and ANZUS—has retained for itself the position of defender of the free world, even though the so-called Nixon Doctrine and the post-Vietnam era have diminished the political import of these treaties. Furthermore, the substance and direction of nuclear strategy continues to come from Washington rather than Brussels. The secretary-general remains locked into a largely European perspective from which he cannot escape without jeopardizing his carefully guarded functions within NATO. In this sense the secretary-general finds himself in a position analogous to that of his predecessors in the League of Nations who found themselves restricted to a primarily European focus while the centers of world power gravitate elsewhere from time to time; who saw major crises occur outside the European continent; and who lacked the means and authority to take independent political action. (The attempt by the United Nations secretary-general—in the Congo crisis—ended in near disaster.) The major difference between the two positions lies in the fact that NATO was not designed to be a universal organ for the promotion of peace. It is a regional coalition designed to deter or, failing that, to prosecute a war.

The Secretary-General and the Council

If the secretary-general cannot function beyond the confines of the alliance, it becomes necessary to ascertain those elements that contribute to his effectiveness within NATO. Because the civilian authority within the alliance is divided between the secretary-general and the Council—with the final power to approve policy residing with the latter—the ability of the secretary-general to act as head of his Council becomes an important factor in determining his capacity to function as an initiator and director of policy.

The Council itself must be examined along two dimensions. First, members of the alliance are legal equals; within the Council no delegation enjoys any greater formal authority than another. Council decisions are therefore made under a rule of unanimity. No state may have any plan or project imposed on it against its will. Or, expressed conversely, each member holds a de facto veto over Council action, which is never formally wielded but which plays a part in the process of consensus formation. France, during the period of de Gaulle's opposition, used this veto as an obstruction and virtually brought alliance political activity to a halt. But behind this formal equality lies the actuality of unequal power. The NATO partners vary in size and power from tiny Luxembourg to the American giant, and this geopolitical-physical inequality translates itself into different degrees of political power within the organization. Because the United States possesses a monopoly of the nuclear weapons on which NATO relies for its deterrent and defense functions, it effectively enjoys a second substantive veto over NATO decisions.

This imbalance of military power carries with it several implications for the decision-making processes within the alliance. First, because of the American preeminence in the nuclear field, NATO military planning becomes an adjunct of American defense planning. Major themes in NATO strategy—massive retaliation, tactical nuclear weapons, forward strategy, flexible response—have originated in Washington. The North Atlantic Treaty was originally conceived as a means whereby American strength could be used to underwrite European security and not as an integrated system of military forces. And from the first, the United States has not coupled its nuclear arsenal entirely with European security needs, in order to protect its overall global independence of action in the military field. Concomitantly, the desire for greater participation in the deployment and possible use of nuclear weapons by the smaller powers has found expression in such American proposals as the MLF or a NATO fleet of Polaris submarines; French demands for greater equality in the possession of nuclear weapons were largely ignored. Thus, NATO military planning is less an Atlantic partnership than an Atlantic debate wherein the United States formulates policy and the Western Europeans serve as critics. The fact that Washington, in the case of MLF, did not achieve what it originally sought demonstrates the limits of the American ability to force its concepts on its European allies. It also demonstrates the ambivalence of the Europeans, who want more of a sense of sharing in nuclear affairs (and resent the American president's ultimate control over the "finger on the trigger"), but who at the same time want an unambiguous American nuclear commitment to their defense. But this does not alter the American domination of the military aspects of the alliance.

Second, this imbalance of power also affects the functions of the Council. The "double veto" exercised by the United States gives that member state the advantage of initiative within the Council. Before making proposals, other delegations must tap American sentiment, either bilaterally or through the secretary-general. The United States may propose more directly. It is no accident that the United States initiates a disproportionate percentage of Council proposals. And as an adjunct of this political advantage, the American permanent representative becomes a powerful political figure whoever he may be. Because he is the representative of the alliance's most powerful member, he enjoys a political advantage not shared by any of his colleagues, and the secretary-general must therefore take this condition into special account.

Thus, this power dichotomy likewise affects the secretary-general. Under the agreements reached at the Lisbon Conference, the secretary-general is empowered to be an initiator in his own right; he may bring before the Council any matter that he feels merits that body's attention. And when he later became chairman of the Council, his ability to influence its proceedings was increased. However, the political reality of the situation requires that the secretary-general work with, or at least not against, the American delegation. And if he is to be successful, the secretary-general cannot be overly partisan; he must serve as a liaison between the United States and the Europeans. Additionally, on occasion he must perform the same function between the larger and smaller European member states themselves. He is expected to act not only as an initiator but also to ensure that smaller voices will be heard. The fact that every secretary-general has come from a small or middle power represents an attempt to grant the smaller members of the alliance access to an advocate before the larger NATO powers.

Superimposed on this legally equal/politically unequal dichotomy in NATO is a second important dimension. The Council itself is really two bodies: the Council of Permanent Representatives, which performs the routine work of the organization and the Council of Foreign Ministers, which meets bi-annually to establish policy guidelines and makes major decisions for the alliance. (The Council can, of course, also meet as a Council of heads of state or governments.) Because of the difference in diplomatic rank between the foreign ministers and the permanent representatives, the secretary-general cannot play the same role in both bodies. Among the latter, with whom he works daily, the secretary-general may try to carve out for himself a creative and dynamic role; among the former, from whom he is quite removed, the secretary-general finds himself limited to the lesser role of presiding officer. The secretary-general may be important within the organization, but he cannot command the same stature above and beyond the organization as can the ministers. Thus, he may be able to play a major role in the day-to-day aspects of NATO affairs, but he is always under threat of being relegated to the sidelines on major issues.

Even this general condition depends on the types of relations the secretary-general is able to establish with his Council(s). Interestingly, the more quiet men of NATO, Ismay and Brosio, enjoyed the best relations with the Council. Ismay, who constantly emphasized his position as the "old boy servant" to the Council, was able to guide that body's actions through quiet persuasion and charm. By deliberately shunning excessive publicity and partisanship among the allies, Ismay created and carefully guarded a reputation as an impartial negotiator and conciliator. Brosio likewise eschewed publicity and relied on quiet diplomacy to establish an effective relationship with the Council. His success as an innovator derived from his thorough mastery of issues, his proposals through the mouths of others, especially the American permanent representative. Through this indirectness, Brosio was able to use the Council as his alter ego in the dialogue with France, thereby removing himself and his office from the exposed position, as Spaak and Stikker had been, as targets for French nationalist policies. Brosio was also able to count on the support of the smaller, nonnuclear, members when changes in the methods of discussion of nuclear affairs threatened to leave the secretary-general out of the picture.

Spaak, the most politically vigorous of the secretaries-general, adopted a radically different approach to his relations with the Council. Always the politician, Spaak treated the representatives much like members of a national parliament. He frequently expressed concern if they failed to agree on innovative policies, for example, those that would lead to greater economic as well as military integration. Spaak dominated Council sessions and sought to lead the alliance by the force of his own personality. His attitude, however, sometimes alienated him from the Council. Toward the end of his tenure, Spaak found himself increasingly isolated from both the Council and national governments and thus was less able either to lead or mediate. He was no longer viewed, as Ismay had been, as the impartial conciliator.

While laboring under the impossible burden of the Franco-American rift, Stikker nonetheless failed to reestablish as secretary-general close relations with the Council and thus weakened his effectiveness within the organization. On one hand he was seen as too closely attuned to the United States to be the impartial spokesman of the alliance. On the other, his penchant for secrecy and his at times brusqueness with the Council (both doubtless exacerbated by ill health) tended to estrange him from that body. For these reasons, it proved difficult for Stikker to work through the Council, which had permitted both Ismay and later Brosio to act as defenders of the alliance and participants in the formulation of Western policy. However, it must also be said that Stikker was the first of the secretaries-general to attempt to get the alliance to face up to the problem of nuclear sharing, command, and control.

The Structure of Power within the Alliance

Another point to be made concerning the secretary-general's

role within the alliance centers on the power relationships within the organization. While the Council possesses the final authority to approve common policy, the parliamentary nature of that body prevents it from fulfilling a leadership function. The role of leader naturally falls on individuals. Within NATO, the secretary-general stands as the most likely individual to assume the role of leader of the alliance. In actuality, however, the secretary-general has had to compete actively for the leadership of the alliance. At several junctures in the history of NATO, the SACEUR and the permanent representative of the United States (to say nothing of de Gaulle) have rivaled the secretary-general as the dominant figure within the organization. Dwight Eisenhower, rather than Ismay, stood as the principal political figure in NATO until his departure to seek political office. Spaak reclaimed the position for himself, but toward the end of his tenure was eclipsed by General Norstad, the brilliant and politically adroit SACEUR. When Norstad in turn departed, the American permanent representative at the time, Thomas Finletter, emerged as the dominant figure. And when Finletter lost the battle over MLF, Stikker moved in to fill the vacancy. Stikker received the strong support of the United States but was compromised in his leadership by ill health, French antagonism, and uneven relations with the Council.

His successor, Manlio Brosio, continued to serve as the dominant, though less visible, figure in NATO. At this point, the split in Washington between the Departments of State and Defense extended in NATO. The military chiefs in the Department of Defense dominated General Lemnitzer, the SACEUR, but Secretary McNamara, with the strong backing of Dean Rusk and the State Department, had a more direct impact on alliance politics through Harlan Cleveland. With its house divided, the United States for a time could not effectively provide unified leadership for the alliance, which enabled Brosio, who enjoyed excellent relations with the Council and with Cleveland, to fill quietly and effectively the role of the leader of the alliance at this critical juncture in NATO's history. As to nuclear affairs and détente, however, Brosio could only chase after events that were being set in motion elsewhere.

Political Consultation

A third measure of the secretary-general's effectiveness within NATO involves his ability to promote consultation among the member states. The report of the "Three Wise Men" following the Suez debacle explicitly recognized the need for active consultation. With the emergence of détente and East-West negotiations as the prime issues for NATO in the late 1960s and 1970s, consultation has been reaffirmed as a necessary element in alliance relations. Consultation has come to be viewed as the cement necessary to hold the alliance together against the potentially divisive issues of nuclear sharing and the dialogue with the Soviet Union over force reductions and the stabilization of Europe.

If indeed consultation is NATO's current challenge, then it should logically follow that the secretary-general should actively seek to foster and encourage the consultative processes within the alliance. But although generally true, it is an overly broad statement that masks several conflicts inherent in the office of secretary-general. As already discussed, since the late 1950s, one of the secretary-general's primary functions has been to serve as a mediator between two of the larger members of the alliance—the United States and France. The French challenge to the organization, the most serious issue in NATO for over a decade, required the secretary-general to act as a conciliator between the disputing parties, if only to preserve the alliance from the divisive forces of nationalism.

At the same time, however, the secretary-general serves as the European "special representative" to the United States. In order to offset partially the constant prospect of American domination of the alliance, the continental member states have coalesced into the Eurogroup. The purpose of this arrangement is to prepare joint positions vis-à-vis the United States rather than deal with the superpower on a bilateral basis. The secretary-general, thanks to the strategic position of his office, has inherited the role of liaison between the two parties; the Europeans look to him to ensure that their position will be heard by the United States, and both sides value his brokerage role. Yet interestingly, the secretary-general performs this same function in a purely European context: he can represent the smaller Benelux and Scandinavian states to the middle European powers to prevent the submergence of their particular needs to the desires of their larger partners.

These three roles which the secretary-general fills are not, however, fully compatible; there exists, therefore, an inherent tension between them. Each group or faction the secretary-general represents wishes him to identify with its position if only to acquire the authority and prestige of his office to support its own position. But the secretary-general cannot do so without compromising his effectiveness elsewhere; he cannot mediate between the United States and France or the United States and Europe if he is viewed, for example, as pro-American. Similarly, he will not be heeded within the Eurogroup if he is suspected of favoring his native country. The secretary-general must, therefore, strive for balance, moderation, and especially impartiality, if he is to participate in alliance consultation. How can he maintain impartiality and still provide leadership through policy initiatives? Spaak tried it one way and Brosio another.

There exists yet a fourth dimension to the office of secretary-general that cuts across all three of his intermediary roles and importantly affects his place in the consultative process. The secretary-general, because of the nature of the office, stands above partisanship as the symbol of the alliance. To him falls the responsibility of representing alliance concerns to all members of NATO. Thus, while performing brokerage functions among various groups of NATO partners, the secretary-general must also stand above intramember divisions and defend the alliance as a whole. This in turn creates a series of dynamic tensions between the secretary-general's internal liaison and mediatory functions—in themselves difficult—and his position as external spokesman for the alliance. The secretary-general must come to grips with these tensions and try to achieve some degree of consonance between them, if he is to achieve personal success and not compromise himself in the eyes of the NATO partners.

Each of the first four secretaries-general adopted a different approach to consultation. Lord Ismay relied on his personal summations of Council discussions as an expression of agreement among the members. In contrast, Spaak did not foster consultation within NATO, but in keeping with his conception of the office, he appealed directly to governments on difficult issues. For him, the secretary-general rather than the Council embodied the concept of consultation.

Both Stikker and Brosio served as intermediaries between the Council and member governments, but moved in different directions. Stikker appeared at times to be acting as an agent between the United States and the other members, and, even though exhaustive in his personal preparation, he did not at times consult widely enough in advance of Council discussions. Brosio sought to maintain the integrity of the alliance by preparing policy in the Council that would be acceptable to all members. He engaged in widespread informal "preparing-of-the-way" before bringing a major item to the Council itself. Again, Ismay and Brosio were the most successful, although for different reasons. By the end of Lord Ismay's term, the immediacy of the Cold War and rearmament began to run second to Franco-American relations as the major issue of the alliance. Under these circumstances, consultation inevitably proved difficult for Spaak. Stikker was caught even more so in the position of being ostracized by the French and embraced by the Americans. Following the cathartic effect of the French withdrawal in 1966, the apparent need for effective consultation to prevent further ruptures in the alliance led to its greater use, and hence Brosio found himself in a different situation from that of his immediate predecessors.

In part, consultation within the alliance can be viewed as the dominance of multinationalism over bilateralism. Bilateralism, however, represents a state's natural tendencies, and NATO members, especially in times of crisis—Suez, Algeria, Cyprus, and Cuba—have tended to revert to bilateral practices. Consultation in NATO has made great progress from Suez to MFR (negotiations for the Conference on European Security and Cooperation took place in a special thirty-five-nation forum), but it is still far from an automatic process. It is truly the current challenge for the alliance. And the measure of the secretary-general's effectiveness within the alliance resides in his ability to keep consultative procedures well oiled and in use.

The United Nations Secretary-General and NATO

The United Nations, at least from the Western perspective, was created as a means to promote and maintain international order. This, in turn, required a multinational statesman. Articles 98 and 99 of the UN Charter embody this concept by granting the secretary-general important political powers beyond those available to the secretaries-general of the defunct League of Nations. Trygvie Lie quickly seized these powers and set out to make the United Nations and its secretary-general an important international political force. Lie, unlike the League's Sir Eric Drummond, was a political activist. He was not above taking positions—as he did on Korea—that might oppose one of the superpowers. Nor was he adverse to taking his own initiatives on important matters.

But Lie's independence and personal intervention engendered the antagonism of both superpowers when each felt the secretary-general's position favored the other. Dag Hammarskjöld represented a reaction to Lie's activism; he was chosen to succeed Lie because of his unobtrusive, international civil servant image. Contrary to expectations, however, Hammarskjöld proved a worthy successor to Lie. After Suez, the secretary-general rejected the concept of the United Nations as "static conference machinery" and strove instead to forge it into a "dynamic instrument" for international diplomacy. Hammarskjöld, like Lie, openly took positions and personally intervened in disputes and crises. And his reward, like Lie's, was a withering attack from the Soviet Union, which accused Hammarskjöld of abusing his office and sought to emasculate the secretary-general through the institution of a three-cornered directorate or "troika."

The experience of Lie and Hammarskjöld closely parallels that of Paul-Henri Spaak in NATO. Spaak, the most "international" of NATO's secretaries-general, also sought to make of his office and organization something more than formal machinery to be used only when its members were so disposed.

Yet his efforts, too, provoked a violent reaction from General de Gaulle. De Gaulle, like the Soviets, opposed the emergence of a multinational political figure over which he had little control, and his triumvirate (or directorate) proposal mirrored the Soviet troika in this respect. Although neither proposal was ever implemented, both had their effect. U Thant and Kurt Waldheim of the United Nations, and Dirk Stikker and Manlio Brosio of NATO were selected as safe candidates agreed upon in advance of their nomination by all concerned parties (with differing levels of enthusiasm, of course). Unlike their predecessors they were not expected aggressively to expand the political horizons of their office but to work instead as intermediaries within the more limited contexts of their own organizations. From the combined experience of the United Nations and NATO, one conclusion clearly emerges: sovereignty and nationalism remain powerful forces and will not permit themselves to be compromised by officials of international organizations engaged in multinational diplomacy.

Détente, NATO, and the Future of the Secretary-General

The logic of détente carries with it certain implications for the office of secretary-general. One possibility involves the partial unilateral disengagement of the United States from Europe. The removal of American troops from Europe without reciprocal cutbacks by the Soviet Union could produce a situation frequently described as the "Finlandization" of Europe. In this milieu, with the Soviet Union the predominant force on the Continent, the secretary-general could assume an increasingly political role as the European spokesman on security affairs to both the United States and the Soviet Union. His ability to function in such a capacity, however, would depend on the support accorded his office and the level of apprehension in Europe over this shift in power relationships.

A second and more probable eventuality looks toward the progressive disappearance of an institutionalized military structure within the alliance. This process began with the French withdrawal from the integrated military commands, and Greece's announcement in 1974 of its intention to withdraw following the Turkish invasion of Cyprus. The winding down of NATO's military structure would undoubtedly mean a substantial reduction—if not the gradual atrophy—of the office of secretary-general. The internal direction of NATO has been a primary purpose for having a secretary-general, and the removal of the "O" would clearly rob him of a substantial part of his raison d'être. But, as this book illustrates, the alliance has come to be at least as much in need of an international (or perhaps, more to the point, a multinational) political manager as it is of a military manager.

NATO was originally conceived as a planning group among the allies. This concept did not foresee the integrated forces, an international civil service, or a secretary-general. The hot and cold wars of the 1950s put the "O" in NATO, and the 1970s at first appeared to witness the reversal of the process. But by the latter part of the decade there has emerged a tendency for France to collaborate more openly in military affairs with NATO and for the United States to reinforce its political and military commitment to NATO.

There is also, of course, the continuing role of the doyen of the Council, who can act as a "conscience" of the alliance when nationalistic impulses are at a high pitch. He is the only permanent representative who, after the secretary-general and deputy secretary-general, can act as chairman of the Council.

As a final note, it should be stressed that in the struggle between personality and events in determining the scope of the office of secretary-general, the balance clearly tips in favor of the latter. How often, for example, has there been an instance in which the personal intervention of a secretary-general, whether of the League of Nations, United Nations, or NATO, ever proved to be the decisive factor in resolving a crisis? The answer seems to be more often negative than otherwise, although some cases exist. The determination of events surrounding such major crises as Manchuria, Ethiopia, Korea, Middle East, Hungary, Suez, Congo, Czechoslovakia, Cuba, Berlin, and Cyprus has been primarily shaped by states. The secretary-general has often been relegated to the sidelines—as in Ethiopia, Manchuria, Cuba, Berlin, Hungary, Suez, and Czechoslovakia—or has stepped in to ratify and give substance to actions taken by states—as in the

Middle East, Korea, and Cyprus. The most dramatic example of a secretary-general's personal intervention—the Congo—ended inconclusively with Hammarskjöld's death, but the prospects were dim at best at the time of the tragic accident. But clearly, in times of crisis, states reserve decision or action for themselves to the maximum extent they can, although they may work through the United Nations or NATO and their secretaries-general if they choose. The fact that the Vietnam conflict was never on the agenda of the United Nations reflects the inability of that body to take action independently of both superpowers; nor did the differing attitude of the United States' NATO allies toward the degree and nature of American involvement in Southeast Asia carry much influence.

But on the other hand, this should not be taken to imply that the secretary-general is excluded from important roles in crisis resolution. His primary contributions have been those of behind-the-scenes mediation and conciliation between states to minimize the effects of a dispute. In NATO during the period under review, perhaps the best example can be found in Brosio's efforts to limit the damage of the Franco-American rift and the subsequent French withdrawal. Paradoxically, it may be the unobtrusive individual and quiet diplomacy rather than the dynamic personality and dramatic intervention that prove most effective in crisis resolution.

At times, when the allies enjoyed a mutual trust or when threatening events brought cohesiveness to the alliance, the secretary-general was able to play a more forceful and independent role. But when calmer moments removed the sense of immediacy, or when the allies were bitterly divided, not even the most dynamic personality could change the course of events. And now, ironically, it appears that NATO's success in preventing war may have produced a chain of events that will, under the general heading of détente, lead to a diminution of the role of the secretary-general.

Appendixes

Appendix 1:
Leading NATO Figures,
1952-1971

Secretary-General

Lord Ismay	1952-1957
Paul-Henri Spaak	1957-1961
Dirk U. Stikker	1961-1964
Manlio Brosio	1964-1971

Office of the Secretary-General

Executive Secretary

Lord Coleridge	1952-1970

Directeur de Cabinet (created 1957)

André Saint Mleux (France)	1957-1961
George Vest (U.S.)	1961-1963
John Getz (U.S.)	1963-1965
Fausto Bacchetti (Italy)	1965-1971

Science Advisor (created 1958)
(Position became Assistant Secretary-General
for Scientific Affairs in 1961.)

Dr. Norman F. Ramsey (U.S.)	1958-1959
Dr. Frederick Seitz (U.S.)	1959-1960
Dr. William A. Nierenberg (U.S.)	1960-1962

Deputy Secretary-General

Jonkeer Henri van Vredenburch (Netherlands)	1952-1956
Adolph Bentinck van Shoonheten (Netherlands)	1956-1957
*Alberico A. Casardi (Italy)	1957-1962
Guido Colonna di Paliano (Italy)	1962-1964
James A. Roberts (Canada)	1964-1969
Osman Olcay (Turkey)	1969-1971
Paolo Pansa Cedronio (Italy)	1971-

Assistant Secretary-General for Political Affairs

Sergio Fenoaltea (Italy)	1952-1955
Guiseppe Cosmelli (Italy)	1955-1956
Alberico A. Casardi (Italy)	1956-1958
Evelyn Shuckburgh (United Kingdom)	1958-1960
Robin Hooper (United Kingdom)	1960-1966
Joachim Jaenicke (Federal Republic of Germany)	1966-1969
Jörg Kastl (Federal Republic of Germany)	1969-

Assistant Secretary-General for Production and Logistics
(In 1961 title changed to Assistant Secretary-General
for Production, Logistics, and Infrastructure.)

David Luke Hopkins (U.S.)	1952-1954
Lowell P. Weicker, Sr. (U.S.)	1954-1956
J. Murray Mitchell (U.S.)	(Feb.-Dec.) 1956
Ernest H. Meili (U.S.)	1957-1959
Robert B. Fiske (U.S.)	1959-1960
Johnson Garrett (U.S.)	1960-1966
John G. S. Beith (United Kingdom)	1966-1967

In 1967 the position was divided into two:

Assistant Secretary-General for Defense Support

A. Tyler Port (U.S.)	1967-

Assistant Secretary-General
for Defense Planning and Policy

Arthur Hockaday (United Kingdom)	1967-1969
Kenneth Nash (United Kingdom)	1969-1971

---

*Served as Acting Secretary-General from 6 March to 21 April 1957.

Assistant Secretary-General for Economics and Finance
(Position was abolished in 1967.)

René Sergent (France)	1952-1955
François-Didier Gregh (France)	1955-1967

(In 1958 Gregh was given the additional title of
Deputy Secretary-General for Defense Coordination.)

Assistant Secretary-General for Scientific Affairs

Dr. William P. Allis (U.S.)	1962-1964
Dr. John L. McLucas (U.S.)	1964-1966
Dr. Rudi Schall (Federal Republic of Germany)	1966-1968
Dr. Gunnar Randers (Norway)	1968-

Permanent Representatives to the NATO Council, 1952-1971

Belgium

**André de Staercke	1952-

Canada

A.D.P. Heeney	1952-1953
**L. Dana Wilgress	1953-1958
Jules Léger	1958-1962
George Ignatieff	1962-1966
Charles S. A. Ritchie	1966-1967
Ross Campbell	1967-

Denmark

**V. de Steensen-Leth	1952-1954
J. A. Westbrik	1954-1956
Mathias Aagaard Wassard	1956-1961
Erik Schram-Nielsen	1961-1966
Henning Hjorth-Nielsen	1966-

France

Hervé Alphand		1952-1954
Maurice Couve de Murville	(Sept.-Nov.)	1954
Alexandre Parodi		1954-1957

**Served previously on the Council of Deputies.

René de Crouy-Chanel	1957-1958
Geoffrey Chondron de Courcel	1958-1959
Pierre de Leusse	1959-1962
François Seydoux Fornier de Clausonne	1962-1964
Pierre de Leusse	1965-1967
Roger Seydoux Fornier de Clausonne	1967-1968
Jacques Kosciusko-Morizet	1969-1970
François de Tricornot de Rose	1970-

Greece

**Panayotis Pipinelis	1952-1954
George Exintaris	1954-1956
Michel Melas	1956-1962
Christian X. Palamas	1962-1967
Phédon Annino Cavalierato	1967-

Iceland

**Gunnlaugur Petursson	1952-1954
Hans G. Andersen	1954-1962
Pétur Thorsteinsson	1962-1965
Henrik Sv. Björnsson	1965-1967
Niels P. Sigurdsson	1967-1971
Tomas A. Tomasson	1971-

Italy

Alberto Rossi Longhi	1952-1954
Adolfo Alessandrini	1954-1958
Umberto Grazzi	1958-1959
Adolfo Alessandrini	1959-1967
Carlo de Ferrariis Salzano	1967-1970
Felice Catalano de Melilli	1970-

Luxembourg

**André Clasen	1952-1953
Albert Wehrer	1953-1954
Nicolas Hommel	1954-1959
Paul Reuter	1959-1967
Lambert Schaus	1967-1972

Netherlands

**Jonkheer A.W.L. Tjarda van Starkenborgh-Stachouwer	1952-1956
Eelco N. van Kleffens	1956-1958
Dirk U. Stikker	1958-1961
Hendrik N. Boon	1961-1970
Dirk P. Spierenburg	1970-

Norway

**Dag Bryn	1952-1953
Arne Skaug	1953-1955
Jens M. Boyesen	1955-1964
Georg Kristiansen	1964-1970
Knut Aars	1970-1971
Rolf T. Busch	1971-

Portugal

**Ruy Ennes Ulrich	1952-1954
Comte de Tovar	1954-1958
Antonio de Faria	1958-1961
Vasco da Cunha	1961-1970
Albano Nogueira	1970-

Turkey

Fatin R. Zorlu	1952-1956
M. A. Tiney	1956-1957
Selim Sarper	1957-1960
Haydar Görk	(May-Nov.) 1960
Muharrem Nuri Birgi	1960-

United Kingdom

**Fredrick Hoyer Millar	1952-1953
Christopher Steel	1953-1957
Frank Roberts	1957-1960
Paul Mason	1960-1962
Evelyn Shuckburgh	1962-1966
Bernard Burrows	1966-1970
Edward Peck	1970-

United States

**William H. Draper	1952-1953
John A. Hughes	1953-1955
George W. Perkins	1955-1957
W. Randolph Burgess	1957-1961
Thomas K. Finletter	1961-1965
Harlan Cleveland	1965-1969
Robert F. Ellsworth	1969-1971

West Germany

Herbert Blankenhorn	1956-1959
Gebhardt von Walther	1959-1962
Wilhelm G. Grewe	1962-1971
Franz Krapf	1971-

Appendix 2:
The North Atlantic Treaty,
April 1949

The Parties to this Treaty reaffirm their faith in the purposes and principles of the Charter of the United Nations and their desire to live in peace with all peoples and all governments.

They are determined to safeguard the freedom, common heritage and civilization of their peoples, founded on the principles of democracy, individual liberty and the rule of law.

They seek to promote stability and well-being in the North Atlantic area.

They are resolved to unite their efforts for collective defence and for the preservation of peace and security.

They therefore agree to this North Atlantic Treaty:

ARTICLE I

The Parties undertake, as set forth in the Charter of the United Nations, to settle any international dispute in which they may be involved by peaceful means in such a manner that international peace and security and justice are not endangered, and to refrain in their international relations from the threat or use of force in any manner inconsistent with the purposes of the United Nations.

ARTICLE II

The Parties will contribute toward the further development of peaceful and friendly international relations by strengthening their free institutions, by bringing about a better understanding of the principles upon which these institutions are founded, and by promoting conditions of stability and well-being. They will seek to eliminate conflict in their international economic policies and will encourage economic collaboration between any or all of them.

ARTICLE III

In order more effectively to achieve the objectives of this Treaty, the Parties, separately and jointly, by means of continuous and effective self-help and mutual aid, will maintain and develop their individual and collective capacity to resist armed attack.

ARTICLE IV

The Parties will consult together whenever, in the opinion of any of them, the territorial integrity, political independence or security of any of the Parties is threatened.

ARTICLE V

The Parties agree that an armed attack against one or more of them in Europe or North America shall be considered an attack against them all and consequently they agree that, if such an armed attack occurs, each of them, in exercise of the right of individual or collective self-defence recognized by Article 51 of the Charter of the United Nations, will assist the Party or Parties so attacked by taking forthwith, individually and in concert with the other Parties, such action as it deems necessary, including the use of armed force, to restore and maintain the security of the North Atlantic area.

Any such armed attack and all measures taken as a result thereof shall immediately be reported to the Security Council. Such measures shall be terminated when the Security Council has taken the measures necessary to restore and maintain international peace and security.

ARTICLE VI[1]

For the purpose of Article V an armed attack on one or more of the Parties is deemed to include an armed attack on the territory of any of the Parties in Europe or North America, on the Algerian Departments of France[2], on the occupation forces of any Party in Europe, on the islands under the jurisdiction of any Party in the North Atlantic area north of the Tropic of Cancer or on the vessels or aircraft in this area of any of the Parties.

---

(1) The definition of the territories to which Article V applies has been revised by Article II of the Protocol to the North Atlantic Treaty on the accession of Greece and Turkey.

(2) On 16th January, 1963, the North Atlantic Council has heard a declaration by

ARTICLE VII

This Treaty does not affect, and shall not be interpreted as affecting, in any way the rights and obligations under the Charter of the Parties which are members of the United Nations, or the primary responsibility of the Security Council for the maintenance of international peace and security.

ARTICLE VIII

Each Party declares that none of the international engagements now in force between it and any other of the Parties or any third State is in conflict with the provisions of this Treaty, and undertakes not to enter into any international engagement in conflict with this Treaty.

ARTICLE IX

The Parties hereby establish a Council, on which each of them shall be represented, to consider matters concerning the implementation of this Treaty. The Council shall be so organized as to be able to meet promptly at any time. The Council shall set up such subsidiary bodies as may be necessary; in particular it shall establish immediately a defence committee which shall recommend measures for the implementation of Articles III and V.

ARTICLE X

The Parties may, by unanimous agreement, invite any other European State in a position to further the principles of this Treaty and to contribute to the security of the North Atlantic area to accede to this Treaty. Any State so invited may become a Party to the Treaty by depositing its instrument of accession with the Government of the United States of America. The Government of the United States of America will inform each of the Parties of the deposit of each such instrument of accession.

---

the French Representative who recalled that by the vote on self-determination on 1st July, 1962, the Algerian people had pronounced itself in favour of the independence of Algeria in co-operation with France. In consequence, the President of the French Republic had on 3rd July, 1962, formally recognized the independence of Algeria. The result was that the "Algerian departments of France" no longer existed as such, and that at the same time the fact that they were mentioned in the North Atlantic Treaty had no longer any bearing.
Following this statement the Council noted that insofar as the former Algerian Departments of France were concerned, the relevant clauses of this Treaty had become inapplicable as from 3rd July, 1962.

ARTICLE XI

This Treaty shall be ratified and its provisions carried out by the Parties in accordance with their respective constitutional processes. The instruments of ratification shall be deposited as soon as possible with the Government of the United States of America, which will notify all the other signatories of each deposit. The Treaty shall enter into force between the States which have ratified it as soon as the ratifications of the majority of the signatories, including the ratifications of Belgium, Canada, France, Luxembourg, the Netherlands, the United Kingdom and the United States, have been deposited and shall come into effect with respect to other States on the date of the deposit of their ratifications.

ARTICLE XII

After the Treaty has been in force for ten years, or at any time thereafter, the Parties shall, if any of them so requests, consult together for the purpose of reviewing the Treaty, having regard for the factors then affecting peace and security in the North Atlantic area, including the development of universal as well as regional arrangements under the Charter of the United Nations for the maintenance of international peace and security.

ARTICLE XIII

After the Treaty has been in force for twenty years, any Party may cease to be a Party one year after its notice of denunciation has been given to the Government of the United States of America, which will inform the Governments of the other Parties of the deposit of each notice of denunciation.

ARTICLE XIV

This Treaty, of which the English and French texts are equally authentic, shall be deposited in the archives of the Government of the United States of America. Duly certified copies will be transmitted by that Government to the governments of the other signatories.

Appendix 3:
Selections from the Report of the Committee of Three on Nonmilitary Cooperation in NATO, December 1956

The Committee on Non-Military Co-operation, set up by the North Atlantic Council at its session of May, 1956, was requested: "to advise the Council on ways and means to improve and extend NATO co-operation in non-military fields and to develop greater unity within the Atlantic Community".

2. The Committee has interpreted these terms of reference as requiring it 1. to examine and re-define the objectives and needs of the Alliance, especially in the light of current international developments; and 2. to make recommendations for strengthening its internal solidarity, cohesion and unity.

3. The Committee hopes that the report and recommendations which it now submits will make NATO's purely defensive and constructive purposes better understood in non-NATO countries, thereby facilitating and encouraging steps to lessen international tension. The events of the last few months have increased this tension and reduced hopes, which had been raised since Stalin's death, of finding a secure and honourable basis for competitive and ultimately for co-operative co-existence with the Communist world. The effort to this end, however, must go on.

4. Inter-allied relations have also undergone severe strains. The substance of this report was prepared by the Committee of Three in the course of its meetings and intergovernmental consultations last September. Subsequent events have reinforced the Committee's conviction that the Atlantic Community can develop greater unity only by working constantly to achieve common policies by full and timely consultation on issues of common concern. Unless this is done, the very framework of co-operation in NATO, which has contributed so greatly to the cause of freedom, and

which is so vital to its advancement in the future, will be endangered.

5. The foundation of NATO, on which alone a strong superstructure can be built, is the political obligation that its members have taken for collective defence: to consider that an attack on one is an attack on all which will be met by the collective action of all. There is a tendency at times to overlook the far-reaching importance of this commitment, especially during those periods when the danger of having to invoke it may seem to recede.

6. With this political commitment for collective defence as the cornerstone of the foreign and defence policies of its members, NATO has a solid basis for existence. It is true, of course, that the ways and means by which the obligation is to be discharged may alter as political and strategic conditions alter, as the threat to peace changes its character or its direction. However, any variations in plans and strategic policies which may be required need not weaken NATO or the confidence of its members in NATO and in each other; providing, and the proviso is decisive, that each member retains its will and its capacity to play its full part in discharging the political commitment for collective action against aggression which it undertook when it signed the Pact; providing also—and recent events have shown that this is equally important—that any changes in national strategy or policy which affect the coalition are made only after collective consideration.

7. The first essential, then, of a healthy and developing NATO lies in the whole-hearted acceptance by all its members of the political commitment for collective defence, and in the confidence which each has in the will and ability of the others to honour that commitment if aggression should take place.

8. This is our best present deterrent against military aggression, and consequently the best assurance that the commitment undertaken will not be engaged.

9. However, this deterrent role of NATO, based on solidarity and strength, can be discharged only if the political and economic relations between its members are co-operative and close. An Alliance in which the members ignore each other's interests or engage in political or economic conflict, or harbour suspicions of each other, cannot be effective either for deterrence of defence. Recent experience makes this clearer than ever before.

10. It is useful, in searching for ways and means of strengthening NATO unity and understanding, to recall the origin and the aims of the Organization.

11. The Treaty which was signed in Washington in 1949 was a collective response—we had learned that a purely national response was insufficient

for security—to the fear of military aggression by the forces of the USSR and its allies. These forces were of overwhelming strength. The threat to Greece, the capture of Czechoslovakia, the blockade of Berlin, and the pressure against Yugoslavia showed that they were also aggressive.

12. While fear may have been the main urge for the creation of NATO, there was also the realization—conscious or instinctive—that in a shrinking nuclear world it was wise and timely to bring about a closer association of kindred Atlantic and Western European nations for other than defence purposes alone; that a partial pooling of sovereignty for mutual protection should also promote progress and co-operation generally. There was a feeling among the governments and peoples concerned that this close unity was both natural and desirable; that the common cultural traditions, free institutions and democratic concepts which were being challenged, and were marked for destruction by those who challenged them, were things which should also bring the NATO nations closer together, not only for their defence but for their development. There was, in short, a sense of Atlantic Community, alongside the realization of an immediate common danger.

13. Any such feeling was certainly not the decisive, or even the main impulse in the creation of NATO. Nevertheless, it gave birth to the hope that NATO would grow beyond and above the emergency which brought it into being.

14. The expression of this hope is found in the Preamble and in Articles II and IV of the Treaty. These two Articles, limited in their terms but with at least the promise of the grand design of an Atlantic Community, were included because of this insistent feeling that NATO must become more than a military alliance. They reflected the very real anxiety that if NATO failed to meet this test, it would disappear with the immediate crisis which produced it, even though the need for it might be as great as ever.

15. From the very beginning of NATO, then, it was recognized that while defence co-operation was the first and most urgent requirement, this was not enough. It has also become increasingly realized since the Treaty was signed that security is today far more than a military matter. The strengthening of political consultation and economic co-operation, the development of resources, progress in education and public understanding, all these can be as important, or even more important, for the protection of the security of a nation, or an alliance, as the building of a battleship or the equipping of an army.

16. These two aspects of security—civil and military—can no longer safely be considered in watertight compartments, either within or between nations. Perhaps NATO has not yet fully recognized their essential inter-

relationship, or done enough to bring about that close and continuous contact between its civil and military sides which is essential if it is to be strong and enduring.

17. North Atlantic political and economic co-operation, however, let alone unity, will not be brought about in a day or by a declaration, but by creating over the years and through a whole series of national acts and policies, the habits and traditions and precedents for such co-operation and unity. The process will be a slow and gradual one at best; slower than we might wish. We can be satisfied if it is steady and sure. This will not be the case, however, unless the member governments—especially the more powerful ones—are willing to work, to a much greater extent than hitherto, with and through NATO for more than purposes of collective military defence.

18. While the members of NATO have already developed various forms of non-military co-operation between themselves and have been among the most active and constructive participants in various international organizations, NATO as such has been hesitant in entering this field, particularly in regard to economic matters. Its members have been rightly concerned to avoid duplication and to do, through other existing international organizations, the things which can best be done in that way.

19. Recently, however, the members of NATO have been examining and re-assessing the purposes and the needs of the Organization in the light of certain changes in Soviet tactics and policies which have taken place since the death of Stalin, and of the effect of the present turmoil in Eastern Europe on this development.

20. These changes have not diminished the need for collective military defence but they have faced NATO with an additional challenge in which the emphasis is largely non-military in character. NATO must recognize the real nature of the developments which have taken place. An important aspect of the new Soviet policies of competitive co-existence is an attempt to respond to positive initiatives of the Western nations aimed at improving, in an atmosphere of freedom, the lot of the economically less-developed countries, and at establishing a just and mutually beneficial trading system in which all countries can prosper. The Soviet Union is now apparently veering towards policies designed to ensnare these countries by economic means and by political subversion, and to fasten on them the same shackles of Communism from which certain members of the Soviet *bloc* are now striving to release themselves. The members of NATO must maintain their vigilance in dealing with this form of penetration.

21. Meanwhile some of the immediate fears of large-scale all-out military aggression against Western Europe have lessened. This process has been facilitated by evidence that the Soviet Government have realised

that any such all-out aggression would be met by a sure, swift and devastating retaliation, and that there could be no victory in a war of this kind with nuclear weapons on both sides. With an increased Soviet emphasis on non-military or paramilitary methods, a review is needed of NATO's ability to meet effectively the challenge of penetration under the guise of co-existence, with its emphasis on conflict without catastrophe.

22. Certain questions now take on a new urgency. Have NATO's needs and objectives changed, or should they be changed? Is the Organization operating satisfactorily in the altered circumstances of 1956? If not what can be done about it? There is the even more far-reaching question: "Can a loose association of sovereign states hold together at all without the common binding force of fear?"

23. The Committee has been examining these questions in the light of its firm conviction that the objectives which governments had in mind when the Pact was signed remain valid; that NATO is as important now to its member states as it was at that time.

24. The first of these objectives—as has already been pointed out—is security, based on collective action with adequate armed forces both for deterrence and defence.

25. Certainly NATO unity and strength in the pursuit of this objective remain as essential as they were in 1949. Soviet tactics may have changed; but Soviet armed might and ultimate objectives remain unchanged. Moreover, recent events in Eastern Europe show that the Soviet Union will not hesitate in certain circumstances to use force and the threat of force. Therefore the military strength of NATO must not be reduced, though its character and capabilities should be constantly adapted to changing circumstances. Strengthening the political and economic side of NATO is an essential complement to—not a substitute for—continuous co-operation in defence.

26. In spite of these recent events Soviet leaders may place greater emphasis on political, economic and propaganda action. There is no evidence, however, that this will be permitted to prejudice in any way the maintenance of a high level of military power in its most modern form as a base for Soviet activity in these other fields.

27. We should welcome changes in Soviet policies if they were genuinely designed to ease international tensions. But we must remember that the weakening and eventual dissolution of NATO remains a major Communist goal. We must therefore remain on guard so long as Soviet leaders persist in their determination to maintain a preponderance of military power for the achievement of their own political objectives and those of their allies.

28. This brings us again to the second and long-term aim of NATO:

the development of an Atlantic Community whose roots are deeper even than the necessity for common defence. This implies nothing less than the permanent association of the free Atlantic peoples for the promotion of their greater unity and the protection and the advancement of the interests which, as free democracies, they have in common.

29. If we are to secure this long-term aim, we must prevent the centrifugal forces of opposition or indifference from weakening the Alliance. NATO has not been destroyed, or even weakened, by the threats or attacks of its enemies. It has faltered at times through the lethargy or complacency of its members; through dissension or division between them; by putting narrow national considerations above the collective interest. It could be destroyed by these forces, if they were allowed to subsist. To combat these tendencies, NATO must be used by its members, far more than it has been used, for sincere and genuine consultation and co-operation on questions of common concern. For this purpose, resolution is more important than resolutions; will than words.

30. The problem, however, goes deeper than this. NATO countries are faced by a political as well as a military threat. It comes from the revolutionary doctrines of Communism which have by careful design of the Communist leaders over many years been sowing seeds of falsehood concerning our free and democratic way of life. The best answer to such falsehoods is a continuing demonstration of the superiority of our own institutions over Communist ones. We can show by word and deed that we welcome political progress, economic advancement and orderly social change and that the real reactionaries of this day are these Communist regimes which, adhering to an inflexible pattern of economic and political doctrine, have been more successful in destroying freedom than in promoting it.

31. We must, however, realize that falsehoods concerning our institutions have sometimes been accepted at face value and that there are those, even in the non-Communist world, who under the systematic influence of Communist propaganda do not accept our own analysis of NATO's aims and values. They believe that while NATO may have served a useful defensive and deterrent role in the Stalinist era, it is no longer necessary even for the security of its members; that it is tending now to become an agency for the pooling of the strength and resources of the 'colonial' powers in defence of imperial privileges, racial superiority, and Atlantic hegemony under the leadership of the United States. The fact that we know these views to be false and unjustified does not mean that NATO and its governments should not do everything they can to correct and counteract them.

32. NATO should not forget that the influence and interests of its members are not confined to the area covered by the Treaty, and that

common interests of the Atlantic Community can be seriously affected by developments outside the Treaty area. Therefore, while striving to improve their relations with each other, and to strengthen and deepen their own unity, they should also be concerned with harmonizing their policies in relation to other areas, taking into account the broader interests of the whole international community; particularly in working through the United Nations and elsewhere for the maintenance of international peace and security and for the solution of the problems that now divide the world.

33. In following this course, NATO can show that it is more than a defence organization acting and reacting to the ebb and flow of the fears and dangers arising out of Soviet policy. It can prove its desire to co-operate fully with other members of the international community in bringing to reality the principles of the Charter of the United Nations. It can show that it is not merely concerned with preventing the cold war from deteriorating into a shooting one; or with defending itself if such a tragedy should take place, but that it is even more concerned with seizing the political and moral initiative to enable all countries to develop in freedom, and to bring about a secure peace for all nations.

34. Our caution in accepting without question the pacific character of any Soviet moves, our refusal to dismantle our defences before we are convinced that conditions of international confidence have been restored, will, particularly after the events in Hungary, be understood by all people of sincerity and good-will. What would not be understood is any unwillingness on our part to seek ways and means of breaking down the barriers with a view to establishing such confidence.

35. The coming together of the Atlantic nations for good and constructive purposes—which is the basic principle and ideal underlying the NATO concept—must rest on and grow from deeper and more permanent factors than the divisions and dangers of the last ten years. It is a historical, rather than a contemporary, development and if it is to achieve its real purpose, it must be considered in that light and the necessary conclusions drawn. A short-range view will not suffice.

36. The fundamental historical fact underlying development is that the nation state, by itself and relying exclusively on national policy and national power, is inadequate for progress or even for survival in the nuclear age. As the founders of the North Atlantic Treaty foresaw, the growing interdependence of states, politically and economically as well as militarily, calls for an ever-increasing measure of international cohesion and co-operation. Some states may be able to enjoy a degree of political and economic independence when things are going well. No state, however powerful, can guarantee its security and its welfare by national action alone.

37. This basic fact underlies our report and the recommendations contained therein which appear in the subsequent chapters.

38. It has not been difficult to make these recommendations. It will be far more difficult for the member governments to carry them into effect. This will require, on their part, the firm conviction that the transformation of the Atlantic Community into a vital and vigorous political reality is as important as any purely national purpose. It will require, above all, the will to carry this conviction into the realm of practical governmental policy.

CHAPTER II
POLITICAL CO-OPERATION

I. Introduction

39. If there is to be vitality and growth in the concept of the Atlantic Community, the relations between the members of NATO must rest on a solid basis of confidence and understanding. Without this there cannot be constructive or solid political co-operation.

40. The deepening and strengthening of this political co-operation does not imply the weakening of the ties of NATO members with other friendly countries or with other international associations, particularly the United Nations. Adherence to NATO is not exclusive or restrictive. Nor should the evolution of the Atlantic Community through NATO prevent the formation of even closer relationships among some of its members, for instance within groups of European countries. The moves toward Atlantic co-operation and European unity should be parallel and complementary, not competitive or conflicting.

41. Effective and constructive international co-operation requires a resolve to work together for the solution of common problems. There are special ties between NATO members, special incentives and security interests, which should make this task easier than it otherwise would be. But its successful accomplishment will depend largely on the extent to which member governments, in their own policies and actions, take into consideration the interests of the Alliance. This requires not only the acceptance of the obligation of consultation and co-operation whenever necessary, but also the development of practices by which the discharge of this obligation becomes a normal part of governmental activity.

42. It is easy to profess devotion to the principle of political—or economic—consultation in NATO. It is difficult and has in fact been shown to be impossible, if the proper conviction is lacking, to convert the profession into practice. Consultation within an alliance means more than exchange of information, though that is necessary. It means more than

letting the NATO Council know about national decisions that have already been taken; or trying to enlist support for those decisions. It means the discussion of problems collectively, in the early stages of policy formation, and before national positions become fixed. At best, this will result in collective decisions on matters of common interest affecting the Alliance. At the least, it will ensure that no action is taken by one member without a knowledge of the views of the others.

II. Consultation of Foreign Policies

A. *Scope and Character of Political Consultation*

43. The essential role of consultation in fostering political co-operation was clearly defined by an earlier NATO Committee on the North Atlantic Community in 1951: " . . . The achievement of a closer degree of co-ordination of the foreign policies of the members of the North Atlantic Treaty, through the development of the 'habit of consultation' on matters of common concern, would greatly strengthen the solidarity of the North Atlantic Community and increase the individual and collective capacity of its members to serve the peaceful purposes for which NATO was established. . . . In the political field, this means that while each North Atlantic government retains full freedom of action and decision with respect to its own policy, the aim should be to achieve, through exchanging information and views, as wide an area of agreement as possible in the formulation of policies as a whole".

"Special attention must be paid, as explicitly recognized in Article IV of the Treaty, to matters of urgent and immediate importance to the members of NATO, and to 'emergency' situations where it may be necessary to consult closely on national lines of conduct affecting the interests of members of NATO as a whole. There is a continuing need, however, for effective consultation at an early stage on current problems, in order that national policies may be developed and action taken on the basis of a full awareness of the attitudes and interests of all the members of NATO. While all members of NATO have a responsibility to consult with their partners on appropriate matters, a large share of responsibility for such consultation necessarily rests on the more powerful members of the Community".

44. These words were written five years ago. They hold true now more than ever before. If we can say that they have not been ignored by NATO we must also recognize that the practice of consulting has not so developed in the NATO Council as to meet the demands of political changes and world trends. The present need, therefore, is more than simply broadening the scope and deepening the character of consultation. There

is a pressing requirement for all members to make consultation in NATO an integral part of the making of national policy. Without this the very existence of the North Atlantic Community may be in jeopardy.

45. It should, however, be remembered that collective discussion is not an end in itself, but a means to the end of harmonizing policies. Where common interests of the Atlantic Community are at stake consultation should always seek to arrive at timely agreement on common lines of policy and action.

46. Such agreement, even with the closest possible co-operation and consultation, is not easy to secure. But it is essential to the Atlantic Alliance that a steady and continuous effort be made to bring it about. There cannot be unity in defence and disunity in foreign policy.

47. There are, of course, certain practical limitations to consultation in this field. They are sufficiently obvious in fact to make it unnecessary to emphasize them in words. Indeed the danger is less that they will be minimized or evaded than that they will be exaggerated and used to justify practices which unnecessarily ignore the common interest.

48. One of these limitations is the hard fact that ultimate responsibility for decision and action still rests on national governments. It is conceivable that a situation of extreme emergency may arise where action must be taken by one government before consultation is possible with the others.

49. Another limitation is the difficulty, and indeed the unwisdom, of trying to specify in advance all the subjects and all the situations where consultation is necessary: to separate by area or by subject the matters of NATO concern from those of purely national concern; to define in detail the obligations and duties of consultation. These things have to work themselves out in practice. In this process, experience is a better guide than dogma.

50. The essential thing is that on all occasions and in all circumstances member governments, before acting or even before pronouncing, should keep the interests and the requirements of the Alliance in mind. . . .

* * *

CHAPTER IV
ORGANIZATION AND FUNCTIONS

88. The Committee considers that NATO in its present form is capable of discharging the non-military functions required of it. Structural changes are not needed. The machine is basically satisfactory. It is for governments to make use of it.

89. At the same time, certain improvements in the procedures and functioning of the Organization will be required if the recommendations

of this report are to be fully implemented. The proposals in this Chapter are submitted for this purpose.

A. Meetings of the Council

90. More time should be allowed for Ministerial Meetings. Experience has shown that, without more time, important issues on the agenda cannot be adequately considered. Decisions concerning some of them will not be reached at all, or will be reached only in an unclear form.

91. Efforts should be made to encourage discussion rather than simply declarations of policy prepared in advance. Arrangements for meetings should be made with this aim in view. For most sessions, the numbers present should be sharply restricted. In order to facilitate free discussion, when Ministers wish to speak in a language other than French or English, consecutive translation into one of these official languages should be provided by interpreters from their own delegations.

92. Meetings of Foreign Ministers should be held whenever required, and occasionally in locations other than NATO Headquarters. Ministers might also participate more frequently in regular Council meetings, even though not all of them may find it possible to attend such meetings at the same time. The Council of Permanent Representatives has powers of effective decision: in other words, the authority of the Council as such is the same whether governments are represented by Ministers or by their Permanent Representatives. Thus there should be no firm or formal line between Ministerial and other meetings of the Council.

B. Strengthening the Links between the Council and Member Governments

93. It is indispensable to the kind of consultations envisaged in this report that Permanent Representatives should be in a position to speak authoritatively and to reflect the current thinking of their governments. Differences in location and in constitutional organization make impossible any uniform arrangements in all member governments. In some cases it might be desirable to designate a high official in the national capital to be concerned primarily with NATO affairs. The purpose would be to help both in fostering NATO consultations whenever national policies impinge on the common interest of the Atlantic Community, and in translating the results of such consultation into effective action within the national governments.

94. To ensure the closest possible connection between current thinking in the governments and consultations in the Council, there might be occasional Council Meetings with the participation of specially designated officials or the permanent heads of foreign ministries.

C. Preparation for Council Meetings

95. Items on the agenda of Ministerial Meetings should be thoroughly examined by Permanent Representatives and relevant proposals prepared before Ministers meet. For this purpose it may be found desirable for governments to send senior experts to consult on agenda items before the meetings take place.

96. The preparation of questions for discussion in the Council should be assisted by appropriate use of the Council's Committees of Political and Economic Advisers (Recommendations on the establishment of these Committees are set forth in Chapter 2, paragraph 56, and Chapter 3, paragraph 72).

97. In the case of consultations on special subjects, more use should be made of senior experts from national capitals to assist permanent delegations by calling them, on an *ad hoc* basis, to do preparatory work. Informal discussions among specialists with corresponding responsibilities are a particularly valuable means of concerting governmental attitudes in the early stages of policy formation.

98. Member governments should make available to one another through NATO 'basic position material' for background information. This would help the Alliance as a whole in the consideration of problems of common concern and would assist individual governments to understand more fully the reasons for the position adopted by any member country on a particular issue which might be its special concern, but which might also affect in varying degrees other members of NATO.

D. The Secretary General and the International Staff

99. To enable the Organization to make its full contribution, the role of the Secretary General and the International Staff needs to be enhanced.

100. It is recommended that the Secretary General preside over meetings of the Council in Ministerial, as he does now in other sessions. Such a change with respect to the conduct of the Council's business would follow naturally from the new responsibilities of the Secretary General, arising out of the recommendations of this report. It is also warranted by the Secretary General's unique opportunities for becoming familiar with the problems and the activities of the Alliance as a whole.

101. It would, however, still be desirable to have one Minister chosen each year as President of the Council in accordance with the present practice of alphabetical rotation. This Minister, as President, would continue to have especially close contact with the Secretary General during and between Ministerial Meetings, and would, as at present, act as the spokesman of the Council on all formal occasions. He would also preside

at the formal opening and closing of Ministerial sessions of the Council.

102. In addition:

a. the Secretary General should be encouraged to propose items for NATO consultation in the fields covered by this report and should be responsible for promoting and directing the process of consultation;

b. in view of these responsibilities member governments should undertake to keep the Secretary General fully and currently informed through their permanent delegations of their governments' thinking on questions of common concern to the Alliance;

c. attention is also called to the additional responsibilities of the Secretary General, recommended in connection with the annual political appraisal (Chapter II, paragraph 52), and the peaceful settlement of disputes (Chapter II, paragraph 57).

Appendix 4:
The "Athens Guidelines,"
May 1962

The regular Spring Ministerial Session of the NATO Council was held in Athens from 4th-6th May, 1962. The meeting was attended by the Foreign Ministers of member countries as well as by the Defence Ministers, who had met separately on 3rd May.

2. In their review of the international situation, Ministers discussed disarmament, and the problem of Germany and Berlin. In addition, various statements were made by Ministers on matters of particular concern to their countries.

3. In reviewing developments at the Geneva Conference, the Council reaffirmed that general and complete disarmament under effective international control is the best means of ensuring lasting peace and security throughout the world. They noted with satisfaction the position taken by the Western Powers in Geneva in order to achieve this goal, and emphasized the importance and urgency of reaching agreement.

4. The Council examined the Berlin question in the light of the basic commitments of NATO in this regard. They took note of the most recent developments in the situation, including the fact that exploratory talks were taking place with the Soviet Union. They took the opportunity to reaffirm their attachment to the principles set forth in their Declaration of 16th December, 1958, on Berlin.

5. The Council noted the progress which has been made in the direction of closer co-operation between member countries in the development of the Alliance's defence policy. In this respect Ministers welcomed the confirmation by the United States that it will continue to make available for the Alliance the nuclear weapons necessary for NATO defence, concerting with its allies on basic plans and arrangements in regard to these weapons. In addition, both the United Kingdom and the United States Governments have given firm assurances that their strategic forces will continue to provide defence against threats to the Alliance beyond the

capability of NATO-committed forces to deal with.

6. So that all member states may play their full part in consultation on nuclear defence policy, it has been decided to set up special procedures which will enable all members of the Alliance to exchange information concerning the role of nuclear weapons in NATO defence.

7. The purpose of NATO is defence, and it must be clear that in case of attack it will defend its members by all necessary means. The Council has reviewed the action that would be necessary on the part of member countries, collectively and individually, in the various circumstances in which the Alliance might be compelled to have recourse to its nuclear defences.

8. The Council noted the progress made during the last twelve months in the defence effort of the Alliance and, in particular, the quantitative and qualitative improvements brought about in the NATO assigned or earmarked forces of member countries. Ministers noted with satisfaction the United States commitment of Polaris submarines to NATO.

9. The Council is convinced that, if the Alliance is to meet the full range of threats to its security, the balance between the conventional and nuclear forces must be the subject of continuous examination. The contribution of member countries towards balanced forces for NATO defence during the coming years is to be examined within the framework of the Triennial Review procedure which is already under way. The Council expects to consider a report on this question at its next meeting in December.

10. At their separate meeting on 3rd May, the Defence Ministers discussed and approved a report from the Armaments Committee which reviewed progress made since their meeting in April 1960 in sharing the burden of research, development and production of military equipment, and made a number of recommendations for improving this co-operation. While there had been certain initial difficulties, Ministers agreed that the programme of co-operative projects launched at that time had made a successful start. Further efforts should now be made to build on this foundation. To obtain speedier results from this co-operation Ministers decided to set up a high-level group to examine the existing machinery, and to make recommendations to the Ministerial Meeting in December 1962 for any improvements necessary to achieve agreement on future military requirements and a better co-ordination of the resources of the Alliance. Meanwhile, special efforts would be made to take final decisions on projects ripe for joint development.

11. The Council reviewed the development of political consultation within the Alliance. It noted the steady and encouraging progress made over the past twelve months in deepening and extending the process of consultation.

12. The Council had before it a detailed analysis of the work of the Alliance in scientific and technical co-operation. They discussed the proposals for fostering international scientific co-operation put forward by a group of eminent scientists appointed by the Secretary General. Ministers requested the Council in Permanent Session to consider these proposals further with a view to making recommendations to member governments.

13. Ministers noted that the Council in Permanent Session had discussed a report by the International Staff on Communist *bloc* activities in the economic field in less-developed countries. It was clear from this report that by far the largest proportion of the aid received by these countries continued to be that contributed by the economically most advanced countries of the Free World, and that the aid extended by the Communist *bloc* was not only substantially smaller than the assistance contributed by the Free World, but was also closely tied to political purposes. Ministers noted with satisfaction the efforts the Free World is making to help developing countries to raise their standards of living while fully respecting their national independence and freedom, and emphasized the importance of continuing and intensifying these efforts.

14. Ministers gave special attention to the economic development requirements of Greece and Turkey. Bearing in mind the contribution of Greece and Turkey to the defence of the Alliance and their continuing efforts to accelerate their economic development in order to improve the living conditions for their peoples, Ministers recognized the need for external assistance to these two countries. With a view to achieving the common objectives in this matter, they agreed that member governments in a position to assist Greece and Turkey should examine urgently the manner of establishing, in an appropriate forum, possibly with other countries and appropriate international organizations, consortia to co-ordinate the mobilisation of resources needed to ensure the economic development of Greece and Turkey at a satisfactory rate. The Ministers also agreed to establish a Study Group to consider further the special defence problems of Greece.

15. The next Ministerial Meeting of the North Atlantic Council is scheduled to be held in Paris in December, 1962.

Appendix 5:
The Ottawa Decisions
(Nuclear Planning), May 1963

The North Atlantic Council met in Ministerial Session in Ottawa from 22nd to 24th May, 1963.

2. In their review of the international situation, Ministers emphasised that in the world of today peace is indivisible. The enduring character of the North Atlantic Alliance, founded on the principles of interdependence and common defence, constitutes a basic guarantee for the maintenance of peace.

3. The Council noted with regret that the Soviet Union had so far shown little interest in seeking equitable solutions for outstanding problems.

4. With regard to Germany and Berlin, the threat has not disappeared. Thanks to the firm attitude maintained by the West, however, developments detrimental to the interests of Berlin and the Alliance have been effectively discouraged. In this connection, the Alliance abides by the terms of its Declaration of 16th December, 1958, on Berlin.

5. Outside the Treaty area too, tensions and difficulties continue to exist which have a profound effect on the Alliance. Soviet military personnel remain in Cuba; and the situation there, with its repercussions in the region generally, still gives cause for concern. Ministers also expressed their disquiet over recent events in Laos, and stressed the importance of sustained efforts to secure respect for the Geneva Agreements.

6. Ministers reaffirmed the importance, in building a peaceful world, of progress towards general and complete disarmament by stages and under effective international control. In this connection, they noted that agreement in principle had been reached between the United States and the USSR on measures to improve communications designed to reduce the risk of war by accident or miscalculation. They expressed the hope that the Soviet Union's attitude would evolve sufficiently to permit genuine progress to be made on key disarmament questions.

7. The growing scope and complexity of the problems facing the

Alliance make it imperative for the Council to ensure that its political consultations are as prompt and effective as they can be made. Ministers noted the progress already achieved in this direction and expressed their determination to secure still further improvements.

8. Ministers discussed NATO defence policy and approved the steps taken to organize the nuclear forces assigned or to be assigned to the Supreme Allied Commander Europe (SACEUR).

These include notably:

(a) assignment of the United Kingdom V-bomber force and three United States Polaris submarines to SACEUR;

(b) establishment by SACEUR on his staff of a Deputy responsible to him for nuclear affairs;

(c) arrangements for broader participation by officers of NATO member countries in nuclear activities in Allied Command Europe and in co-ordination of operational planning at Omaha;

(d) fuller information to national authorities, both political and military.

Ministers welcomed these measures to increase the effectiveness of the nuclear capability at the disposal of the Alliance and to improve co-ordination and control of its nuclear deterrent forces.

9. Ministers recognised the need to achieve a satisfactory balance between nuclear and conventional arms. They directed the Council in Permanent Session to undertake, with the advice of the NATO military authorities, further studies of the inter-related questions of strategy, force requirements and the resources available to meet them.

10. The Council noted progress made in the implementation of earlier resolutions concerning the defence problems of Greece and reaffirmed its interest in the effective application of these resolutions.

11. The North Atlantic Alliance seeks peace. It deplores the diversion into the military field of resources which might be used for the betterment of mankind, and in particular for increased efforts to raise living standards in developing countries. But the Free World remains faced with a continuing threat and the members of the North Atlantic Alliance have both the right and the duty to protect their freedom and independence.

12. The next Ministerial Meeting will be held in Paris in December 1963.

Appendix 6:
The Future Tasks of the Alliance
(Harmel Report), December 1967

1. A year ago, on the initiative of the Foreign Minister of Belgium, the governments of the fifteen nations of the Alliance resolved to "study the future tasks which face the Alliance, and its procedures for fulfilling them in order to strengthen the Alliance as a factor for durable peace". The present report sets forth the general tenor and main principles emerging from this examination of the future tasks of the Alliance.

2. Studies were undertaken by Messrs. Schütz, Watson, Spaak, Kohler and Patijn. The Council wishes to express its appreciation and thanks to these eminent personalities for their efforts and for the analyses they produced.

3. The exercise has shown that the Alliance is a dynamic and vigorous organization which is constantly adapting itself to changing conditions. It also has shown that its future tasks can be handled within the terms of the Treaty by building on the methods and procedures which have proved their value over many years.

4. Since the North Atlantic Treaty was signed in 1949 the international situation has changed significantly and the political tasks of the Alliance have assumed a new dimension. Amongst other developments, the Alliance has played a major part in stopping Communist expansion in Europe; the USSR has become one of the two world super powers but the Communist world is no longer monolithic; the Soviet doctrine of "peaceful co-existence" has changed the nature of the confrontation with the West but not the basic problems. Although the disparity between the power of the United States and that of the European states remains, Europe has recovered and is on its way towards unity. The process of decolonisation has transformed European relations with the rest of the world; at the same time, major problems have arisen in the relations between developed and developing countries.

5. The Atlantic Alliance has two main functions. Its first function is

to maintain adequate military strength and political solidarity to deter aggression and other forms of pressure and to defend the territory of member countries if aggression should occur. Since its inception, the Alliance has successfully fulfilled this task. But the possibility of a crisis cannot be excluded as long as the central political issues in Europe, first and foremost the German Question, remain unsolved. Moreover, the situation of instability and uncertainty still precludes a balanced reduction of military forces. Under these conditions, the Allies will maintain as necessary, a suitable military capability to assure the balance of forces, thereby creating a climate of stability, security and confidence.

In this climate the Alliance can carry out its second function, to pursue the search for progress towards a more stable relationship in which the underlying political issues can be solved. Military security and a policy of détente are not contradictory but complementary. Collective defence is a stabilising factor in world politics. It is the necessary condition for effective policies directed towards a greater relaxation of tensions. The way to peace and stability in Europe rests in particular on the use of the Alliance constructively in the interest of détente. The participation of the USSR and the USA will be necessary to achieve a settlement of the political problems in Europe.

6. From the beginning the Atlantic Alliance has been a co-operative grouping of states sharing the same ideals and with a high degree of common interest. Their cohesion and solidarity provide an element of stability within the Atlantic area.

7. As sovereign states the Allies are not obliged to subordinate their policies to collective decision. The Alliance affords an effective forum and clearing house for the exchange of information and views; thus, each Ally can decide its policy in the light of close knowledge of the problems and objectives of the others. To this end the practice of frank and timely consultations needs to be deepened and improved. Each Ally should play its full part in promoting an improvement in relations with the Soviet Union and the countries of Eastern Europe, bearing in mind that the pursuit of détente must not be allowed to split the Alliance. The chances of success will clearly be greatest if the Allies remain on parallel courses, especially in matters of close concern to them all; their actions will thus be all the more effective.

8. No peaceful order in Europe is possible without a major effort by all concerned. The evolution of Soviet and East European policies gives ground for hope that those governments may eventually come to recognise the advantages to them of collaborating in working towards a peaceful settlement. But no final and stable settlement in Europe is possible without a solution of the German question which lies at the heart of present

tensions in Europe. Any such settlement must end the unnatural barriers between Eastern and Western Europe, which are most clearly and cruelly manifested in the division of Germany.

9. Accordingly the Allies are resolved to direct their energies to this purpose by realistic measures designed to further a détente in East-West relations. The relaxation of tensions is not the final goal but is part of a long-term process to promote better relations and to foster a European settlement. The ultimate political purpose of the Alliance is to achieve a just and lasting peaceful order in Europe accompanied by appropriate security guarantees.

10. Currently, the development of contacts between the countries of Western and Eastern Europe is mainly on a bilateral basis. Certain subjects, of course, require by their very nature, a multilateral solution.

11. The problem of German reunification and its relationship to a European settlement has normally been dealt with in exchanges between the Soviet Union and the three Western powers having special responsibilities in this field. In the preparation of such exchanges the Federal Republic of Germany has regularly joined the three Western powers in order to reach a common position. The other Allies will continue to have their views considered in timely discussions among the Allies about Western policy on this subject, without in any way impairing the special responsibilities in question.

12. The Allies will examine and review suitable policies designed to achieve a just and stable order in Europe, to overcome the division of Germany and to foster European security. This will be part of a process of active and constant preparation for the time when fruitful discussions of these complex questions may be possible bilaterally or multilaterally between Eastern and Western nations.

13. The Allies are studying disarmament and practical arms control measures, including the possibility of balanced force reductions. These studies will be intensified. Their active pursuit reflects the will of the Allies to work for an effective détente with the East.

14. The Allies will examine with particular attention the defence problems of the exposed areas e.g. the South-Eastern flank. In this respect the present situation in the Mediterranean presents special problems, bearing mind that the current crisis in the Middle-East falls within the responsibilities of the United Nations.

15. The North Atlantic Treaty area cannot be treated in isolation from the rest of the world. Crises and conflicts arising outside the area may impair its security either directly or by affecting the global balance. Allied countries contribute individually within the United Nations and other international organisations to the maintenance of international

peace and security and to the solution of important international problems. In accordance with established usage the Allies, or such of them as wish to do so, will also continue to consult on such problems without commitment and as the case may demand.

16. In the light of these findings, the Ministers directed the Council in permanent session to carry out, in the years ahead, the detailed follow-up resulting from this study. This will be done either by intensifying work already in hand or by activating highly specialized studies by more systematic use of experts and officials sent from capitals.

17. Ministers found that the study by the Special Group confirmed the importance of the role which the Alliance is called upon to play during the coming years in the promotion of détente and the strengthening of peace. Since significant problems have not yet been examined in all their aspects, and other problems of no less significance which have arisen from the latest political and strategic developments have still to be examined, the Ministers have directed the Permanent Representatives to put in hand the study of these problems without delay, following such procedures as shall be deemed most appropriate by the Council in permanent session, in order to enable further reports to be subsequently submitted to the Council in Ministerial Session.

Appendix 7:
Final Communiqué of the
Ministerial Meeting of the North
Atlantic Council (Czechoslovakia),
November 1968

1. The North Atlantic Council met in Ministerial session in Brussels on 15th and 16th November. The meeting was attended by Foreign, Defence and Finance Ministers. The Council had moved forward from mid-December its normal year-end meeting so that Ministers might discuss at an earlier date the serious situation following the armed intervention in Czechoslovakia and the occupation of that country by forces of the Soviet Union and of four of its Warsaw Pact Allies.

2. Ministers reaffirmed the inviolability of the principle, which has been invoked on numerous occasions by every country, including the USSR, that all nations are independent and that consequently any intervention by one state in the affairs of another is unlawful.

They noted that this principle has been deliberately violated by the Soviet leaders with the backing of four of their allies. World opinion has been profoundly shocked by this armed intervention carried out against the wishes of the Government and people of Czechoslovakia. All the members of the Alliance have denounced this use of force which jeopardises peace and international order and strikes at the principles of the United Nations Charter. Like all other peoples, the people of Czechoslovakia must be free to shape their future without outside interference. Agreements concluded under the pressure of occupying forces can provide no justification for challenging this basis concept.

3. The contention of the Soviet leadership that there exists a right of intervention in the affairs of other states deemed to be within a so-called "Socialist Commonwealth" runs counter to the basic principles of the United Nations Charter, is dangerous to European security and has inevitably aroused grave anxieties. It gives rise to fears of a further use of force in other cases.

The use of force and the stationing in Czechoslovakia of Soviet forces not hitherto deployed there have aroused grave uncertainty about the situation and about the calculations and intentions of the USSR. This uncertainty demands great vigilance on the part of the Allies.

4. Applied to Germany the policies which the USSR derives from its doctrine of a so-called "Socialist Commonwealth" raise new obstacles to the rapprochement and ultimate unification of the two parts of Germany. Moreover, they would be contrary to the letter and spirit of the Four Power agreements relating to Germany as a whole. In this situation, and bearing in mind the special responsibilities of the United States, the United Kingdom and France, the Ministers reaffirm the determination of the Alliance to persevere in its efforts to contribute to a peaceful solution of the German question based on the free decision of the German people and on the interests of European security. Their Governments do not recognize the "GDR", and they reject all claims which would tend to perpetuate the division of Germany against the will of the German people.

Referring to their communiqué issued in Reykjavik on 25th June, 1968, the Ministers confirm the support of their Governments for the declared determination of the Three Powers to safeguard Berlin's security and to maintain freedom of access to the city. They recall the declaration of the North Atlantic Council of December 16, 1958 on Berlin and the responsibilities which each Member State assumed with regard to the security and welfare of Berlin. They note with satisfaction the important measures taken by the Federal Republic of Germany in conformity with the status of Berlin for the purpose of maintaining the viability of the city. They associate themselves with the position of the Three Powers as regards the legitimate concern of the Federal Government for the welfare and viability of Berlin and as regards the resulting ties which exist between the two on the basis of the arrangements in force.

The Ministers associate themselves with the call made upon the Soviet Union by the Three Powers to respect the quadripartite agreements concerning Berlin and the decisions taken pursuant to these agreements by the United States, France and the United Kingdom.

5. The new uncertainties resulting from recent Soviet actions also extend to the Mediterranean basin. This situation requires that the Allies continue by every available means their efforts to promote stability and a just and equitable peace, as well as mutual co-operation and understanding, in the area. The expansion of Soviet activity in the Mediterranean, including the increased presence of Soviet naval units, requires vigilance to safeguard allied security.

6. The members of the Alliance urge the Soviet Union, in the interests of world peace, to refrain from using force and interfering in the affairs of other states.

Determined to safeguard the freedom and independence of their countries, they could not remain indifferent to any development which endangers their security.

Clearly any Soviet intervention directly or indirectly affecting the situation in Europe or in the Mediterranean would create an international crisis with grave consequences.

7. So long as the Soviet leaders adhere to a policy of force, these new uncertainties will remain. The Allies are convinced that their political solidarity remains indispensable to discourage aggression and other forms of oppression. Above all, they stand wholly determined to meet their common responsibilities and, in accordance with the North Atlantic Treaty, to defend the members of the Alliance against any armed attack.

8. The Allies participating in NATO's integrated defence programme have, therefore, been obliged to re-assess the state of their defences. They consider that the situation arising from recent events calls for a collective response. The quality, effectiveness, and deployment of NATO's forces will be improved in terms of both manpower and equipment in order to provide a better capability for defence as far forward as possible. The quality of reserve forces will also be improved and their ability to mobilise rapidly will be increased. Renewed attention will be directed to the provision of reinforcements for the flanks and the strengthening of local forces there. The conventional capability of NATO's tactical air forces will be increased. Certain additional national units will be committed to the Major NATO Commanders. Specific measures have been approved within these categories of action for improving the conventional capability of NATO's forces. Ministers agreed that the co-ordinated implementation of these measures and the provision of additional budgetary resources to the extent necessary to support them would form part of the NATO Force Plan for 1969-1973 which will be submitted in January 1969. They also acknowledged that the solidarity of the Alliance can be strengthened by co-operation between members to alleviate burdens arising from balance of payments deficits resulting specifically from military expenditures for the collective defence.

9. A year ago Ministers affirmed in the Report on the Future Tasks of the Alliance that, while maintaining adequate military strength and political solidarity to deter any aggressor, the Alliance should work to promote a policy of détente. The Soviet intervention in Czechoslovakia has seriously set back hopes of settling the outstanding problems which still divide the European continent and Germany and of establishing peace and security in Europe, and threatens certain of the results already achieved in the field of détente. Indeed, in view of the action of the five members of the Warsaw Pact, the scope and level of Allied contacts with them have had to be reduced.

10. More specifically, prospects for mutual balanced force reductions have suffered a severe set back. Nevertheless, the Allies in close consultation are continuing their studies and preparations for a time when the atmosphere for fruitful discussions is more favourable.

11. In any event, consistent with Western values the political goal remains that of secure, peaceful and mutually beneficial relations between East and West. The Allies are determined to pursue this goal, bearing in mind that the pursuit of détente must not be allowed to split the Alliance. The search for peace requires progress, consistent with Western security, in the vital fields of disarmament and arms control and continuing efforts to resolve the fundamental issues which divide East and West.

12. The North Atlantic Alliance will continue to stand as the indispensable guarantor of security and the essential foundation for the pursuit of European reconciliation. By its constitution the Alliance is of indefinite duration. Recent events have further demonstrated that its continued existence is more than ever necessary. The Foreign Minister of France recalled that, for its part, unless events in the years to come were to bring about a radical change in East-West relations, the French Government considers that the Alliance must continue as long as it appears to be necessary.

13. The next Ministerial Meeting of the Council will be held in Washington on 10th and 11th April, 1969.

14. The Defence Planning Committee which met in Ministerial Session on 14th November will hold its next Ministerial Meeting in Brussels on 16th January, 1969.

Index